MONTAIGNE'S DECEITS
The Art of Persuasion in the *Essais*

MONTAIGNE'S DECEITS

The Art of Persuasion in the *Essais*

Margaret M. McGowan BA, PhD

University of London Press Ltd

35666

ISBN 0 340 18114 1
First published 1974
Copyright © 1974 Margaret McGowan

University of London Press Ltd
St Paul's House, Warwick Lane, London EC4P 4AH

Printed and bound in Great Britain
by W & J Mackay Limited, Chatham, Kent

CONTENTS

INTRODUCTION

IT is virtually impossible to judge Montaigne's *Essais* in a detached way; their style establishes a familiar relationship between author and reader, and elicits a personal response. While Montaigne constantly reminds me that he did not seek to teach anything, I nevertheless find, when reading the *Essais*, that they make a moral impact—though not in an ordinary way. Two images of Montaigne dominate my thoughts: the first pictures him preoccupied with ways of living comfortably in 'un siècle si gasté'; the second shows him absorbed in the workings of the human mind and in trying to solve the problems of communicating complex thoughts and feelings to others. And the two images seem to be connected.

In this book I have tried to present this double picture of Montaigne by examining the means he used to project such a view. The extent of his defensive writing, and his frequent references to style, encouraged me to concentrate upon his oblique presentation of ideas which I have called 'Montaigne's Deceits'. The word 'deceit' was used by contemporary writers on rhetoric to describe those indirect ways of writing or speaking which commanded greater emotional response from the reader or listener than 'natural' or direct means of presenting ideas. Montaigne was, I believe, aware of this definition and extended its use to include a wide variety of oblique methods which writers on rhetoric had not adequately defined. In order to clarify how Montaigne adapted the rhetorical devices known to his contemporaries, I have provided in some chapters (4–6) details of sixteenth-century interpretations of specific techniques as well as evidence from contemporary writers to illustrate how they were commonly used before analysing the ways Montaigne exploited them. No systematic account of these rhetorical traditions is given here since recent work has made them readily available to us.[1] Chapters 1 and 2 examine Montaigne's attitude to the problems of writing more generally, while Chapter 3 sets out the oblique approaches to persuasion as they were understood by writers in the Renaissance.

To engage in a coherent account of a writer's method, such as I have attempted, poses many difficulties. And I am aware that I might have fallen into the trap recognised by Montaigne himself of making him seem more complex, more self-conscious, and more consistently 'craftie', than he really was: 'Est-il possible qu'Homere aye voulu dire tout ce qu'on luy faict dire?' (II: 12, 570). It is probably impossible to avoid creating such an impression in a work which deliberately concerns itself with style and methods of argument. I wish to stress, however, that I am presenting a view of Montaigne's work which in no way excludes or diminishes the contribution to his thought made by his own *primesautier* temperament—and, indeed, I try to take some account of this in Chapter 7. Nevertheless, since Montaigne's spontaneity has always attracted critical attention, I have primarily concerned myself with Montaigne's use of rhetorical devices for I feel that, conversely, too little attention has been given to the secret ways by which he arouses interest.

Earlier criticism of Montaigne suggests a greater awareness of the effects of this dissimulating art. In the seventeenth and eighteenth centuries, for instance, writers were disturbed by his ability to persuade readers in ways difficult to pin down. Pascal and his Jansenist friends, and Malebranche, in particular, were fascinated and exasperated by Montaigne's methods. Diderot extolled them because they provided a constant stimulus to thought, and his description of Montaigne's art suggests obvious parallels to the methods of argument employed by Socrates. These oblique approaches to truth, their effectiveness, and their abundance provide the matter for this book which ends, appropriately, with a discussion of the striking affinities between Socrates and Montaigne.[2]

ACKNOWLEDGEMENT

I am very grateful to Professor Alan Boase and to Dr Peter France for having read the manuscript of this book, and for their many valuable suggestions.

M. McG.

1

MONTAIGNE'S MODESTY

No one has protested more eloquently or more frequently about the triviality of his writings than Michel de Montaigne; while few authors have been more seriously concerned to arouse specific responses in the reader. Expressions such as 'toute cette fricassée que je barbouille icy' (III: 13, 1056)* abound in the *Essais* which he describes variously as 'ce fagotage' (II: 37, 736), 'ces inepties' (II: 37, 763), 'ces sotises' (II: 37, 764), 'cette sotte entreprise' (II: 8, 364), 'cette rapsodie' (I: 13, 48)[1] and 'la farcissure de mes exemples' (I: 20, 88). Montaigne's own inconsistent views on the nature of his work, however, should warn us away from accepting his disclaimers too seriously. They hardly agree with such proud assertions as: 'C'est le seul livre de son espèce au monde', or with the affirmative stance which Montaigne increasingly adopts as he gains confidence in himself and his enterprise.

Contradictions in Montaigne are usually accounted for by an assumption that his ideas changed significantly between 1572 and 1592. Yet references to such an evolution cannot satisfactorily explain his apparently vacillating attitude both towards himself and to his work.[2] From a detailed examination of the chronology of the *Essais* two facts emerge: first, that additions have the function of strengthening and clarifying ideas already held rather than of introducing new discoveries; secondly, that Montaigne's confidence in his powers of communication is deepened. Modest disclaimers appear as frequently in the last essays as in the first. Because it is true that the motives for assuming diffidence seem sometimes different in late additions to the *Essais* (where expressions of modesty, for instance, are used to hide genuinely increasing self-assurance), it has proved impossible to establish a clear, coherent

*All references are to the Pléiade edition of the *Essais*. Ed. A. Thibaudet & M. Rat, 1962.

pattern in Montaigne's retreat into confessions of inadequacy. Each expression needs to be seen in its context. And then it becomes apparent that modesty for Montaigne spans a vast terrain.

Throughout the *Essais* Montaigne is concerned about the image of himself which he is projecting, and this concern is in large part reflected through expressions of modesty. It may merely be assumed for social and professional reasons; or it may arise from a much more fundamental sense of the difficulty of what Montaigne is trying to do, and of the inadequacies of language as a means of self-investigation and expression. There are times when modesty is linked paradoxically with self-assertion. It is then that Montaigne discovers its moral value, and this in turn seems to heighten his awareness of its advantages as a means of persuasion. Thus, from an art used in self-defence, modesty becomes a method of involving the reader in Montaigne's most profound pre-occupations. It is the purpose of this chapter to explore the principal features of Montaigne's modesty; and especially in so far as it relates to his Art of Persuasion.

It was, of course, part of a well established tradition for writers wishing to hide their intentions, or to avoid the charges always levelled at professionals by their colleagues, to declare that their work had been botched up in half an hour, or composed at high speed—as Castiglione is at great pains to remind us in his epistle to *The Courtier* 'the which I accomplished in a few days'. Alternatively, they could cover themselves by suggesting that their work was not serious—that it was a mere game to be enjoyed at a moment of leisure, a sport which could be justi-fied because ancient writers had similarly indulged themselves. Thus Erasmus self-consciously defends himself in the Prefatory Dedication of *The Praise of Folly*,

> Homer wrote of no more weighty a subject than of a war between the frogs and mice; Virgil of a gnat and a pudding-cake; and Ovid of a nut. Polycrates commended the cruelty of Busiris; and Isocrates, who corrects him for this, did as much for the injustice of Glaucus. Favor-inus extolled Thersites, and wrote in praise of a quartan ague. Synesius pleaded in behalf of baldness; and Lucian defended a sipping fly. Seneca drollingly related the deifying of Claudius; Plutarch the dialogue betwixt Gryllus and Ulysses; Lucian and Apuleius the story of an ass. And somebody else records the last will of a hog, of which St Hierom makes mention.[3]

Marguerite de Navarre, for similar protective reasons, specifically excludes from her story-tellers 'ceux qui auroient étudié et seroient gens de lettres', since they spoilt the story by too much attention to style, and would undermine the amateur status of her gentlewomen and their noble companions.[4]

The fate of La Noue's *Discours militaires* is especially revealing of the attitudes of French nobles towards professional writing in the six-teenth century. La Noue composed them to while away the time he was forced to spend in prison. Once they had served their purpose, he thrust them aside as unworthy, useless and to be forgotten, until a friend (Monsieur de Fresnes) discovered them: 'un monceau de papiers iettez pesle-mesle en un coin, comme chose qui n'estoit gardee que pour estre perdue'.[5] The unwilling La Noue was eventually persuaded to have his manuscript published; but to the last this military hero bewailed the fact that the printed work should carry his name 'lequel il se contente d'avoir rendu si celebre par les armes, n'estimant peut-estre à Honneur (suyvant l'ancien erreur de la Noblesse Françoise) qu'on sçache combien il aime et honnore les lettres'.[6] It is indeed difficult to find a French sixteenth-century book in which one does not encounter such preliminary dis-claimers.[7] At the beginning of the century Castiglione had ridiculed the ignorance of French noblemen, and at the end even the most enlightened among them, clinging to their military ideals, felt uncomfortable about wielding a pen publicly.

A powerful current of thought lent authority to those who wished to cultivate a modest public image. It reached back to Plutarch and beyond; and it is precisely to this Greek historian that Montaigne turned when he sought confidence and a reason for writing, acknowledging, in *A demain les affaires* (II : 4, 344), 'sa mercy [grâce à lui] nous osons à cett' heure et parler et escrire'. Plutarch had examined at some length, in his *Moral Works*, the justifications for writing about oneself, without incurring envy or blame. In Amyot's translation (published in 1572) Montaigne would doubtless have noted the opening sentence of that chapter: 'Il n'y a celuy qui ne die de bouche, que parler de soy-mesme en se donnant la louange d'estre ou de valoir quelque chose, amy Herculanus, ne soit fort odieux, et mal seant à toute personne bien apprise'.[8] Such strictures must have caused Montaigne to pause and reflect carefully upon his self-confessed project of exploring his own person and publish-ing his findings in a work destined for public consumption. How could he avoid the kind of censure, the accusations of vain glory, which Plutarch has in mind? The grounds on which the Greek historian defends self-talk seem at first glance hardly applicable to Montaigne: he has not been attacked, and is not therefore required to defend himself; he is not under sentence of death; nor is there any military advantage to be gained from confession of his virtues.[9] When, however, Plutarch begins to discuss the ways of talking about oneself in public, then one begins to recognise the same flavour of modesty as that which characterises Montaigne's manner: 'est adroit, de bon jugement, et de bonne grace celuy, qui allegue contre soy-mesme quelque oubliance, quelque ignorance, ou quelque desir de iouir et d'apprendre'.[10]

*   *   *

It is within these traditions that the *Essais* should first be considered. In 1572, when Montaigne began to write, his only claim to expertise was that of a magistrate—and, as a lawyer, he had been trained to apologise to the judge in advance for the weakness of his arguments so that the latter might be favourably disposed towards his case.[11] He had been trained to recognise the advantages of humility. To class his work as 'fantasies' or even 'bizarreries' removed his writing from important areas of attack: as long as he stressed his lack of qualifications, he was safe from the criticism of the professionals. In fact, one might say that his modesty initially reflects a lack of experience. Though he dealt with matters of behaviour and of education, he did not have the self-assurance or the skill of the much-travelled diplomat Castiglione. He could nevertheless imitate the Italian's *sprezzatura*, and pretend that he was only trying out his ideas without expecting them to be taken seriously. More particularly, he wanted to emphasise that he was not writing for gain 'car une fin si abjecte est indigne de la grace et faveur des Muses' (i: 26, 149). Such a thing was unworthy of the nobleman he thought himself to be. In spite of extensive reading and detailed commentaries on the work of contemporary historians,[12] Montaigne did not have the military experience of Monluc or La Noue, and, though this did not deter him from considering matters of soldiery, he was careful to present his views in such a way that experts would not think to challenge him. Similarly, he was no theologian and he is quick to assure us of this fact at the beginning of the *Apologie* (ii: 12, 417)[13] before he embarks on his long disquisition on man's relationship (or rather lack of it) with God.

Traditions of defensive writing not only made him more secure as a writer, they also offered him another kind of shelter. Temperamentally, Montaigne the lawyer was torn between the desire to depict himself as a noble gentleman enjoying his retirement by writing on various matters as a mere dilettante, and the need to shape another sort of image of himself which would arouse the interest of readers. Idle leisure was a mark of the ageing members of the noble class to which Montaigne's family had recently gained admittance.[14] Montaigne was fearful of cutting a figure of fun before the gaze of nobles of longer standing than himself: 'car de servir de spectacle aux grands et faire à l'envy parade de son esprit et de son caquet, je trouve que c'est un mestier tres-messeant, à un homme d'honneur' (III:8,901). Montaigne is careful to note in *De l'Oisiveté* that the self-reflexion which came with quiet solitude at first brought inchoate, disordered thoughts, and that he wrote the *Essais* in the hope that he might give them some coherence, and thereby profit from them. But as his thoughts accumulated, even over the first eight years of composition, he realised that writing was not only needful as an ordering and enriching process, but that it was an occupation as necessary to him as food, and that he cared very much about public response to his work. Already by 1580 he seems to be aware that claims of modesty, frequently repeated, allowed him to maintain that double image of himself not only as noble dilettante but also as committed writer. And later, in *De la vanité* (III:9,958), he is even more explicit: 'la confession genereuse et libre enerve [affaiblit] le reproche et desarme l'injure'.

The first comment Montaigne offers the reader about his book is that it is 'un livre de bonne foy'.[15] This expression of good faith is immediately defined by statements about the private nature of the work, limited, as it is, to an exploration of himself in all his inadequacies, and intended only for a small band of friends. And as if these warnings were not enough, he multiplies, throughout his first two books, assurances of sincerity, of frankness and honesty; and phrases like 'de vray', 'en vérité', 'à la vérité', 'sans mentir', are scattered unsparingly through the pages of the *Essais*. Montaigne's frequent and violent attacks upon lying can also be seen as a means of gaining the confidence of the reader.[16] It seems that the latter's good will is important to Montaigne who tries to encourage it both by assertion of frankness, and by admission of uncertainty. Whenever his anecdotes, for example, touch upon the extraordinary he hurriedly unloads responsibility upon vague and impersonal 'à ce qu'on dit', 'dict le précepte'; or he supplies tentative remarks such as 'il me semble ouy dire' (I:48,276). Laudable hesitation, such as his use of paradox introduced by 'il semble',[17] frequently gives way to frank avowals of inadequacy, and these seem to be made in order to flatter the reader. In *De la vanité*, for instance, Montaigne parades the advantages of weaknesses: 'Les imperfections mesme ont leur moyen de se recommander' (III:9,942); they are advantageous since they disarm the common reader.

The man who protests that he is an ordinary chap speaking a simple language often seems much more persuasive than the professional who adopts a special language and obviously assumes artificial forms to manipulate his audience. Montaigne stresses the natural approach and derides the artificial. He talks of his sincerity, and of his ordinariness, and he prefers to see himself 'vivoter en la moyenne region' (I:54,300), away from the dangers of the over-subtleties of the schoolmen. It is not, of course, always easy to distinguish the natural from the artificial in sixteenth-century writing. J. B. Gelli, who is similarly concerned with exploratory and confessional writing, deliberately adopts a character 'en si basse condition, et mourri en si vil mestier' that he might speak naturally, untidily, and without being 'fort versez aux lettres et sciences humaines'. Having chosen the plainest of men to compose a discourse on the soul, Gelli then pretends that his character is to be excused all his faults and his presumption for speaking at all, since his words were 'pour s'entretenir soy-mesmes à loisir', and that 'il ne pensoit estre ouy ni entendu de personne'.[18]

Montaigne's technique was less obviously deceptive; and that he did indeed succeed (at least in large part) in projecting the desired image of sincerity might be gauged by the reactions of some contemporaries. Pasquier, it is true, is somewhat doubtful. He questions Montaigne's sincerity, particularly as far as his titles of essays are concerned. He suggests that Montaigne deliberately leads us into error, 'il s'est voulu du propos délibéré moquer de nous, et par aventure de lui-même, par une liberté particulière qui lui était née avec lui'.[19] Bouchet and Lestoile, on the other hand, praise Montaigne's frankness and forthrightness, and both declare that they aspire to imitate the completeness with which he was able to write about himself.[20] Montaigne actively sought certain reactions; even in *De la ressemblance des enfans aux peres* (II:37,765–6) he admits that he is concerned to preserve a certain image of himself. And in *De la praesomption* (II:17) he tries to justify this concern. First he assures us that he prefers those philosophers who expose the weaknesses of man (II:17,616–7). He follows this up by insisting on his own poor opinion of himself (*Ibid*, 618), excusing his talk of self on the grounds that, first, he does not have the same opportunities of self-exposure as those men of eminence who are constantly in the public eye; and secondly that, although he is a weakling, some of his characteristics are better than those of others which are nevertheless admired (*Ibid*,

619–20). In order to escape the accusation of vainglory, Montaigne is forced to emphasise his inadequacies—an attitude which reveals something of the extent to which he was concerned about the kind of response he was eliciting.

We do know from Montaigne's dedicatory epistle in his edition of La Boëtie's *Règles de mariage* (1572) that he was alive to the consoling power latent in any contemplation of one's good reputation (particularly if one's active life is as short as that of his friend to whom he refers here): 'I'estime toutefois que ce soit une grande consolation à la foiblesse et brieveté de ceste vie, de croire qu'elle se puisse fermir et allonger par la reputation et par la renommée; et embrasse tres volontiers une si plaisante et favourable opinion engendree en nous, sans m'enquerir curieusement, ny comment, ny pourquoy'.[21] It seems unlikely that Montaigne would not want to preserve his own portrait from criticism in any way he could.

It might well be felt, however, that Montaigne's insistent modesty is carried too far. His presentation of self is almost always hedged around by adjectives such as 'bas, privé, sot, inepte', by terms such as 'chose de néant' and 'particulier bien mal formé (III: 2, 782). At times he seems to derive a kind of melodramatic delight from painting himself 'rampant au limon de la terre' (I: 37, 225), and from referring to his mental achievements as 'folie, rêverie, chimères, monstres fantasques' and 'étrangetés', or as the blubberings of an old and useless man (II: 28, 682), and to his writing as 'excremens' or as wrapping paper for butter (II: 18, 647). To insist in this way that your writing is foolish and worthless must arouse a sense of protest in any reader who is, otherwise, favourably impressed by your views. It also has other effects, for, as Montaigne seems to assume, it allows you complete freedom to say what you like about anything. As Landi discovered in his *Paradoxes*, 'Le sot . . . n'est aucunement subject a personne, et vit en plaine franchise et liberté. Il luy est permis et licite, de dire ce que bon luy semble, touchant le faict des princes, et personnes privees'.[22] Whatever we might feel about the truth of this assumption, that Montaigne appreciated the benefits of striking such an attitude is apparent from the manner in which he refers to his enterprise of self-revelation as something audacious, new, startling, and even shocking: 'qui ose tant dire de moy', he asserts rather coyly (I: 14, 65); 'si j'osois' he adds in another place (I: 32, 214). Hesitant expressions—even blatant self-deprecation—serve to whet the reader's appetite further. But they also reveal a mind very seriously involved with its subject.

*   *   *

Modesty in Montaigne is much more complex than I have so far shown. While Montaigne's awareness of social prejudice and anticipation of possible criticisms led him to adopt modes of defensive writing of an obvious kind, other modest disclaimers are prompted by much more fundamental considerations. The exploration of the 'moi' which became his all-absorbing preoccupation—as he stated in 1580: 'je suis moy-mesmes la matière de mon livre . . . subject si frivole et si vain'—was difficult and complicated, and no one realised this more forcibly than Montaigne himself. It was not simply a question of the elusive nature of human personality constantly changing with every instant of experience, as he describes in *Du repentir*; it was, even more, a matter of communication. How to find the words to describe each moment of being in all its diversity was Montaigne's major problem: 'Et quand seray-je à bout de representer une continuelle agitation et mutation de mes pensées, en quelque matière qu'elles tombent' (III: 9,923). The task seemed insurmountable when he considered that the mind which controlled the use of words was subject to the effects of the imagination, of climate, emotions, health, and a host of other disturbing influences, and when language itself seemed inadequate and was ever at the mercy of the distorting interpretative processes of other human minds. For instance, in the more general context, until 1561, Catholics and Protestants had sought mutual understanding with some confidence. They had thought it possible to find a language in which they could discuss their problems, free from prejudice, personal motives and political interest. All attempts at such a dialogue, however, had proved impossible since the Colloque de Poissy. To avoid a similar impasse Montaigne insisted on man's overriding need to be honest with himself and others. Telling lies about oneself is much more than a lack of dignity: it corrupts one's nature (I: 51,292 and II: 18,649). Furthermore, there was his own need to replace his friend, La Boëtie. To talk to someone, and to know that someone would respond, was compulsive for Montaigne, and it seemed that only by assuming a modest role, and by constantly reminding himself and his interlocutor of his inadequacies, could he begin to tackle the enormous difficulties of exploring and exposing his inner self.

At all moments of his writing career Montaigne showed himself conscious of the detailed problems involved in communication, though he was not the only writer at this time to concern himself with this topic. It is interesting to compare a similar comment made by Etienne du Tronchet in 1572: 'il n'y a de plus grande difficulté au monde, que de donner à autruy vraye notice de ce que l'on est'.[23] The idea is the same as that of Montaigne; although its formulation is more abstract, less personal, and infinitely less striking. In *De l'institution des enfants* (I: 26, 145) Montaigne discusses the incompleteness of his articulation of ideas in this way: 'mes conceptions et mon jugement ne marche qu'à tastons, chancelant, bronchant et chopant; et, quand je suis allé le plus avant que je puis, si ne me suis-je aucunement satisfaict: je voy encore du païs au delà, mais d'une veüe trouble et en nuage, que je ne puis desmeler'. He does not merely state the fleeting nature of his thoughts as Du Tronchet did, he demonstrates their flight. Thoughts are frequently so vague that they defy expression; and even those which do find form often do so only inadequately. Throughout his essay on *Praesomption* (II: 17) he argues from a similar angle. He perceives an idea in his mind only momentarily and thus he can never catch its real nature. Quickly gone is the opportunity for giving it concrete form: 'J'ay tousjours une idée en l'ame et certaine image trouble, qui me presente comme en songe une meilleure forme que celle que j'ai mis en besongne, mais je ne la puis saisir et exploiter' (II: 17, 620).

So pronounced a sense of inadequacy explains, in part, his modest claims for his ideas. They are his alone: 'car aussi ce sont ici mes humeurs et opinions' (I: 26, 147); and he declares that he has no intention of dressing them up to impose them upon other people. But he does not run away from the effort of giving shape to his ideas; indeed he despises those who try to find excuses for imperfect formulations (I: 26, 168–9). He recognises more fully in Book III that his natural bent is for communication: 'ma forme essentielle est propre à la communication et à la production' (III: 3, 801), and it is this compulsive need to reveal which at times gives him the impression that he does indeed expose his inner person fully to the reader. Yet there is always that nagging doubt that his conscious apparatus for expressing thoughts is not altogether in control. Indeed, many of his best ideas come to him in sudden moments of insight when he least expects them, and disappear before he has time to give them form: 'Mais mon ame me desplait de ce qu'elle produict ordinairement ses plus profondes resveries, plus folles et qui me plaisent le mieux, à l'improuveu et lors que je les cerche moins; lesquelles s'esvanouissent soudain, n'ayant sur le champ où les attacher' (III: 5, 854). On another occasion, however, he remarks confidently 'ce que je ne puis exprimer, je le montre au doigt . . . Je ne laisse rien à desircr et deviner de moy' (III: 9, 961). Nevertheless, in one of the final additions he gives to *De l'experience*, he reminds himself of the ever present difficulty of giving a coherent form to anything so shifting as man (III:

13, 1054). The clearer, the more categorical the language you use, the
more you misrepresent what you are trying to show. It does not matter
what sphere of human endeavour you consider, you are always confronted with the same problem: the inadequacy of language. It is at the
root of most of the injustices in law (III : 13, 1047).[24] It is the cause of
contemporary religious quarrels: 'nous ne faisons que nous entregloser'
(III : 13, 1045), or 'la plus part des occasions des troubles du monde sont
Grammariennes' (II : 12, 508). It even constitutes the mask which doctors
use to cover up their ignorance (II : 37, 749–50). In order to teach man to
be humble God had allowed languages to multiply and, within the same
language, interpretations to proliferate (II : 12, 535). Inadequacy of
language is the biggest obstacle to Montaigne's self-confidence. How
can he be sure that he has said what he wants to say in a way that cannot
be misunderstood? His basic tool is a dangerous one and it is scarcely
aided by Montaigne's changing temper, and the extraordinary diversity
he perceives when in *De l'experience*, for example, he looks back on the
span of his life (III : 13, 1081).

In *De la ressemblance des enfans aux peres* (II : 37) he tries to give us
some idea of the difficulties involved in any attempt at self-analysis, by
exposing, in detail, a parallel problem of greater magnitude. Doctors are
ridiculed, and the patients who believe their diagnosis are criticised, not
so much because Montaigne thought of them as ignorant, but rather because they did not appreciate the enormous complexities of their art.
Having exposed the pride and the stupidity which lie behind their sense-
less jargon, Montaigne, in an address to Madame de Duras which ends
the essay, writes of his own 'inepties' and his 'sottises' (II : 37, 763–4)
and insists that 'mon art et mon industrie ont esté employez à me faire
valoir moy-mesme'. He recognises pitfalls in his task which the doctors
did not see in theirs. Self-investigation, of body or of mind, is extraordinarily difficult. It is an art which takes years to acquire, and, even
then, it is scarcely adequate. For this reason, Montaigne shows himself
reluctant to pronounce on any other person, and is critical of anyone who
presumes to do so.

Such recognition of obstacles probably caused the prolific number
of protestations of modesty to which we have pointed: and this kind of
protest seems by no means a device but a genuine and fundamental
expression of difficulty. Nevertheless, Montaigne's awareness of the
magnitude of the problems that confronted him did not close up his
sources of inspiration. In fact, a contrary effect is produced. He determined to break down the resistances of language, temperament, and

other distorting influences, for he was more and more convinced that thoughts are of little worth if they are kept to yourself: 'les biens mesmes de l'esprit et la sagesse nous semble sans fruict, si elle n'est jouie que de nous, si elle ne se produict à la veüe et approbation estrangere' (iii:9,932). As he contemplated the problems of communication to be overcome, Montaigne's writing became increasingly excited: 'je suis affamé de me faire connoistre' (iii:5,824). He issued self-imposed rules such as daring to say everything about himself: 'je me suis ordonné d'oser dire tout ce que j'ose faire' (iii:5,822); and, by giving as complete a coverage of himself as possible—'je dois au publiq universellement mon pourtrait' (iii:5,866)—he tried to overcome the difficulties posed by insufficiency of judgement or by diversity of thought and action.

*   *   *

Thus, we are confronted by insistent self-assertion side by side with the modest disclaimers. Such juxtaposition may also be explained by the particular political conditions in which Montaigne was writing. Measured against the multitude of ills which surround him, his own seem trivial; yet the recognition of them gives him the means of building up resources which can resist the pressures of civil war. This interpretation of his self-analysis is more explicitly stated in Book III and in the later additions to earlier essays. Useless writing, though a symptom of bad times, is defended as something praiseworthy by comparison with more active sources of disaster (iii:9,923). Exploration of self was, of course, rendered very much more difficult in the noise and confusion of civil war (iii:13,1059), yet Montaigne assures us of the moral advantages of pursuing self-knowledge: 'nostre guerre a beau changer de formes, se multiplier et diversifier en nouveaux partis; pour moy, je ne bouge' (ii:15,601).

The context of war in which Montaigne was writing transforms his expressions of modesty into discussions on the advantages of self-reliance. Discourses upon himself are offered as a counterbalance to the disputes of Protestants and Catholics; leisure for study is thrust forward as a substitute for civil peace. It is noticeable that already in one of the earliest essays—*De l'Oisiveté* (i:8,34)—there are glimmerings of the possibility of achieving a fruitful state of tranquillity. He compares his mental activities both to the ground which is rich and fertile, and to the soil on which only useless, wild things grow: and the essay ends with the hope that his present wild and infertile mind will grow enriched, ordered, and useful. As his self-awareness increases and he perfects his means of

analysis, so the conviction grows that he has a duty to publish his findings: 'qui se connoistra ainsi', he adds to *De l'exercitation* (ii:6,360),
referring to knowledge of self, 'qu'il se donne hardiment à connoistre par
sa bouche'. This battle cry could be said to herald most of the assumptions behind the celebrated essay *Du repentir*, where Montaigne not
only insists on the necessity to talk about himself, but about the whole of
himself—Michel de Montaigne and 'son estre universel'.

While recognising the problems involved in projecting the
entirety of his person onto the pages of a book, Montaigne nevertheless
insists that his self-portrait is as complete, as exact, and as faithful as he
can make it. In fact, he considers that he has achieved a degree of penetration and revelation never before attained: 'jamais aucun ne penetra en sa
matiere plus avant, ny en esplucha plus particulierement les membres et
suites; et n'arriva plus exactement et plainement à la fin qu'il s'estoit
proposé à sa besoingne' (iii:2,783). Modest disclaimers in the essays
frequently give way to a dominant note as he asserts the singularity of
his achievement. In the later essays, particularly, Montaigne's tone rises
to confidence, to enthusiasm and even to blatant self congratulation:
'J'ose non seulement parler de moy, mais parler seulement de moy', he
affirms. In other places he had discussed the difficulties involved in self-
study, and had drawn a picture of a mind, hesitating, gropingly aware of
the relative nature of everything contained within constantly shifting
horizons. This ever changing world is still there for Montaigne, but he
is rather proud of the manner in which he has come to terms with the
intricacies involved: 'C'est une espineuse entreprinse, et plus qu'il ne
semble, de suyvre une alleure si vagabonde que celle de nostre esprit;
de penetrer les profondeurs opaques de ses replis internes; de choisir et
arrester tant de menus airs de ses agitations. Et est un amusement
nouveau et extraordinaire . . .' (ii:6,358). Montaigne's very style
reveals the extent to which he savours the whole process of delving into
his inner complexities. It is truly an 'amusement', and all feelings of inadequacy have disappeared. Indeed many of the terms which we had first
assumed had a deflating critical sense, because Montaigne had placed
them in a context of apparent disapproval, acquire a different flavour
within the perspective we have been trying to establish. The words
'resveries' and 'folles', for instance, in the example 'Mais mon ame me
desplait de ce qu'elle produict ordinairement ses plus profondes resveries, plus folles qui me plaisent le mieux' (iii:5,854), are rather the
flippant adjectives used a little ironically by the confident writer to
mean the opposite of what they normally imply.

Montaigne had always been conscious of feeling different from other people: 'Je n'ay point cette erreur commune de juger d'un autre selon que je suis', he announced at the beginning of the essay *Du jeune Caton* (i: 37, 225)—a sentiment which he expanded considerably in later additions. He writes differently (iii: 5, 851), uses his sources differently, and handles his unique subject differently (*Des livres*, ii: 10). He takes pleasure in showing how his mental activities run counter to the 'occupations communes du monde'; in enumerating even the most trivial of personal quirks which set him at a distance from others; and, especially, in emphasising the distinctions separating his style and conceptions from those of specialist writers. 'Les autres forment l'homme; je le recite', so begins *Du repentir* (iii: 2, 782), and so Montaigne defines by contrast his intention. But even his affirmations of singularity assume a defensive air. Montaigne always expects to be attacked, he anticipates reactions, and he has his answers ready before one has had time to formulate the question or the criticism. Constantly before his eyes, as he writes, he sees a reader responding to his words. He is conscious of the figure he is cutting in front of a public gaze, and many of his expressions of modesty might well be in the nature of nervous reactions to such an audience. He feels an overpowering need to explain, and to justify his enterprise, even when he is at his most jaunty and ebullient. He is no professional amuser but one 'homme d'honneur' speaking to another (iii: 8, 901). Swaggering is quickly tempered by apology. And it is at these moments that Montaigne frequently makes his most valuable discoveries both about himself and about man.[25]

He is himself aware that chance, the sub-conscious, and the process of writing itself, are frequently more effective sources of subtle thought than conscious judgement: 'je ne me trouve pas où je me cherche; et me trouve plus par rencontre que par l'inquisition de mon jugement. J'aurai eslancé quelque subtilité en escrivant' (i: 10, 41–2).[26] So absorbed is he with defending his enterprise, and with explaining why he devotes so much time and space to the elaboration of his portrait from all aspects, that the kind of revelations he makes about his being, in *Du repentir* or *De l'experience*, seem almost incidental. His analyses on the nature of vice in the first of these essays do less to establish some objective criteria by which to distinguish vice from virtue than to reveal Montaigne's notions of self-reliance and of the virtues of contradiction, and his emphasis on the importance of the present instant of being as opposed to a cumulative view of experience. His discourse on law at the beginning of *De l'experience* is equally excited and insistent, but it divulges more about the workings of the human mind than about the process of law. In *Sur des vers de Virgile*, while defending the extent to which he reveals himself to others, he discovers the moral consequences of his own audacious enterprise 'qui s'obligeroit à tout dire, s'obligeroit à rien faire de ce qu'on est constraint de se taire' (III: 5, 822). His own private responses to any subject, emphatically stated and vigorously defended, begin as modest comments and develop into novel and persuasive arguments. Although such writing might seem uncontrolled and haphazard, and for this reason is quickly condemned by Montaigne as naïve and not to be listened to, it is precisely this kind of self-appraisal which Montaigne expects to be appreciated.

Such confidence in his own ability to counteract the effects of war by exposing his person on the pages of the *Essais* seems strange after the extraordinarily extended confessions of inadequacy we have already examined. The matter seems even more curious when one considers that Montaigne's essays not only become more confident in tone, but also that even his expressions of modesty and ignorance in later essays seem couched in immodest tones. Self-reflexion—'l'entretien de nous à nous-mesmes' (I: 39, 235)—engendered modesty which, in its turn, became a sort of remedy to the times. Perhaps even before the extent of the remedy had been recognised, modest appraisal of self became a source of pride. Montaigne places himself among the weakest, and then shows that these are the most virtuous (III: 1, 768).

The move from modesty to proud self-assertion can best be illustrated if one considers the specific contexts in which Montaigne speaks so modestly of himself. It then becomes apparent that his assessment is often made in comparison to something infinitely great. In this, he is mirroring the tradition of declared ignorance which has most frequently been associated with Nicolas of Cusa's *De Docta Ignorantia* (completed 1440) where the writer struggled to express what he knew while being conscious of how little he did know.[27] Following on from such demonstrations on the relativity of human knowledge with its multiple, complex, and approximate nature, writers had developed diverse strands extending from Lefèvre's virtual repetition of Nicolas of Cusa's words[28] to Agrippa's accumulations on the vanity of knowledge,[29] and onto Sanchez' discourse on the impossibility of knowing anything.[30] Many of Montaigne's protestations of ignorance are placed in the same contexts as these earlier developments.

Modesty and caution are always advocated where any discussion of God occurs (for example, I: 56, 302–3, 308). In early essays, when comparing himself with La Boëtie, he is insistent that his own powers of thought are weak and yet, in spite of this, he notes that the kind of friendship and intellectual exchange which they enjoyed together was so rare that it only occurred once in three centuries (i : 28, 183). In later essays, Socrates is taken as his model, and whereas at first he measures the distance between the ancient philosopher and himself, he subsequently seems to find traits worthy of comparison: as, for example, their similar attitude to others' assessment of themselves (iii : 8, 903), or their naturalness (iii : 12, 1031). A parallel development can be traced as far as Montaigne's attitude to his style is concerned. 'Je ne cognois personne si sottement sterile de langage que moy' (i : 40, 247), he states, though in a context where such strictures on himself are demonstrably more apparent than real, since, in the same essay, he acknowledges that he cannot perform in a way which he despises. It seems clear that, for all his statements about sincerity and modesty, Montaigne is not concerned finally to leave the reader with a modest impression of himself.

*   *   *

Genuine feelings of inadequacy and initial apprehensions about self-exposure in print, an acute awareness of his social status and the insufficiencies of language to communicate without fear of misunderstanding, together with the complex nature of what had to be said—these are all factors which explain the extent of Montaigne's defensive writing. The shift from feelings of modesty to self-assertion paradoxically made the need for modest expression even more acute. As Montaigne grew more confident in his self-discovery, so he wanted to convince others of the value of what he had found. It is then that modesty became not so much a reflexion of feelings of inadequacy or notions of difficulty, but rather an effective means of persuasion. And it is to this concern for effective communication that we must now turn.

Montaigne is concerned that his words make the precise impact he desires: 'a toutes avantures, je suis content qu'on sçache d'où je seray tombé' (iii : 2, 796). Above all, he wants to gain a hearing, and he wants to be liked. From this twin desire stem all his efforts to disarm the reader. Expressions of modesty are merely one of his means of attracting attention; they serve as pointers to an attitude which is much closer to moral intention than Montaigne dared admit publicly. He knows that neither straight talking, nor obvious efforts to persuade, convince anyone. He therefore adopts a somewhat different course. He repeats, tirelessly, that he prescribes nothing, 'je n'enseigne poinct, je raconte' (iii : 2, 784), and that while he cannot control his own activities, he is not worthy to suggest action for others. He himself is not appreciative of a writer who talks at you from a lofty height. Yet, as we have seen, he does not count his experience as worthless. Behind his discovery of self lies the urge to tell others about his finds. How then does Montaigne envisage his relationship to the reader?

In the first place one might take Montaigne himself as a model. He hates to be bored, and what he fears most of all as a writer is that he should be accused of being boring. In order to escape such a charge, he followed the advice of his mentor Plutarch: he countered self-praise by subtly transferring the compliments to the reader: 'car l'auditeur secrettement ainsi gaigné par ses propres louanges, en reçoit plus volontiers, et avec plaisir, le dire de l'orateur'.[31] Furthermore, with the same aim in mind, he strove to keep the reader on the alert. He sought to arouse him, even to produce a reaction of anger if necessary, 'j'aymerois mieux poindre que lasser' (III:9,942); he tried to amuse him, 'je desire de contenter chacun, chose pourtant tres difficile' (III:5,867). Often he will state that he is boring so that the reader might protest to the contrary, as at the end of the *Apologie pour R. Sebond* (II:12,588). Always in the forefront of his mind is a hypothetical reader, someone who, because of Montaigne's skill, will be susceptible to manipulation. He tried hard to accommodate his material to the taste of his reader whom he assumes from the outset to be 'un esprit vigoureux et reiglé', taking the reader's assumptions into account and often using them as matter for discussion—those of the princess in the *Apologie* (II:12), for example, and of women generally in *Sur des vers de Virgile* (III:5). Their presence acts as a stimulus to Montaigne who needs to be ever mindful of a public in order to reveal himself fully to himself (II:10,387–8). Far from being passive or quiescent, Montaigne's reader is expected to take an active part in the creative process, discovering for himself elements of which the author might well be ignorant: 'un suffisant lecteur descouvre souvant ès escrits d'autruy des perfections autres que celles que l'autheur y a mises et apperceuës, et y preste des sens et des visages plus riches' (I:24,126).

To ensure that such scrutiny is observed, Montaigne initiates a deliberate campaign to arouse the reader, 'qui est celuy qui n'ayme mieux n'estre pas leu que de l'estre en dormant ou en fuyant' (III:9,974). Like Du Bellay in *La Deffence et Illustration de la langue françoyse*, he hopes to emulate the writer 'qui me fera indigner, appaiser, ejouir, douloir, aimer, haïr, admirer, estonner: bref, qui tient la bride de mes affections, me tournant çà et là à son plaisir'.[32] Modesty is simply one

of the voices he assumes to achieve such an aim, and in this, Montaigne
is by no means running counter to common practice or advice. Erasmus
had shown him the way in both *The Praise of Folly* and the *Colloquies*. In
the first work Folly, conscious of an audience to please, adopts many
voices. She first gives a humble definition of her own stupidities, but
under the same name and in a different voice she discourses on the
excesses of war and religion.[33] Another voice, mock-learned, is then
assumed to drub the scholars, while some few pages earlier the tone and
manner of the first voice had been used, only to be changed again and
fused with the voice of madness in the discussion on poets' and philosophers' attitudes to Folly.[34] In these instances the tone has shifted from
mild disapproval, to blatant satire of pedants and priests, and then to
benevolent tolerance. Such self-consciousness had been more than
adequately prepared for by the extended defence of allowing Folly to
speak which ended 'For who can set me forth better than myself? or who
can pretend to be so well acquainted with my condition?'.[35] Montaigne
virtually translated Erasmus' words in *Du repentir*—'au moins j'ay cecy
selon la discipline, que jamais homme ne traicta subject qu'il entendit ne
cogneust mieux que je fay celuy que j'ay entrepris, et qu'en celuy- là je
suis le plus sçavant homme qui vive' (III : 2, 783)—and he learned many
more lessons from the same source.

If Montaigne could not succeed in forcing interest through weight
of argument, then he would do it 'par mon embrouilleure'(III : 9, 974).
He was willing to make people think by deliberate obscurity, and by
variety of style and content. He proposed to induce reflexion through
understatement: 'celuy qui craint à s'exprimer nous achemine à en
penser plus qu'il n'en y a' (III : 5, 858). Oblique approaches, unresolved
argument, inconclusive discussions, and a hesitant manner of writing and
thinking, all serve to bring the reader into the work. Montaigne's
silence and his refusals to conclude (*De la moderation*, I : 30, 200) force
the reader to come to a decision himself. Then, frequently, he punctures
expectation by a surprise twist in argument or anecdote (*Des vaines
subtilitez*, 1 : 54, 300). It is hard but pleasurable work reading Montaigne
since he seems convinced that effort and enjoyment go together. For this
reason he cannot tolerate a stupid reader; he imagines 'un homme
vigoureux' (III : 8, 915), one of ingenious mind, set apart from the dull,
credulous foolishness which he felt dominated his century (III : 9, 923).
Most especially, he hoped for someone who could look all round a
problem before making up his mind: 'voilà pourquoy, quand on juge
d'une action particulière, il faut considerer plusieurs circonstances et

l'homme tout entier qui l'a produicte, avant la baptizer' (ii: 11, 406).

It seems then, in spite of his disparaging remarks about his work, that Montaigne does think that he has something to communicate, if only because he goes to such elaborate and varied lengths to do so. One must remember that his first comment in the Preface to the Reader is to assure him of his good faith. What better way of arousing, at one and the same time, the reader's sympathy and his curiosity. We are put on our guard by so much talk in defence of self, while dismissive comment immediately removes standards, makes us make up our own minds, and turns our attention to the manner in which Montaigne is expressing his thoughts.

A consideration of technique in its turn reveals the extraordinary diversity of Montaigne's ways of talking about himself: he runs the whole gamut from ridicule to enthusiastic, almost over-persistent, praise. There is no doubt that he wants to be known; but he also wants this knowledge to take a certain course: 'Je propose une vie basse et sans lustre, c'est tout un. On attache aussi bien toute la philosophie morale à une vie populaire et privée que à une vie de plus riche estoffe: chaque homme porte la forme entiere de l'humaine condition' (iii: 2, 782). Modesty, and all his other techniques of communication (which will be discussed in the next chapter), hide a complex, self-conscious person whose urge to communicate his discovery of his own inner resources is powerful. (iii: 8, 899). He had realised the strength self-knowledge gives to men in times of adversity, and he was willing to tarnish his noble honour, if need be, in order to show others how to acquire a similar insight into themselves.

Modesty had the merit of being able to harmonise attitudes in Montaigne which had seemed irreconcilable. He wanted, as he explains in *De l'Oisiveté* (i: 8), to withdraw as much as he could from public life, and thus escape the lies and necessity to deceive which beset all servants of king, court, and country. Yet, as his self-knowledge increased, he felt the urge to tell the truth about himself for the benefit of others, knowing full well that the kind of truth he had to communicate would only prove of solid interest if the reader were made to participate fully in the discovery of self, and that this last desire would only prevail through those very methods of persuasion which he despised in the courtier he had fled.

A very sophisticated kind of moral intention lies, I feel, within Montaigne's manner of writing.[36] And he himself directs our attention to it: 'qu'on ne s'attende pas aux matieres, mais à la façon que j'y donne' (ii: 10, 387). He gives us a hint to look for it when he wrote of 'good faith', and he shows us the way as he defined the demands he knew he was making upon the reader whom he sees in the closest possible relationship with himself. He does not want to create a succession of Montaigne models, but he obviously hopes that we will be enlightened, and encouraged to think for ourselves by sharing as actively as possible in his thoughts and emotions. His aim is to communicate the *feel* of an idea or emotion, to allow you, as it were, to take it within your hands, turn it round, observe it from all angles, and to *know* it intimately. Such was the effect of fear generated in *De la peur* (1:18), and such too was the thorough knowledge he hoped to communicate of himself. On his own admission, he consciously adopted varied stylistic techniques to assault the reader, and keep him ever on the watch. Modesty is only one type of dissimulation so employed. There are others.

2

CONSCIOUSNESS OF STYLE

IT is always dangerous to write about an author's consciousness of style since it is a difficult matter to assess, and, indeed, one frequently tends to overestimate such self-awareness. Montaigne, however, positively encourages this approach by giving great prominence in the *Essais* to discussions on style. While it is true that he composed his essays in many different moods and in many different places, sometimes dictating to a secretary, and sometimes correcting his own printed copy of the *Essais*, it should be recognised that these two activities were not so disparate for Montaigne as they might seem to us. As a lawyer he had been trained to compose fairly complicated arguments orally, and to anticipate the mental excitement of engaging in discussion with similarly trained minds; as an avid reader he recognised the persuasive force of a show of accuracy and of a simple style. It is not surprising, therefore, that he should try to combine the sum of this experience in the *Essais* where his preferences for particular types of style are unequivocally stated.

Over the whole range of the work his opinions on this subject are remarkably consistent. Let us first consider the following:

> Le parler que j'ayme, c'est un parler simple et naïf, tel sur le papier qu'à la bouche; un parler succulent et nerveux, court et serré, non tant delicat et peigné comme vehement et brusque . . . plustost difficile qu'ennuieux, esloingné d'affectation, desreglé, descousu et hardy: chaque lopin y face son corps; non pedantesque, non fratesque, non pleideresque, mais plustost soldatesque. (1:26, 171)

Here, Montaigne sets out clearly his version of the ideal style; that is, a manner of writing which is forthright, frank, and entirely free from artifice of all kinds. He gives a schoolman's twist in the echoing suffixes at the end of this definition to emphasise, through irony, what his ideal style is not. It is precisely the specialists—schoolmen, priests, lawyers, and courtiers too—whom he has in mind. They are ignominiously bundled together since they all display the same significant flaw: their language is consciously removed from the reality it pretends to describe. Courtiers are, by the nature of their position, affected liars. The schoolmen, with their artifice, so transform experience that their definitions and descriptions bear no relation to feelings actually sustained: 'Mon page faict l'amour et l'entend. Lisez luy Leon Hébreu et Ficin: on parle de luy, de ses pensées et de ses actions, et si il n'y entend rien. Je ne recognois pas chez Aristote la plus part de mes mouvemens ordinaires, on les a couverts et revestus d'une autre robbe pour l'usage de l'eschole' (III: 5, 852).

That Montaigne feels very strongly about the distorting tendencies of their technical jargon is not only apparent in the irony latent in the passage just quoted, but it is also clear from the terms he always opposes to such artifice. 'Scholastique' and 'artiste' are directly contrasted with 'naturel' and 'sain' (III: 8, 904). Everything on the side of naivety is loaded with approval, while on the side of artifice, Montaigne goes to the length of borrowing Cicero's own judgement of the two verbose lawyers—Amafarius and Rabirius—in order to condemn the great Roman orator from his own mouth. The 'definitions', 'partitions', and 'conclusions' which Cicero criticised (but used himself) are very deliberately set by Montaigne against 'un parler informe et sans regle, un jargon populaire' (II: 17, 620)—the natural style adopted by his hero, Socrates (III: 12, 1031). Thus, everything which has to do with the distinctions, definitions, rhetorical divisions and intellectual niceties of the professionals is presented critically.

To take but one example: for more than half a century theologians and philosophers had argued about the meaning of the simple demonstrative term 'hoc' in the phrase 'hoc est enim corpus meum', surrounding it with mysterious definitions and incomprehensible terminology. Montaigne boldly takes them to task, attributing the greater part of the world's troubles to their arrogant affirmations. He goes so far as to point out that not only their method of reasoning but Language itself is fundamentally inadequate to say anything for certain, and, in an affirmative statement of his own, he asserts, 'Je ne trouve pas bon d'enfermer ainsi la puissance divine soubs les loix de nostre parolle' (II: 12, 507–8).[1] The theologians' quarrels about meaning, and their extraordinary ability to reduce every argument to a question of applying the cumbersome

methods and barbarous terms of contemporary logic aroused the criticism of many readers. Montaigne was certainly not alone in thinking
that their very procedure prevented serious discussion, or led to strange
distortions of the truth. Charles de la Ruelle in 1574, for instance, stated
in trenchant terms that 'souvent es oeuvres des doctes et habiles hommes,
se treuvent erreurs et hallucinations si lourdes, et ineptes, qu'il n'est
possible de plus'.[2] While the 'doctes' and 'habiles' had prepared the way
for civil war by insisting that the solution to religious strife lay in agree-
ing on the use and meaning of terms, Montaigne—convinced of the
wrong-headedness of this approach—sought to discover his spiritual
peace elsewhere. The degree to which he feared that religious upheaval
had been extended (and might be magnified further) by the discussion of
doctrinal problems in French, is confirmed by his friend Florimond de
Raemond who virtually repeats Montaigne's own words: 'Car la plus-
part de nos disputes en la religion sont Grammeriennes, Plaisantes gens
que les Pretendus Reformez, dict un bel esprit de nostre aage, (Montagne) qui pensent avoir desvoué les difficultez de la saincte parole,
pour l'avoir mise en langage populaire'.[3] It is not surprising, therefore,
that Montaigne struggled so obviously to distance his own way of
writing from the methods of the theologians and philosophers.

No less impassioned was his attack upon the schools which had
been responsible for training these specialists, and others: the lawyers,
for example, whose job (it seemed) was to exert all their efforts, regardless of the truth, to produce the beautifully rounded phrase and the
telling aphorism at the right moment. They had been taught to draw
attention to themselves and to their rhetorical skill, while their client's
interests remained incidental to their main purpose. In many respects,
the revival of learning had encouraged the view that style was more important than matter. And even Erasmus, for all the venom of his attacks
upon the Ciceronians, and his positive suggestions for the education of
children, had been unable to eradicate from the schools imitative methods
of learning which turned the student's mind away from thought and towards performance.[4] This point can perhaps be illustrated by La Ruelle
who devotes many pages of his short work to a severe attack on the
praises which were so liberally bestowed upon Erasmus's *Adages*. He
ridicules his friends who thought to have profited from accumulating
several hundred of such sayings, summing up their work and that of
their master as 'peine et labeur perdu, si onques il y en eut': their efforts
were no more than 'ravauderie pedantesque'.[5] Montaigne would have
agreed with these sentiments, for although he appreciated the usefulness

of pithy phrases for provoking thought and used them himself, he objected to thoughtless and uncritical accumulation of the aphorisms of others. In addition, he could not have ignored the sixteenth-century controversies over Cicero's style since they raised the very same problem which he found so disturbing : namely, the fact that words used merely for their own sake had a stultifying effect on the mind. He was convinced that the schools catered well for their professional clientele, but did nothing for the non-specialist. They taught you to talk, but not to communicate.[6]

There is an interesting passage in *Considération sur Cicéron* (1:40, 246) where Montaigne sets his own style—describing it as 'comique et privé . . . trop serré, desordonné, couppé, particulier'—beside the grandiloquence of Cicero's speech which he dismisses, along with many of his own contemporaries, as 'abjecte et servile prostitution de présentations'. In most contexts one would interpret the adjectives which Montaigne uses to describe his own performance as somewhat derogatory in tone : yet it will be noticed that not only do they contrast specifically with the dismissive tone used to describe Cicero's art, but that they also accord very well with the 'natural look' lauded by Montaigne in the passage cited at the beginning of this chapter.[7] Eloquence is nearly always defined as verbosity in Montaigne, and it is rejected precisely because it does not fulfil the demands he made upon style. It could not communicate. The architect, for instance, when he mouths 'ces gros mots de pilastres, architraves, corniches, d'ouvrage Corinthien et Dorique' conjuring up the beauties of the 'palais d'Apolidon' is, in fact, merely describing 'les chetives pieces de la porte de ma cuisine' (1:51, 294). Ficino's writing on love bears no resemblance to actual experience (III:5,852). The orator meddles with people's emotions, rouses their laughter or their tears through the force of his false rhetoric (III:4, 816); or, alternatively, he sends you to sleep with his long-windedness, with his 'prefaces, definitions, partitions, etymologies', and with his scintillating 'ordonnances logiciennes et Aristoteliques' which have no relevance to the matter in hand. Eloquence flourishes, Montaigne affirms, in states which are on the point of collapse, and at times when civil war rages rampant. Such, he reminds us in an oft-repeated truism, was the case when Rome had lost all her moral fibre, and such is the case now in France (1:51,293). It is against the background of civil strife, brought about by specialist verbal quarrels, that Montaigne sought an unpretentious language which would neither confuse nor act as a soporific. He needed, above all, a manner of writing which would keep his readers on the alert : 'Ny les subtilitez grammariennes, ny l'ingenieuse contexture de parolles et d'argumentations n'y servent' (II:10,393).[8]

Unequivocal, truthful, frank, spontaneous, brusque, natural, colloquial, lively—these are the terms Montaigne most often applies both to his ideal of style, and to that which he himself employs. The word 'natural' occurs most frequently, and seems to sum up his thought on the best manner of writing for his own particular purposes, since it both describes what he tries to do with words, and it points to the appropriateness of this conception of writing for him. A simple style is 'natural' to him; it is becoming (I:40,243); it belongs to his mind and temperament as well as to his aim. This plea for the personal, and for an individuality which reflects his personality faithfully, doubtless explains such insistence as 'J'ai faict ce que j'ay voulu; tout le monde me reconnoit en mon livre, et mon livre en moy' (III:5,853). He seems less concerned here with possessive claims for originality than with accuracy. The tone of affirmation and satisfaction convey his sense of achievement at having rendered his thoughts, feelings, and observations with clarity.

It is important to realise that Montaigne's view of the natural style does not mean that he believes in spontaneous writing, or in some unthinking exercise. In the statement about the individual nature of his style, he shows himself fully conscious of the need for one particular style rather than another. Furthermore, his fondness for controlling his mental and stylistic activities would preclude any impulsive record of them: 'Je n'ay guere de mouvement qui se cache et desrobe à ma raison' (III:2,790). Though he admits that much happens within us over which we have no power, and about which we have little understanding, he is adamant in his refusal to accord any value to such movements; 'Or ces passions qui ne nous touchent que par l'escorse, ne peuvent se dire nostres. Pour les faire nostres, il faut que l'homme y soit engagé tout entier' (II:6,356). In fact, total commitment necessarily involves the mental control and judgement which Montaigne prizes above all.[9] Although such insistence on the value of consciousness sometimes limits Montaigne's field of discovery,[10] the ever-present controlling 'I' of the narrator or thinker gives to his work an impression of frank communication. In the *Essais* there is a considerable distance between the spontaneity which Montaigne initially wants the reader to imagine as giving form to his ideas, and the studied naivety which, in fact, he used.

One might think, when reading Montaigne's comments on style, that he alone among sixteenth-century writers had this particular ideal of naivety. It is true that such a view of style was not particularly common to prose writers (though after the 1580 publication of the *Essais* it was to become more so). Naturalness was nevertheless one of the criteria of good style set by the Pléiade poets, and both Du Bellay and Ronsard refer to 'un art caché qui ne semble pas art'.[11]

Montaigne seems at great pains to achieve this effect of a style which disappears, as it were; of a manner which is not noticed by the reader; so that, when he does draw attention to his way of writing, he can do so at moments when it is convenient to stress its naivety. 'Mon stile et mon esprit vont vagabondant de mesme' (III:9,973) says Montaigne, telling us how haphazard his compositions are. He makes the same claim in *Du parler prompt ou tardif* (I: 10,41): while the work of others 'puent l'huyle et la lampe', his own spoken style (he insists) owes its power to the secret workings of chance: 'l'occasion, la compaignie, le branle mesme de ma voix'. When Montaigne is overcome by the concern to project this natural image of himself, he seems virtually to contradict all the claims he has made for the importance of being consciously in control of thoughts. Thus it is that, in the process of defending his untidiness, Montaigne insists that the ideas which are produced spontaneously and without effort are the most to be admired; 'les moins tandues et plus naturelles alleures de nostre ame sont les plus belles' (III: 3,798), and he goes on to ward off possible criticism by maintaining that he has many times proved the truth of this statement through his own experience. 'I throw myself onto the page', he contends literally, 'with such eagerness that I've no idea of the impression that I've created'. It is not easy to accept the truth of such a statement when one considers the care taken by Montaigne to launch the idea that his writing was truly simple and artless. Indeed in one place he is sufficiently incautious as to admit that he was not always successful in his efforts 'de vouloir eviter l'art et l'affectation' (II: 17,621).

Rarely forgetting to remind us that his arguments wander all over the place, Montaigne litters his essays with expressions such as, 'pour revenir à mon propos' (II: 11,409), 'reprendre le fil' (II: 37,765), 'à ma fantaisie' (I: 23,113), and even more pointedly 'retombons à nos coches' (III: 6,894). In other places he will compare his work to a patchwork quilt, or to a poor piece of marquetry, brought together by chance. Equally self-consciously, he pin-points the innumerable times his arguments take a side-turning from his main theme: 'à gauche de mon theme' (II: 27,677), or 'Cette farcisseure est un peu hors de mon theme. Je m'esgare, mais plustot par licence que par mesgarde' (III: 9,973). He defends licence—such as introducing information which has nothing to do with his subject—by suggesting that order is unimportant, and that significance rests in facts alone, regardless of the moment at which such facts appear in the argument (ii:27,678). And again, he will inform you that he has three facts to communicate, and then add 'd'où d'ay perdu la troisiesme et en suis bien marry' (i:31,212). As Du Plessis remarked, some years later, 'Confusion de matières desennuie l'esprit, et le contente plus qu'un ordre exact, et exquis'.[12] Whether we agree with Du Plessis or not, Montaigne's wanderings do suggest that we are communing with a mind revealing its thoughts at the moment of their conception, entirely free from the shaping process which the conscious artist gives to his work. This impression of closeness to a mind thinking aloud on the page is further enhanced by Montaigne's apparently careless statements: 'poursuivons donc, puis que nous y sommes' (i:48,278); 'en voici d'un autre cuvée' (i:23,117), as though he just thought of it at that second—a tendency which seems almost lackadaisical in such a comment as 'a propos ou hors de propos, il n'importe' (iii:11,1011). It is rare to read a page of Montaigne which does not contain some self-conscious parenthesis designed to interrupt the even flow of thought, some jerky or disjointed phrase which arrests the reader and sets him thinking. There is no doubt that such a style rivets attention; we make sure that we are following the argument which Montaigne tells us is wandering; and we are immediately involved in deciding for ourselves whether something is relevant or not, revealing or otherwise. It is as though we are there in Montaigne's study, listening to his words as they come now stuttering, now streaming from his head.[13]

That Montaigne himself was aware of this impression can be judged from the number of times he compares writing and speaking. For a lawyer, there might well have been little distinction between these two activities, especially when he is thinking about style. 'Je parle au papier comme je parle au premier que je rencontre' (iii:1,767) he states, deliberately underlining the point which seems to recur again and again: that a reading of the *Essais* is no more or less than partaking in a real conversation with the author. He says so in as many words when talking of himself in the passage addressed to Madame de Duras at the end of *De la ressemblance des enfans aux peres* (ii:37,763): 'Vous y reconnoistrez ce mesme port et ce mesme air que vous avez veu en sa conversation'.

There are times when this feeling of presence is made more acute, such as when Montaigne begins a proposition with 'considérez', or ends it with an expression such as 'prenez-y garde' (iii:10,991), or when he addresses you directly, or confidentially, with a 'voulez-vous voir cela' and continues 'sentez', 'voyez', 'oyez' (ii:12,487–8), as though you were indeed there to feel, see, and hear.[14] Occasionally, however, he achieves such a degree of contact with the reader that it is difficult to decide whether he is speaking in his own voice or whether he is assuming that of the reader. He moves with disconcerting ease through all the personal pronouns, 'tu', 'vous', 'nous', 'on': only the context allows one to discover whether he is speaking for himself, for all men, or whether he has a specific reader in mind. Is he merely talking to himself when, referring to his state of health, he declares 'mon bon homme, c'est faict' (III: 13, 1067)? Is he not speaking for the reader as well as himself when he states 'pauvre fol que tu es' (1: 20, 83)? That he does sometimes assume a kind of complicity between himself and the 'suffisant lecteur' seems clear from the number of times (increasingly in Book III) that he whispers: 'entre-nous' (III: 13, 1095).[15]

Montaigne himself realized that the Essay form gave him a much greater freedom to adjust his language to the needs of each idea and to the expectation of his potential readers than the Discourse, Dialogue, or the Letter forms which were so popular with his contemporaries.[16] Without limiting himself to the specific demands of any one of these forms, he could integrate them—and other forms such as the Socratic dialogue—into the looser structures of the Essay, when he needed them. He was, he admitted, attracted to the Letter form, precisely because it implied the closest possible contact with, and knowledge of, the reader: 'et eusse prins plus volontiers ceste forme à publier mes verves, si j'eusse eu à qui parler' (1: 40, 246).[17] He coveted the stimulation which comes from lively discussion, and this was how his contemporaries defined the letter form: 'toute epistre ou lettre missive n'est autre chose que aux absens *parler comme presens*'.[18] Yet, as Fabri himself goes on to stress, you need to know your correspondent intimately in order to adjust your style to his way of thinking.[19] That Montaigne knew no such person is fortunate for us in so far as he was obliged to develop an infinitely flexible writing instrument, capable of making each individual reader feel that the author is speaking personally to him.[20]

Floyd Gray has shown how important Montaigne's syntax is in this process of drawing the reader into a much closer contact with the material of the *Essais*.[21] The slow build-up of fragments of sentences keeps the reader's curiosity engaged. The instance which Professor Gray examines in detail concerns the Black Prince:

> Edouard, prince de Galles, celuy qui regenta si longtemps nostre
> Guienne, personnage, duquel les conditions et la fortune ont beaucoup

de notables parties de grandeur, ayant esté bien fort offencé par les Limosins, et prenant leur ville par force, ne peut etre arresté par les cris du peuple, et des femmes, et enfans abandonnez à la boucherie, luy criants mercy, et se jettans à ses pieds, jusqu'à ce passant tousjours outre dans la ville, il apperceut trois gentils hommes François, qui d'une hardiesse incroyable soustenoyent seuls l'effort de son armée victorieuse. La consideration et le respect d'une si notable vertu reboucha premierement la pointe de sa cholere: et commença par ces trois, à faire misericorde à tous les autres habitans de la ville. (I: 1, 11)

What the critic failed to mention, however, is that the procedure which keeps the reader in suspense (since the resolution of the first long sentence is delayed to the very end) seems to have been a feature of sixteenth-century prose. Lestoile, for instance, often indulges in such long sentences.[22] The device was also frequently employed by story-tellers who wished at once to please the reader by a swift and economical way of presenting facts, and to give as much information as possible. We know that Montaigne had a large collection of anecdotal literature in his Library, and he doubtless appreciated that the humour of a Des Periers tale, for example, often depended on the attributes of a character being quickly given.[23] Or, to take another instance of a similar technique, consider the thirty-third story told by the Queen of Navarre, which begins thus:

Le comte Charles d'Angoulême, père du roi François, premier de ce nom, prince fidèle et craignant Dieu, étant à Cognac, quelqu'un lui raconta qu'en un village près de là, nommé Cherves, y avoit une fille vierge, vivant si austèrement, que c'étoit une chose admirable; laquelle toutefois étoit trouvée grosse, ce qu'elle ne dissimuloit point, assurant à tout le peuple que jamais n'avoit connu homme et qu'elle ne savoit comme le cas lui étoit advenu, sinon que ce fût oeuvre du Saint-Esprit; ce que le peuple croyoit facilement, et la tenoit et réputoit comme une seconde vierge Marie; car chacun connoissoit que, dès son enfance, elle étoit si sage, que jamais n'eut en elle un seul signe de mondanité.[24]

This long sentence speedily gives all the information necessary for a correct appreciation of the story. First the credentials of the listener are established: Charles d'Angoulême, as both a prince and a faithful Christian, hears the story in a specific place at a specific time. No one is going to doubt the veracity of such a figure. Then the saintly gullibility of the girl has to be underlined, if the sophisticated reader is to swallow the fact that she believed herself pregnant through the agency of the Holy Ghost. A final touch is added, assuring us of the fact that everybody who knew the girl believed the story and even thought of her as a second Virgin Mary, so that all doubt about the truth of the story might be removed. Now Marguerite can, with confidence, elaborate her story. If we return to the example from Montaigne, which occurs in the very first essay of Book I, it will be seen that he has already mastered the technique of so ordering his words that the reader's attention may be engaged and directed. The story he has to recount is similarly incredible. It is, nevertheless, a fact; and from this fact Montaigne derives the maximum effect of surprise by preparing for it slowly and methodically. Such control over the pattern of a long sentence argues the opposite of a 'natural' style; and yet, when this anecdote is first read, its effect *seems* spontaneous.

This juxtaposition of anecdotes is not intended to reduce Montaigne's originality. It is simply a means of trying to consider Montaigne's remarks on style, and his own performance, within their contemporary context. Montaigne has told us so often that his style is unlettered and non-professional that we are inclined to believe him. Such belief should not, however, obscure the fact that Montaigne has engineered this impression, and that he has been able to do it not only through the natural gift of genius, but through a knowledge of the sources, ancient and contemporary, dealing with methods whereby a reader might be affected. Anecdote, accumulation, and similitude, were recognised means of persuasion, frequently used by story-tellers, moralists, and historians.[25] Familiar taps on the shoulder, such as those we have examined at some length, are enjoyed as frequently by the 'benevoles lecteurs' of Rabelais as by the 'graziosissime donne' of Boccaccio. And it is no coincidence, I think, that Montaigne praises both these authors because they are 'simplement plaisans'.[26] They both arouse the reader, and they both have a natural air: two qualities which Montaigne prized above all else in a writer.[27]

Like all writers who set out to provoke a reaction, Montaigne studies closely the expectation of his readers. Thus *Sur des vers de Virgile* (III:5) is, as its title suggests, largely concerned with style not so much because Montaigne was afraid to shock the delicate ears of an assumed female audience—they were doubtless avid readers of the large numbers of editions of the *contes* and *facéties* of Du Fail, Des Periers, and others—nor simply because he wished to titillate them, but rather because a full realization of the proper manner of speaking about such things as sex was fundamental to an understanding of Montaigne's intention. In this

essay we catch Montaigne at the heart of his main problem: what is the
best language to convey thoughts and feelings to others? He feels that
even the most intimate details of love should be talked about with frankness and accuracy; his open-minded temperament constantly told him so.
Yet, he knows, from his own response to literature, that the most forceful
impact is not always made through such directness. The verses which he
quotes from Virgil suggest the highest point of passion: yet details such
as nakedness and gesture are omitted, 'Venus n'est pas si belle toute nue,
et vive, et haletante, comme elle est icy chez Virgile' (III:5,826). Thus,
for all his talk of nakedness, naivety, and naturalness, Montaigne app-
reciates that these qualities are not always the most effective.

Montaigne did not exclude himself from the general run of human
beings whom he saw so peculiarly susceptible to the power of words.
Rather, he frequently displayed a highly emotional response to the force
of another's writings. In *De la phisionomie*, for example, (III:12,1016–7)
he compares the styles of Seneca and Plutarch when they write about
death. The first impresses him by reason of its emotive force as Seneca
sweats and heaves, and desperately tries to steel himself against death.
But Plutarch's manner, cool and calm, is the more convincing: 'celuy-
là ravit nostre jugement, celuy-ci le gaigne'. This aesthetic sense, which
we also observed in his comments on Virgil, shows how quickly he was
impressed by the style of an author, and how he judged the effectiveness
of impact and aesthetic worth together.[28] And it is interesting to note
that the bulk of his considerations of ancient authors are concerned with
effect. Seneca and Plutarch are admirable because of the degree to which
they impinge upon the mind: 'Celuy là vous eschauffe plus, et vous
esmeut; cestuy-cy vous contente davantage et vous paye mieux. Il nous
guide, l'autre nous pousse' (II:10,393). Their work is equally 'belle'
and 'profitable'. Terence is appreciated for the effectiveness, and for the
force, with which he renders the movements of the human mind (*Ibid*,
391); the affected notes of Italian and Spanish poets are rejected in
favour of Martial and Catullus who 'se font assez sentir' (*Ibid*, 391). In a
late addition to this same chapter Montaigne finds the confidence to
commit 'cette sacrilege audace'—of disliking the dialogue manner of
Plato—simply because he finds this particular style of argument long-
winded and boring. Montaigne is here making explicit an attitude which
has guided both his response to the work of others, and the writing of
his *Essais:* you must mould your style in such a way that the reader's
attention is caught, and that his thinking mechanism is set in motion.

Montaigne's admiration of poetry can probably be explained in the same way. Convinced of the intensity of its effects, of its power of persuasion through the degree of emotion generated, he gave it a very high status: 'on peut faire le sot par tout ailleurs, mais non en la Poesie' (ii: 17,618). He frequently returns to the power poetry exerted over him, describing its effect most strongly, perhaps, in *Du jeune Caton*: 'Dès ma premiere enfance, la poësie a eu cela, de me transpercer et transporter' (i: 37,228).[29] His own comment on those lines of Virgil speaks for itself: 'Quand je voy ces braves formes de s'expliquer, si vifves, si profondes, je ne dicts pas que c'est bien dire, je dicts que c'est bien penser' (iii: 5,850-1). Polish the style and truth is perfected. Moreover, something well said leaves its mark,[30] and this was no sudden 'volteface'. Montaigne does not mean that he now approves of ideas which stressed exclusively the importance of style over matter; he was convinced that they went together, and from their union, pleasure—and possibly persuasion—would naturally follow.

It should not surprise us, therefore, to find in the *Essais* (almost alongside statements of disorder and naivety) lapidary phrases, turned and polished to clinch an argument or sum up a position. He shared his contemporaries' admiration for the pithy phrase, the motto or the proverb which, through its conciseness, stimulated both pleasure and thought.[31] This style was emulated by the courtiers, used by the diplomats, and cherished by the schoolmen. The most artificially contrived formulation, it was recognised, frequently controlled the maximum effect. In Montaigne, such sayings range from virtual translations of Senecan maxims—'Il est incertain où la mort nous attende, attendons-la partout. La premeditation de la mort est premeditation de la liberté. Qui a apris à mourir, il a desapris à servir' (i: 20,85),[32] which echo throughout the sixteenth-century literature devoted to such considerations—to the more personalised: 'Je voudrois . . . luy choisir un conducteur qui eust plutost la teste bien faicte que bien pleine' (i: 26,149). This tendency to coin a memorable phrase declared itself early in Montaigne's writing, and these two examples are taken from essays composed in 1572 and in 1578. His ability to write such phrases becomes more and more pronounced. He takes care to balance his words perfectly, giving them force by making concrete and abstract notions depend upon the same element of syntax, 'et plus je m'estois chargé de monnoye, plus aussi je m'estois chargé de crainte' (i: 14,65); or by repetition of all the words in the first part of the construction except two: 'Chacun fuit à le voir naistre, chacun suit à le voir mourir' (iii: 5,856). Sometimes, he reinforces their impact by straight alliteration, as when he writes—

half-playfully, half-solemnly—of God's promises: 'pour dignement les imaginer, il faut les imaginer inimaginables, indicibles et incomprehensibles' (ii: 12,499). Or sometimes the alliteration might suddenly change, as in 'cette morne, muette et sourde stupidité' (i: 2,16) where the three adjectives are chosen to give multiple meaning and emphasis to the word we had waited for: 'stupidité'.

Balanced antitheses, and play upon the sound of words or upon their meaning, seem rarely in Montaigne the products of a mind merely indulging its love of a phrase happily made; although he obviously likes manipulating words as, for example, when describing philosophy as 'cette lacheté voyelle . . . ny cordiale . . . ny stomacale' (ii: 37,739). On such a subject Montaigne can hardly resist the temptation to indulge in Rabelaisian tricks of satire, where one word suggests another, and so on. Most often, however, he binds together very firmly his intention and the manner of his expression—the manner, indeed, implying the thought. Emphasis, succinctness, and even emotion is contained in the alliteration (added later) 'Combien ay—je veu de condemnations, plus crimineuses que le crime' (iii: 13, 1048). The pleasure we derive from the play on words, 'Il faict laid se battre en s'esbatalnt' (iii: 8,918)—although it was another late addition to the essays—becomes for us the first step in the thought process which Montaigne is trying to encourage. There are times when the brevity of a phrase renders the meaning difficult of access; and, although Montaigne believed that something which resists is a source of pleasure and therefore a means of learning, he was not willing to accept obscurity as the price of a fine phrase. For this reason he explains the implications of 'ils laissent là les choses, et s'amusent à traiter les causes' (iii: 11, 1003), and pinpoints the meaning of the opposition 'nous nous preparons aux occasions eminents plus par gloire que par conscience' (iii: 2,787). When he refers to Death, as 'bien le bout, non pourtant le but de la vie' (iii: 12, 1028), he is not just coining a phrase which Seneca would have been pleased with, he is pulling sharply into focus the fact of his complete change of attitude towards Death. A similar fine distinction in the meaning of words which assonate together can be seen in: 'La curiosité est vicieuse par tout, mais elle est pernicieuse icy' (iii: 5,847). The reader is made to reflect upon the different degrees of intensity given in the two adjectives, and, at the same time, to appreciate their difference in general and particular terms.

It is, of course, impossible to say for certain whether such well-turned phrases were natural to Montaigne's way of thinking and writing; or whether, while pondering on the right word to use, he suddenly

alighted upon a 'jeu de mots' which would make his point most forcibly;
or, again, whether he deliberately sought out such a manner. Any sixteenth-century writer whose knowledge and use of Latin was as considerable as his ability to write in French would naturally reproduce the
syntactical symmetry and echoing sounds which especially characterise
that language. What one can say is that there are literally hundreds of
brief, compact, and suggestive phrases in the *Essais*. Most of them unite
thought and expression so successfully that they might well argue the
conscious control of their author.[33] Others—and these are fewer in
number—contain a certain obviousness, together with a note of self-
satisfaction, such as 'que les haires ne rendent pas tousjours heres ceux
qui les portent' (ii:33,706), or 'je m'esgare, mais plustot par licence
que par mesgarde', (iii:9,973) suggesting that Montaigne was possibly
searching intently for such a formulation. Where the wordplay is the
result of a later modification to the *Essais*, one is tempted to argue that
Montaigne was consciously drawing our attention to a specific point.
There are many instances of this process as, for example, in his expressed
wish that there were more writers like Diogenes Laertius: 'Ou qu'il ne
soit ou plus estendu ou plus entendu' (ii:10,396). The addition of 'entendu' encourages the reader to think more about the implications of the
whole phrase, since he is asked to distinguish clearly between 'estendu'
and 'entendu'. I suspect that there are other times when some of Montaigne's most significant discoveries come from a pondering upon the
right word, the correct tense, the best mode of argument. 'Veut-elle
tousjours ce que nous voudrions qu'elle vousist?' (i:21,101) seems to
me to be such a case, where the artistic urge plays as large a role in the
making of thought, as does conscious meditation of the thought itself.
Here we have Montaigne who sets such store upon being able to control
his thoughts, who sets such a premium upon being conscious of mental
activity, suddenly discovering—because of an artistic need—that the
mind works independently of our conscious will.

The urge to awaken the reader to a serious state of affairs ob-
scured by habit or sentiment often explains the rather careful structuring
that Montaigne gives to certain phrases. In the following example he is
anxious to make the full force of the triple nouns 'cruauté', 'tyrannie',
'trahison', strike deeply. Realising that the meaning of these terms—
through the use made of them in the civil wars—had been considerably
diluted, he prepares for their impact very deliberately:

C'est passetemps aus meres de veoir un enfant tordre le col à un poulet, et s'esbatre à blesser un chien et un chat; et tel pere est si sot de prendre à bon augure d'une ame martiale, quand il voit son fils gourmer injurieusement un païsant ou un laquay qui ne se defend point, et à gentillesse, quand il le void affiner son compagnon par quelque malicieuse desloyauté et tromperie. Ce sont pourtant les vrayes semences et racines de la cruauté, de la tyrannie, de la trahyson. (i: 23, 107-8)

A series of contrasts, 'passetemps/tordre le col', 's'esbattre/à blesser', 'sot/bon augure', are presented. The two examples of the mother's reaction are quickly given; but the father's response is more long-drawn-out, and consequently more insistent. Montaigne gives us time to reflect on the oppositions, and, by the time we come to the triple nouns, we are ready to seize their serious implications. This example was added very late to the essay, and there is ample evidence in the *Essais* to suggest that Montaigne arrived at this degree of skill through imitation—an acknowledged artificial means of perfecting one's style.

He admits freely that, in speech, 'j'ay une condition singeresse et imitatrice' (iii: 5, 853), and it is easy to see that his awareness of many different styles, and appreciation of their effects, made him equally susceptible to imitation when writing. Although it has been well argued[34] that straight stylistic confrontation of Seneca and Montaigne, for example, is dangerous since the former's aphoristic manner of writing was held in esteem and copied by many sixteenth-century writers, the essayist nevertheless does seem at times to model his manner very consciously upon that of the ancient Stoic. In the essay, *Que le goust des biens et des maux dépend en bonne partie de l'opinion que nous en avons*, Montaigne, at moments, not only translates Seneca and Cicero almost verbatim or arranges their phrases of comfort in a different order—the kind of transforming imitation praised by the generation of the Pléiade— but, in the disjointed phrases describing pain ('tu ne la sentiras guiere long temps, si tu la sens trop; elle mettra fin à soy, ou à toy: l'un et l'autre revient à un. Si tu ne la portes, elles t'emportera', i: 14, 57) he seems to be mirroring what he called the 'pointes et saillies' of Seneca much more closely. What is important, however, is not so much that Montaigne wilfully copied Seneca's manner because he liked a jerky style, but that he copied it because the style was appropriate to his present needs. He was prepared to take over, absorb, or modify, any style which most perfectly expressed his matter. In another place, *De l'inconstance de nos actions*, the same copying technique is apparent:[35]

the quickly shifting moods of the Senecan original is adopted by Montaigne to underscore the constantly changing nature of the human mind.[36] 'Ce que nous avons à cett' heure proposé, nous le changeons tantost, et tantost encore retournons sur nos pas . . . Nous n'allons pas; on nous emporte, comme les choses qui flottent, ores doucement, ores avecques violence' (II: 1, 316). Once more, manner and matter are inextricably bound together.

If we examine briefly other examples of Montaigne's ability to assume different styles as the moment called for them, we shall begin to appreciate the kind of training Montaigne had given himself, and which he sought nonchalantly to hide. Thus, his experience as a lawyer stood him in good stead when he needed to accumulate evidence against the philosophers and their manner of writing. At many points in the *Apologie* he sustains, relentlessly, the same construction; and, like a gramophone needle caught in a groove, he continues until we are moved to beg him to stop, to tell him that we agree, if only for the sake of peace. We are virtually battered into submission by the infinitive constructions, the conditional clauses, and the repeated questions (II: 12, 428-9). The same technique has a different effect later in the essay, where Montaigne adopts the formal register of the very style he criticises in order to reduce it and its method to ridicule: the reiterated 'ainsi' over three pages (II: 12, 585–8) and the obsessive 'donc' over two (II: 12, 511–12) are used, maliciously, to expose the dangers of syllogistic logic-chopping which is solely concerned with the form of an argument and not its content, and to prove conclusions as absurd as 'nous avons besoing de nourriture, aussi ont donc les Dieux'. The entire sequence of 'donc's' is neatly rounded off with Montaigne simultaneously asking for admiration for his virtuoso performance while not excluding himself from the criticism: 'enfle toy, pauvre homme, et encore, et encore, et encore'. Unlike La Fontaine's frog, Montaigne, the self-conscious artist and the satirist, can stop at the critical moment. Like all good writers of satire Montaigne has to be able to imitate seriously the style he seeks to ridicule. His virtuosity has convinced us, and he rarely asks for more;[37] though it might be argued that his love of accumulation sometimes gets the better of him and that the original purpose of the lists and reiterations is lost as he strives, for instance, to imitate the 'tintamare de tant de cervelles philosophiques' (II: 12, 496).[38] Far from adopting the philosophical position of Sextus Empiricus, he had simply imitated his method. And I imagine that Montaigne was much more influenced by the lively mockery in Sextus's attack on the *Matematicos* than by the more arid formulations of the *Pyrrhoniarum Hypotyposes*.[39] A similar satirical effect is engineered when Montaigne allows Mexican natives to imitate the hollow eloquence of the Spanish style. When the conquerors 'à la queste de leurs mines . . . firent . . . leurs remonstrances accoustumées' (III:6,889) they found the tables neatly turned upon them as each point of their speech was systematically answered and countered with a series of 'Quant à' which start off as measured and logical, but which acquire a more menacing tone as they accumulate. The Spaniard has been outplayed at his own game.

Syllogism, considered by contemporary writers on dialectic as the most important feature of their skill,[40] was thought by Montaigne to be the biggest obstacle to thought. Students were made to master series of barbarous terms such as 'Barroco' which Montaigne demonstrates could more easily be used to arrive at such inane conclusions as: 'le jambon fait boire, le boire desaltere, parquoy le jambon desaltere' (I:26,170). Not many years before Montaigne composed this syllogism, Ramus had defended this form of dialectic as being the only means of ensuring good judgement. Man, he had said,

> est souvent troublé et trompé par erreur d'opinion, car, par amour, hayne, envie, crainte, cupidité et autres trompeuses affections nous concluons bien souvent plustost que par solide et constant jugement du syllogisme, il fault doncques exciter et remettre, sus ce tant grand jugement de l'esprit et l'establir par constance et verité du syllogisme, autrement nostre conclusion sera légiéreté, erreur, témérité, non jugement.[41]

It is precisely on the grounds that Ramus chose to place his argument that Montaigne mounts his attack. Far from guaranteeing sound judgement, as Ramus claimed, syllogisms, in Montaigne's view, distort the truth. And to make his points most convincingly he has recourse to parody using the structures advocated by contemporary rhetoric and abused by the professionals. By playing their logical game ruthlessly, he exposes the weaknesses of their method.

Indeed, there seems scarcely a role which Montaigne is unwilling to assume as long as he can keep his reader interested. He admired Plutarch because he was 'le seul autheur du monde qui n'a jamais soulé ne dégousté les hommes, se montrant aux lecteurs tousjours tout autre, et fleurissant tousjours en nouvelle grace' (II:36,731), and he himself had no difficulty in adding diversity to the list of contemporary criteria of good style (simplicity, brevity, imitation) which he already practised.[42]

Indeed, it would not be difficult to find all the most obvious feats achieved by contemporary writers of French prose in the *Essais:* ideas, for example, which depend on the constant repetition of one element of syntax. The famous list of sixty-eight verbs, which Montaigne used to describe the complexity of man's gestures, had been equalled by Sebillet in his *Paradoxe contre l'Amour*, and no doubt by many others.[43] Amyot was as addicted as Montaigne to the use of triple nouns, adjectives, and verbs which were considered elegant as well as emphatic. And even Ambroise Paré showed himself equally concerned to catch the sound of the spoken voice or the noise of battle.[44] They were all aware of, and excited by, the expressive resources of the French language. But it is not my purpose to try to prove that Montaigne wrote like his contemporaries, or to challenge the truth of his own remarks when he insists that his style is different from theirs. It seems obvious that his emphasis on difference is made against the background of professional abuse of forms of the language. It is enough to show that Montaigne diversified his use of the possibilities of expression which were available to him both in French and in his favourite Latin authors, and that his handling of them argues not a naïve practitioner but a consummate artist who, nearly always, knew exactly what he was doing. A thought well-expressed— that is, expressed appropriately—can appear 'natural' or 'contrived' according to Montaigne's purpose.

Amid the myriad examples which one might quote to illustrate the range of Montaigne's stylistic ability, let us consider two important areas: the image, and Montaigne's narrative skill. The image is fundamental to Montaigne's methods of discussion, and he uses it in a variety of ways.[45] It can crown an argument, as when he sums up his views on knowledge, 'en quelque main, c'est un sceptre; en quelque autre, une marrotte' (III:8,905). It can clinch another by giving such an air of finality that any contradiction seems impossible—an effect which acquires even more bite when the metaphor is personalised, as in 'je marche plus seur et plus ferme à mont qu'à val' (I:26,149). It can equally well clarify a point which might otherwise be difficult to accept: Montaigne's description of his attitude to thought and decision-making is made convincing by his comparison 'tout ainsi que des chemins, j'en evite volontiers les costez pandans et glissans, et me jette dans le battu le plus boueux et enfondrant, d'où je ne puisse aller plus bas, et y cherche seurté'(II:17, 627-8). Most often it seems to circumvent the need for discussion altogether, acting of itself, as a proof or confirmation of the arguments Montaigne is putting forward, such as this image, 'L'archer qui outrepasse

le blanc, faut comme celuy qui n'y arrive pas' (1:30, 195), which seems
to offer the best reason to the reader for not over-reaching himself. By
means of the image Montaigne can ensure the reader's pleasure in a
comparison which might be both apt and delightful—as, for instance, his
reference to the gaiety which the reflective power of the mind can bring
to old age: 'qu'il verdisse, qu'il fleurisse ce pendant, s'il peut, comme le
guy sur un arbre mort' (III:5, 821). Or it can bring the reader as close
as possible to the author's own state of mind. In the following example
our response to the image of the fly and the *ventouse* has been calculated
in advance, for Montaigne knows that we find them unpleasant, dis-
agreeable things. Playing on this knowledge, and with an acute sense
of observation, he makes the fly's activities immediate, and makes us feel,
distastefully, the sucking of the *ventouse*, so that we easily share the
strength of his disapproval:

> Je hay un esprit hargneux et triste qui glisse par dessus les plaisirs
> de sa vie et s'empoigne et paist aux malheurs: comme les mouches,
> qui ne peuvent tenir contre un corps bien poly et bien lissé, et s'attach-
> ent et reposent aux lieux scabreux et raboteux; et comme les van-
> touses qui ne hument et appetent que le mauvais sang. (III:
> 5, 822)

Such proximity of reader and author is made even more sharp
when one considers Montaigne's anecdotes. These frequently seem to
lose their argumentative function and take on an air of entertainment,
for the characters are quickly brought to life, whether it be the old man
whose presence is sketched in by the narrator—'C'est injustice de voir
qu'un pere vieil, cassé et demi-mort, jouysse seul, à un coin du foyer'
(II:8, 367); or whether Montaigne himself takes on the role and speaks
in the voice of a king (1:42, 258). Yet the entertainment is part of the
argument. The old man is not depicted sympathetically, and Montaigne
loads our response. He ensures that we enjoy his anecdotes by beginning
his tale in a leisurely way, and then by suddenly injecting a sense of
excitement which we hardly expected so soon: 'Passant avant hier dans
un vilage, à deux lieues de ma maison, je trouvay la place encore toute
chaude d'un miracle qui venoit d'y faillir, (III:11, 1006). These are the
opening words of the story about the ease with which people believe in
miracles. It will be noticed that the expression 'encore toute chaude' not
only communicates the excitement of the inhabitants of the village, and
rouses similar expectation in us, it also carries a touch of the irony which becomes, almost immediately, the dominant note of the story. Sometimes

Montaigne bounces into the middle of his narration with a comment which takes all the grimness out of the story, as when he slips 'qui pis est' into his tale of the Sieur de Licques who got himself made prisoner on his wedding day. On other occasions, he will self-consciously interrupt his argument, reminding you that he knows what he's doing, and thus forestalling all criticism. It is in this way that he excuses an extended Latin quotation with the parenthesis '(j'use en liberté de conscience de mon Latin, avecq. le congé que vous m'en avez donné)' (II:12,453) which also, since he never asked permission, punctures the serious tone and makes his points more digestible. From the very first essay, as we saw, he has mastered the technique of story-telling. There is no straight third person narrative; instead, he lightens his tale with changes to the first person, dialogue, and exclamation. Just as it was sometimes difficult in earlier discussion of the *Essais* to distinguish the voice of Montaigne from that of his hypothetical reader, so, in his stories about himself, only the closest examination of the text can reveal the speed with which he changes angles of narration—the ease with which he passes from 'Je' to the objectivised 'le petit homme' (II:6,353) in the account of his fall. It is the same feeling of exhilaration which dominates his tale about the projected attack upon his château: playing on the reader's suspense, he gradually builds up the number of the intruders, first 'un quidam', then four or five, and finally twenty or twenty-five. Though he throws out plenty of hints about the disposition, friendly or otherwise, of his visitors —with words like 'fable', with his own initial artless reaction to their words, and then his subsequent elaboration of his suspicions—he keeps us in suspense and we fear the worst. Once Montaigne has got us into this state he can tell the climax of his tale: his trusting face has saved both his life and his goods (III:12, 1037-8). There are, no doubt, a thousand ways to recount such a happening, but it would be difficult to find one which is so engrossing.

To my mind his narrative skill can best be illustrated in his account of Messalina's amorous wiles:[46]

Elle fit au commencement son mary coqu à cachetes, comme il se faict; mais, conduisant ses parties trop ayséement, par la stupidité qui estoit en luy, elle desdaigna soudain cet usage. La voylà à faire l'amour à la descouverte, advouër des serviteurs, les entretenir et les favoriser à la veüe d'un chacun. Elle vouloit qu'il s'en ressentit. Cet animal ne se pouvant esveiller pour tout cela, en luy rendant ses plaisirs mols et fades par cette trop lâche facilité par laquelle il

sembloit qu'il les authorisat et legitimat, que fit elle? Femme d'un
Empereur sain et vivant, et à Romme, au theatre du monde, en plein
midy, en feste et ceremonie publique, et avec Silius, duquel elle jouy-
ssoit long temps devant, elle se marie un jour que son mary estoit
hors de la ville. Semble il pas qu'elle s'acheminast à devenir chaste
par la nonchallance de son mary, ou qu'elle cerchast un autre
mary qui luy esguisast l'appetit par sa jalousie, et qui, en luy
insistant, l'incistast? Mais la premiere difficulté qu'elle rencontra
fut aussi la derniere. Cette beste s'esveilla en sursaut. (III: 5,
849-50)

At the outset, Montaigne the narrator is obvious, controlling the shape
of his story, and slipping in the odd remark 'comme il se faict' to intro-
duce a note of familiarity and even of ordinariness. Messalina is defin-
itely apart from us. With the phrase 'Elle vouloit qu'il s'en ressentit',
however, Montaigne enters the mind of his character and comments on
her thoughts. 'Cet animal' could equally well describe her view of her
husband, as well as Montaigne's. Such ambiguity is useful for it will
allow Montaigne later to slip in his moral observations naturally and
unobtrusively. He then resumes his account of her deeds with drawn-out
emphatic detail to arouse our astonishment. Then comes the moral
comment—the real point of the narrative—an ironical probing into the
motives for such strange behaviour. And, almost before we have had
time to absorb such reflections, the story is abruptly over, 'ceste beste
s'esveilla en sursaut'. The rest is left to the imagination.

　　This ability to control the gradations of tone from the narrative
to the reflective (and in some cases through dialogue and exclamation),[47]
to vary the speed of a phrase according to the effects he wants to produce,
to emerge and disappear again (at times obviously, at others almost
secretly), is not limited to Montaigne's anecdotal style. He uses all
these means of keeping us close to his thought, and of directing our
own thinking processes along the lines which he controls. By pretending
he had an easy, natural, accessible style, and by insisting on the qualities
which distinguished it from that of others, he attracted his readers. Once
they were within his net, as it were, then he could manipulate their
reactions with all the skill he had acquired from his own highly aesthetic
response to the writings of others, ancient and modern. His methods of
alerting our minds are not always as obvious as in his satirical pastiches,
or in his obtrusive literary tools—the image and the anecdote—although
these means are themselves far removed from the untidy, haphazard

style he had laid claim to. It is the aim of the following chapters to invest-
igate these less apparent means, used by Montaigne to provoke strong
feeling and incite thought, encouraged by a note to *De l'art de conférer*
which warns: 'mon humeur n'est propre, non plus à parler qu'à escrire,
pour les principians'.

3

OF THE
'CRAFTIE & SECRETE
METHODE'

I T is virtually impossible to open any sixteenth-century book of rhetoric without finding advice on the art of dissimulation. Pierre Fabri (1521), Pierre de Courcelles (1557), and all editions of Peter Ramus' work (to name but a few representative theorists), advocate its use and set out its persuasive advantages.[1] Their ideas had largely been suggested by Cicero and elaborated by Quintilian who placed what was often called 'the craftie and secrete methode' firmly in the tradition of persuasion. The prudential or 'craftie' method sought to inculcate a known position by indirect means, seeing obliqueness as a more effective means of persuading someone caught in entrenched opinions, than the direct or natural method. A 'craftie' writer would rouse his reader's suspense by starting *in medias res*, for example, by keeping his main points to the end, or by suspending his argument with anecdotes, and so on. Within the wider definition which I shall adopt here, protective masks, understatement, and, above all, irony, may be included since they work in a similar indirect way to produce a calculated response in the reader. This last trope in particular was especially popular: Fouquelin gives it much space; Fabri examines the many different ironic methods then available; Ramus—quoting Aristotle—writes eloquently on the 'sagesse de cette methode'; and the lawyer Gribaldus devotes a chapter to advocating its frequent use.[2] Such consensus of opinion came, doubtless, not only from writers' experience of this particular method, but also from Quintilian's remarks: 'By far the most artistic device is to indicate one thing by allusion to another'.[3]

In the view of these rhetoricians, the art of dissimulation offers a writer numerous advantages. Both Fabri and Courcelles recommend it 'pour faire les auditeurs ententifs', and Courcelles adds that mastery of 'insinuation' argues a successful control of the whole range of devices contained in the art of rhetoric.[4] Ramus is more precise: he prescribes its use 'pour gaigner l'intelligence, la grace et l'attention':[5] while Fabri notes that it may enable the author to avoid giving offence to any member of his audience. From the disguises adopted by many sixteenth-century writers, one can guess how far they appreciated the protection afforded by wrapping up their thoughts in ambiguous guise. In the *Cymbalum mundi* Bonaventure des Periers hid his most outspoken accusations in the voice of a horse or a dog;[6] De la Primaudaye in his *Académie françoyse* pleaded that it was more convenient to adopt 'masques empruntez' as his main spokesmen;[7] and the arch defender of the protestant cause —Du Plessis Mornay—at the Etats de Blois in 1576 spoke up for peace, incredibly, 'sous la personne d'un catholique romain'![8] Obviously at times of civil strife, the art of disguising oneself in order to speak one's true thoughts was especially necessary. Moreover, Pasquier thought that it was the best way to get people to swallow nasty medicine: 'pour vous faire present après, des remedes et preservatifs que je pense necessaires aux maladies de nos esprits'.[9]

Self-protection and moral intention were both at the centre of sixteenth-century preoccupation with oblique methods of persuasion; and no one understood the intricacies of such an approach better than Erasmus. The multiplication of Follies in *The Praise of Folly*, for instance, makes it difficult to weigh up his real position. Even the closest attention to shifts of tone reveals only a few clear lines of attack as, for example, against monks and the excesses of the Church—though, here too, Erasmus protects himself from counter-attack by insisting that it is Folly who speaks and that, therefore, one cannot take her criticisms seriously. And yet, the opening lines to the work had warned the reader that 'trifles may be a whet to more serious thoughts, and comical matters may be so treated of, so that a reader of ordinary sense may possibly thence reap more advantage than from some big and stately argument'.[10] In other words, you can read into his work virtually whatever you like, but he will take no responsibility for your interpretation. In the *Colloquies* Erasmus uses dialogue for similar purposes, allowing the reader to identify himself with one, both, or neither of the interlocutors.[11] The weight of interpretation is placed firmly on the shoulders of the reader.

There were other writers, too, who advocated a similar method; and their suggestions on equally subtle forms of disguise probably filtered through to a much larger reading public. These were the authors of the hand-books on social behaviour which proliferated throughout

Europe at this time. Castiglione's *Courtier* talks of the need to acquire *sprezzatura*—a mixture of grace, aplomb and studied nonchalance—so that (as Guazzo was to emphasise later in the century) 'the whole seemeth to be done by chance, that he may thereby be had in more admiration'.[12] Even more important than this elegant stance, is the positive profit to be gained from a dissimulating art in writing. Sir Frederick discusses the usefulness of what he calls 'covered subtiltie [which gives] a certaine authoritie to writing, and makes the reader more heedefull to pause at it, and to ponder it better, and he taketh a delyte in the wittinesse and learning of him that wryteth, and with a good judgement, after some painestaking, he tasteth the pleasure that consisteth in hard things'.[13] French adaptations of these two authors repeat and elaborate the same points, with the exception of that intelligent critic of Castiglione, Philibert de Vienne; but even he admits, when referring to the dissimulatory skill of Socrates, that such a method is admissible, if it is for 'le profit des autres'.[14]

To a reader familiar with Montaigne's insistence upon his honesty, and with his reputation as being the man who always tells the truth, it might seem strange to find him placed in such a flourishing tradition of deceit. However, it can be shown that he knew this tradition well, and appreciated its persuasive advantages: indeed, he extends its use considerably, and it is for this reason that I define the 'craftie methode' in a much broader sense than those provided by contemporary handbooks of rhetoric. In the *Essais*, oblique presentation of ideas was to become both an effective means of communicating a complex response to natural phenomena, as well as disarming prejudice, and it was to turn into a method of discovery.[15]

*   *   *

As we have seen, Montaigne was prepared to use the most varied means possible to impress the reader. This included an oblique approach which, as he himself freely admits, strikes 'd'autant plus picquammant que plus obliquement' (1:40,245). In this phrase, Montaigne connects, very obviously, force of impact with an indirect means of achieving it. This relationship is spelt out further on the same page when he claims that the anecdotes he uses, and the allegations which he makes

> ne servent pas tousjours simplement d'exemple, d'authorité ou d'ornement. Je ne les regarde pas seulement par l'usage que j'en tire. Elles portent souvent hors de mon propos, la semence d'une matiere plus

riche et plus hardie, et sonnent à gauche un ton plus delicat, et pour moy qui n'en veux exprimer d'avantage, et pour ceux qui rencontreront mon air. (i:40,245)

In this way, he summarises the two main advantages—grace and profit—claimed by the long tradition which had stressed the great utility of an insinuating art. Montaigne knew *The Courtier* (i:48,281) and obviously appreciated the *sprezzatura* which Castiglione and his contemporaries so prized. He realised, too, that the indirect and the understated pointed the way to the 'matière plus riche et plus hardie'—the exact nature of which he preferred to leave his readers to discover. The process of thinking and discovery is linked very closely by Montaigne to that of aesthetic appreciation which itself depends, in his mind, on an oblique presentation of subject-matter. His use of the 'craftie methode' is less concerned with self-protection and more with finding ways of getting the reader's mind actively in play. Once you admit that you want to persuade your readers of something and even wish to improve them, then Montaigne argued, deception is often necessary, and is, indeed, the only course to success: 'car il n'est pas nouveau aux sages de prescher les choses comme elles servent, non comme elles sont. La verité a ses empeschemens, incommoditez et incompatibilitez avec nous. Il nous faut souvent tromper afin que nous ne nous trompons, et siller nostre veüe, estourdir nostre entendement pour les dresser et amender' (iii:10,983).

It must be made clear that Montaigne accepts 'lying' only as far as the manner of presentation is concerned; and, even then, he would not admit any excess in its use. He firmly rejected obscurity used for the sake of mystifying (i:11,45); and, with equal force, he argued against that finesse which set out thoughts ingeniously, simply to elicit admiration from the reader (i:21,99). On moral grounds, he unequivocally condemned 'lying', but was forced to admit its frequent effectiveness as a means of persuasion. In *Sur des vers de Virgile*, for instance, he comments ironically on the numerous times women have recourse to disguising, while at the same time he acknowledges: 'le mentir y est en siege d'honneur: c'est un destour qui nous conduit à la verité par une fauce porte' (iii:5,845). And to this admission he adds another: that 'lying' is especially successful when a state of mutual distrust exists. Now, although it is true that Montaigne had worked hard to build up a feeling of trust between the reader and himself, the knowledge that the feeling itself had been founded upon methods of deception made him doubt its reality.

Montaigne's own experience had taught him to appreciate the advantages of an oblique approach. From his observations upon his own reading he noted that he responded more to Plutarch, who left you something to discover for yourself, than to a writer who tells you all (I:26, 156). This belief in the persuasive force of understatement, is most cogently argued for example in *Sur des vers de Virgile* (III:5,858), where Montaigne sums up: 'celuy qui dict tout, il nous saoule et nous desgoute'. He adds this warning, however: 'celuy qui craint à s'exprimer nous achemine à en penser plus qu'il n'y en a'; thus reminding us that, whatever the advantages of understatement, it is a dangerous course which easily leads to misinterpretation. For this reason, he makes it clear that in his own writing he always shows us the way and hints at the right direction: 'ce que je ne puis exprimer, je le montre au doigt' (III:9,961). Obviously, Montaigne does not intend that the reader should have a completely free hand. The kind of limits he had in mind might well be gauged from his own response to other writers' works, where close reading became a source of inspiration: 'un suffisant lecteur descouvre souvent és escrits d'autruy des perfections autres que celles que l'autheur y a mises et apperçeües, et y preste des sens et des visages plus riches' (I:24, 126). While pondering upon this enriching experience, it must have occurred to Montaigne that his own work could similarly provoke thought in others. Confirmation that his work did, indeed, arouse such response which, in turn, initiated a chain reaction on the *Essais*, comes from a late addition to *Du parler prompt ou tardif* (I:10,42). There he writes that another—'l'estranger'—found the real thread of his thought while he himself did not know 'ce qu['il a] voulu dire'. Given this additional evidence, it is not surprising that Montaigne willingly adopted a manner of writing which seems at first sight to run counter to the frank image of himself which he had so elaborately constructed.

His discussion on the merits of diversion is relevant in this context, since it helps us to understand how Montaigne envisaged the detailed working out of his oblique approach. He recognised that the human mind naturally seeks to protect itself. In trying to escape pain, it tries to occupy itself by diverting its thought elsewhere; in attempting to escape the spectacle of civil war, it proposes travel; in an effort to avert its gaze from problems of old age or death, it dwells on the past and the pleasures of youth. Montaigne agrees in *De la diversion* (III:4) that he frequently employs these tricks, which he called variously 'gauchir', 'decliner' or 'detourner'. In this essay, he describes the imperceptible manner in which the mind is drawn to diversion; and he suggests that deeper pleasure and profit may be gained by turning this process into a conscious exercise. This effort is similar to that demanded of the reader in *De la vanité* (III:9) and *Sur des vers de Virgile* (III:5), where the very process of diversion provides the fundamental structure of each essay. In the first, Montaigne is himself engaged in a vain effort to withdraw from the turmoil of civil strife; in the second, he seeks to bridge the gap between his youth and his old age in order to subdue the claims of the latter. In the first, Montaigne's thought ranges between notions of vanity and desire for consolation; in the second, he tends to distort memories of youth in his struggle to quieten the demands of age; and, in both, the reader is warned that Montaigne's 'fantaisies se suyvent, mais parfois c'est de loing, et se regardent, mais d'une veüe oblique'. If you do not take heed of Montaigne's hints, then you deserve his criticism: 'c'est l'indigent lecteur qui pert mon subject, non pas moy' (III:9,973). The extent to which Montaigne had committed himself to the notion that the reader must work, for pleasure and profit, now becomes clearer. He saw the *Essais* as offering resistance to all but the most determined readers, who, like his own thoughts, progress 'comme les tireurs d'aviron qui s'avancent ainsin à reculons' (III:1,772). It is now time to examine, more closely, the nature of this resistance.

*   *   *

'Me voicy devenu Grammairien', Montaigne begins his chapter on Horses (I:48), pointedly drawing attention to a profession he has more than adequately satirised elsewhere: a joke, used a little at his own expense, in order to direct our minds to the fact that the horse is merely an excuse for writing on the diversity of nations' habits. His essay on Liars also begins halfway along an apparent side-road, with a long disquisition on memory. Knowing that popular opinion of this faculty was high, and that his fellow lawyers considered it a necessity, he ostentatiously demeans himself, first by the affirmation: 'Il n'est homme à qui il siese si mal de se mesler de parler de memoire' (I:9,34), and further by the additional information, proudly given, that his memory is execrable. 'What has all this to do with lying?' the startled reader might well enquire. Yet it is through consideration of memory that Montaigne brings us to reflexions on the true nature and implications of not telling the truth: you need a good memory to lie successfully. Then we realise that his bad memory is a virtue, and that the irony with which the essay began was false.

Incomplete or inappropriate titles are another obvious means of engaging attention: even if the response proves merely to be the kind of exasperation voiced by Montaigne's contemporary Pasquier.[16] The title of the very first essay indicates that Montaigne envisages a complex subject matter: *Par divers moyens on arrive à pareille fin*. The second, *De la tristesse*, seems explicit enough, yet the essay is really about human imbecillity, a preoccupation confirmed by later additions to the essay. The link between the two themes—sadness and imbecillity—is, however, made perfectly clear. Titles which give little clue to the content of the essay both tease the reader's mind and provide a cautious cover for audacious thoughts. Such is the case of the essays on suicide, euphemistically called: *De juger de la mort d'autruy* (II:13), or *Coustume de l'isle de Cea* (II:3). In other essays, like *Si le chef d'une place assiegée doit sortir pour parlementer* (I:5), the title suggests that Montaigne is going to provide some useful conclusion. Such expectation is not fulfilled; instead, he demonstrates the complexity of the problem through a series of anecdotes which show the different habits and priorities of different nations, and concludes that, in practical terms, he is unable to conclude, for there is no general rule of thumb which will fit each individual circumstance. The anecdotes, far from playing their conventional illustrative role, tend to render the discussion more problematic and less easy of solution.[17] Similarly, in *Divers evenemens de mesme conseil* (I:24), the title suggests one thing and Montaigne concludes on its opposite: 'un conseil pour tout evenement'. Such procedures require the reader to look hard at Montaigne's mode of argument.

Other devices encourage greater participation. Many comments, for instance, end inconclusively, either with elliptical expressions such as 'ainsi du reste' (I:26, 157) or 'peu de nouvelles' (I:25, 135) bringing the reader's mind up short, and making him search around for his own evidence. On such occasions we rarely question what we are searching for: we are caught by Montaigne in a trap where, for example, his abrupt cutting off of an accumulation encourages agreement because it stimulates us to add to his list. As we have noted, Montaigne had a declared preference for the tentative, unresolved formulation: 'J'ayme ces mots, qui amollissent et moderent la temerité de nos propositions: A l'avanture, Aucunement, Quelque, On dict, Je pense et semblables' (III: 11, 1007). Such an irresolute manner of presenting arguments tends to disarm criticism; and the arguments themselves are, perhaps, frequently accepted precisely because they seem so hesitant. In *Du pedantisme* (I:25, 143), Montaigne showed his appreciation of the socratic method of argument which ridiculed Hippias by letting him guess, from what the philosopher did not say, the uselessness of his (Hippias') reasoning power. In many other instances there is evidence that Montaigne's appreciation was not merely intellectual, and that he himself employed a similar studied reticence. The sudden breaking off of an argument, a metaphor not developed (III : 1, 781) or a story left unfinished (1 : 30, 200) has the same mental effect. We concentrate on the silence, fill it for ourselves, and find, that by doing so, we have accepted Montaigne's own assumptions, and agreed with his comment.

Agreement is rather more delayed when Montaigne engineers (as he frequently does) a surprise reversal of commonly-held assumptions. His most blatant, if most conventional use of this technique occurs when he wishes to make his satire of man's pretentions particularly virulent in the *Apologie* (II : 12). Here beasts are elevated in the same see-saw movement which debases man, so that the latter's fall seems all the more desperate. Although the blunting of man's pride by a comparison with animals was a frequent device of sixteenth-century moralists, and readers might well anticipate it in the same context in Montaigne, their natural impulse would still be to reject the comparison, and to cling to their sense of superiority. Only a total reversal of the relationship between man and animal would urge them to reconsider their assessment of themselves. Montaigne's object here is not merely of a satirical nature :[18] he wants to alert us to a more realistic appraisal of man's possibilities.

A reversal of men's common view of kings is used by Montaigne for a like purpose in *De l'inequalité qui est entre nous* (1 : 42). The chapter is really concerned to elaborate Seneca's question 'Pourquoy, estimant un homme, l'estimez vous tout enveloppé et empaqueté?' (1 : 42, 251). Montaigne loosens, little by little, the glorious packaging which clothes our ideas of what it is to be a king. Gradually, he strips his monarch of all his outward splendour, demonstrating that a king is just a man. His examination does not stop there, however, as he proceeds through the inconveniences and difficulties of the duties of kingship, to the suggestion that a king, for these reasons, is less than a humbler man. Such reversal could challenge the entire social order which depended on the acceptance of neat hierarchies conventionally surmounted by kings: but a Latin quotation, 'Mores cuique sui fingunt fortunam', throws the whole discussion back onto a moral plane. Montaigne's prime concern in this essay is moral not social inequality: and he reaches his main theme through consideration of the obvious external advantages enjoyed by kings, while underlining, at every opportunity, the moral disadvantages of wealth and position. Throughout, the intermingling of the two planes—moral and social—together with the reversal of the automatic expectation that it is good to be a king, forces the reader to consider for himself what is of real value in being a man, divorced from externals and social complication.

*　　　*　　　*

Montaigne's main discussion of what constitutes *Virtue* is achieved through a similar process—that is, by arguing the opposite of what was unthinkingly accepted as the proper definition of virtue.[19] Naturally, Montaigne returns to the theme of virtue frequently; and, on almost every occasion, conventionally-agreed notions are used as yardsticks against which he could measure his own opinion. In *De la vertu* (II:29, 683), for instance, the extraordinary physical courage shown at moments of crisis, which epitomised *virtue* for the ancients and for many of his military-minded contemporaries, is set aside, to be replaced by a view which prefers consistency of behaviour in the ordinary happenings of everyday life. Only constant evidence of virtue defines virtue, he adds, in *L'inconstance de nos actions* (II:1). Military prowess is made to bow before that calm, dependable, and constant power of spirit, which not only withstands the accidents of Fortune but even seems indifferent to them: 'force et asseurance de l'ame, mesprisant également toute sorte d'accidens enemis: equable, uniforme et constante' (II:7,362). Although, like his contemporaries, Montaigne admired the astonishing virtuous acts of Cato or Seneca he did not find their deeds instructive for his own mode of life; such acts were certainly ill-suited to the world of affairs where private virtue had vicious effects (II:18,649); and, moreover, they were inappropriate to his own times when vice was taken for virtue (III:9,969).

From the number of times Montaigne returns to this theme it is obvious that he would have liked to offer a neat, easily recognisable and universally acceptable code of virtue. But he knew, all too well, its complexities, and its strange outward manifestations which often seem more like the accompaniments of vice. Significantly, it is in *De la cruauté* (II:11), apparently at the opposite extreme from virtue, that Montaigne gives his most detailed account of this theme, recording his own unbounded enthusiasm for the virtuous, and demonstrating the difficulties of recognising and appreciating their true worth. As can be seen from the implications of the title, it is difficult to be virtuous. Indeed, one can only define it with any degree of accuracy, Montaigne goes on to maintain,

if one sets it against its opposite—vice. Only constant temptation nour-
ishes the truly virtuous man. Virtue, or that impulse in man which urges
him to do good, needs some obstacle by which to prove itself: 'elle ne
peut s'exercer sans partie' (II:11,401). Thus, Montaigne argues, virtue
is known by its opposite. Then suddenly, into the discussion, Montaigne
inserts the figure of Socrates. He is presented just freed from chains and
rubbing his sore ankles; and this gesture is immediately interpreted not
as a symbol of his misfortune but as a sign of,

> je ne sçay quel contentement nouveau et une allegresse enjoüée en ses
> propos et façons dernieres. A ce tressaillir, du plaisir qu'il sent à grat-
> ter sa jambe apres que les fers en furent hors, accuse il pas une pareille
> douceur et joye en son ame, pour estre desenforgée des incommodités
> passées, et à mesme d'entrer en cognoissance des choses advenir ? (II:
> 11,404)

'Contentement, plaisir, allegresse, douceur, joye': with Socrates, virtue
has acquired a new status and commands a new enthusiasm. Through
the simple gesture of rubbing sore ankles, Montaigne sees a kind of mental ascension. In his mind, virtue is no longer confined to the realm of
behaviour; it defines a permanent attitude of mind in a singular man—
something nearer the expression 'sublime'. Once virtue has been defined
as something more than the mere disposition to do good—as a mental
activity which, through its enjoyment of simply being, gives proof of
great potential—then qualities often referred to as 'virtues' can be seen
in their true light. Chastity, sobriety, and temperance, have no mental
counterpart in virtue; they are most frequently the consequence of mental or physical weakness. Similarly, fear and stupidity, are at the root of
apparent virtues such as conforming to convention, and are, lamentably,
habitual sources of cruelty: the frightened man obeys a leader's order
(apparent virtue) by committing an atrocity (vice). And so, Montaigne
sums up, appearances must not be allowed to provide the criteria by
which we judge virtue, since these may equally well be the consequences
of vice.

This discussion about virtue has brought Montaigne very close to
those notions about consciousness and individual self-assessment which
he was to elaborate more fully in *Du repentir* (III:2). The joyous assurance which he saw mirrored in Socrates' gesture, and the calm spirit he
desired so fervently in *Des recompenses d'honneur* (II:7), are both indic-
ative of the necessary conditions which the virtuous man must have (or
must cultivate) in order to establish that individual code of behaviour:

'un patron au dedans, auquel toucher nos actions' (III : 2, 785). The consciousness which this pattern implies is taken up again in *Des coches*
(III : 6), where Montaigne shows that even the effects of real virtue (i.e.
that which is not founded upon weakness) can often be most vicious, if
its exercise is not accompanied by the ability to distinguish the right
time for its use. He comments rather ruefully on the treatment of the
virtuous Mexicans by the vicious Europeans: 'Mais, quant à la devotion,
observance des loix, bonté, liberalité, loyauté, franchise, il nous a bien
servy de n'en avoir pas tant qu'eux : ils se sont perdus par cet advantage,
et vendus, et trahis eux mesme' (III : 6, 887).

Finally then, Montaigne's notions of Virtue are clear. They are
accumulated through abstract, assertive comments; through the measuring of opposites; and through detailed examples and anecdotes which, in
the end, lead us to a separation of the true from the apparent. He has
provided us with no solutions; but he has shown, conclusively, the importance he attached to virtue, while suggesting to us that we look with
due penetration at human behaviour; that we consider motives along
with appearances; that we take account of time; and finally, that we resist sloppy judgements, born of habit.

*   *   *

The sort of difficulty which presents itself when one discusses an
abstract notion, like virtue, extends to all such words as Montaigne uses
them. It is not, I think, simply a question of the somewhat fluid state of
the French language in the sixteenth century. Commentators have, perhaps, exaggerated the elasticity of sense in words precisely because
writers like Montaigne allowed the context to give exact meanings.
Montaigne demonstrated, time and again, that such concepts as Virtue,
Nature, Judgement, Opinion, Constancy, Honesty, and so on, cannot be
strictly defined outside specific contexts, nor can they be assumed unthinkingly as belonging to some neatly established moral code which
functions perfectly in every situation. In his *Essais*, by presenting such
terms from an unexpected angle, Montaigne can surprise us into reconsidering what precisely is involved when we use notions such as virtue
or cruelty, while at the same time uncovering a wealth of insights into
human motivation.

The meaning of words, then, slides and shifts according to a
specific moment of experience; and Montaigne introduces yet further
complexity by using the same word in a variety of contexts, frequently
without signalling his passage from one plane of discussion to another. In

Du pedantisme (1 : 25, 142), for example, his argument moves easily from what is good in an individual to what is strong in the State. The opening paragraphs of *Du repentir* (III : 2, 782) elaborate the theme of inconstancy, and Montaigne introduces a new approach to this well-known sixteenth-century talking point by treating the problem on several different levels, almost simultaneously. In successive sentences, he first describes the general instability of the visible universe, then passes to a general moral comment, 'La constance mesme n'est autre chose qu'un branle plus languissant', before introducing his own personal difficulties in maintaining any steady gaze upon the fleeting nature of world and self. His analysis of drunkenness (II : 2) moves from general moral statements about how the world is made up of variety, and how vice can be relatively great or small according to its context, to considerations upon types of drunkenness, anecdotes about the Ancients' praise of this state, to his own personal denunciation of anything which removes from man conscious control of his thoughts and acts. At first, it seems that Montaigne is merely concerned with fairly traditional statements on drunkenness. Then, suddenly, he presents a series of anecdotes, recounted by his father, giving examples of physical endurance and deprivation, pretending by a 'revenons à noz bouteilles' (II : 2, 326) that these are mere parenthetical entertainments, irrelevant to his main theme. But nothing could be further from the case. These anecdotes anticipate and parallel the 'fureur' of the martyrs, who from the tortures they were made to endure, derive a certain voluptuous pleasure akin to drunkenness. They also mirror the 'folie' and 'eslancement' of the poets drunk with inspiration. Montaigne deliberately used the word 'ivrongnerie', with its overtones of moral disapproval, to link these apparently very different planes of experience: excessive physical courage; the smug satisfaction Stoics derived from their constancy; and mental excitement over which the active mind has no real control. In the end, it becomes clear (and Montaigne makes it more obvious by later additions to the essay) that, through a discussion of varying forms of drunkenness, spanning different levels of experience, he is coming towards an idea of what constitutes wisdom. Quoting Socrates's idea that 'le principal office de la sagesse estoit distinguer les biens et les maux', Montaigne suggests that 'nous autres, à qui le meilleur est tousiours en vice, devons dire de mesme de la science de distinguer les vices'. This sorting-out process has, in fact, lead him to a definition of what is good.

The same shifting series of contexts is used to explore the nature of opinion and its hold over men's thoughts and activities. Montaigne gives it various names: in people's response to death it can be seen as unthinking habit, or a part of the faculty of imagination; in the context of religion its sense is close to that of indoctrination; at moments of adversity there seems little distinction between opinion and fear, between anticipating the worst and one's idea of disaster. Loose association of different contexts allows for a more complex view of the moral world: it also makes Montaigne's points more forcibly.[20] Our ideas of virtue are exposed as mere habits of mind with little to support them in reality. In Montaigne's eyes, putting up with pain for the sake of beauty, appearances, or even devotion, undermines the value of such motives. In fact, his various attempts in this essay (*Que le goust des biens et des maux dépend en bonne partie de l'opinion que nous en avons*, I: 14) to bring the ravages wrought by opinion to the forefront of our minds, convince him of its extraordinary force and range. There is little which can counteract its action: except perhaps this clear-sighted appraisal of its power.

*   *   *

A popular way of communicating your thoughts in the sixteenth century, judging from the number of surviving examples, was the dialogue form.[21] It had certain advantages in that it could present sometimes difficult material in a lively and accessible way, and in an urbane atmosphere which delighted admirers of Castiglione's *Courtier*. Furthermore it enjoyed the authority of Plato whose accounts of Socrates's conversations with his friends revealed the skill with which such a form could be handled. Writers, like Erasmus, had demonstrated how successfully and tantalisingly ambiguous this form could be: only discovering the author's real intention to the initiated reader, and even he, in the end, is not entirely freed from doubt.[22] Montaigne was clearly attracted by the possibilities of this way of writing, since it had an in-built system of keeping the reader awake by question and answer: two voices, two minds capable of producing arguments for and against a problem, and (in the case of Erasmus) able to suggest more complex approaches. While appreciating these advantages, Montaigne must also have considered the fact that most writers of dialogue did not manage to exploit these possibilities properly; their speakers were all too frequently the same mind and voice discoursing under another name; or the dialogue rapidly degenerated into a monologue with one character asking a pointed question, and the other producing a long disquisition in reply.[23] In the end, he must have decided that such a form was too rigid for his purposes.

De l'art de conférer (III: 8) recognised the value of a lively discourse with another, since it helps both to shape arguments more clearly, to discover new ideas by the force of opposition, and to sift out the truth.[24] Montaigne's definition of 'conférer' includes the sense 'disputer'. There is not such a considerable distance between scholarly disputation as it might be handled and Montaigne's idea of conversation, when one considers the stimulating effect they both have on thought.[25] Yet, for Montaigne, the formal patterns of disputation and dialogue were too clear-cut. Within the looser structure of the essay, Montaigne preferred to use dialogue as the need arose; in *De la vanité* (III:9), for example, where he imagines the voice of the reader questioning his motives for wanting to embark on a journey at his age: and in *Sur des vers de Virgile* (III:5,853), where the dialogue form allows him to distance the discussion of his style from himself, and to deal with it as though he were criticising the style of another work. It seems that Montaigne did not want to over-use forms whose structures were so set. In *De l'institution des enfants* he declared 'Je n'ayme point de tissure où les liaisons et les coutures paroissent' (I:26,171)—preferring to hide the bone structure of his arguments from the reader. Nevertheless, Montaigne was able to use the dialogue form to great effect; and perhaps the most interesting example occurs in *De l'experience* (III:13) where Montaigne divides himself into two parts, his mind in conversation with his body. After a series of affirmations, when Montaigne's real mind has tried to convince his ailing frame of the necessity of accommodating itself to the inevitability of pain, he invents a kind of fictive mind which enters into disputation with his body—though the argument is somewhat undermined by Montaigne's initial statement: 's'il persuadoit comme il presche, il me secourroit heureusement' (III:13,1068). What Montaigne is really doing is presenting the reader with a possible way of coping with painful illness. The arguments of the fictive mind might not convince, but they do divert attention, and prevent the real mind from dwelling on pain, from enhancing its attacks, and from anticipating pain even before it arrives. When it does occur, the mind is helpless. But Montaigne encourages us to use it positively when we have the chance; just as he resorts to the dialogue form at the end of the same essay—in direct conversation with the reader this time—to urge as earnestly as he knows how: 'avez-vous sceu mediter et manier vostre vie? vous avez faict la plus grande besoigne de toutes' (III:13,1088). This meditation and control, which he covets above everything else, he tries to inculcate by allowing the reader's mind no rest.

Montaigne's legal training had, of course, taught him to sustain a for and against argument without recourse to another voice. At the beginning of *De l'incertitude de nostre jugement* (1:47), he is explicit about his approval of this form which he most faithfully demonstrates in his chapter on Democritus and Heraclitus—a favoured sixteenth-century confrontation. Antonio Fregoso, who published perhaps the best-known account of the contrary views of these philosophers, set out their positions clearly, but made it obvious that his aim was one of moral instruction since Democritus interrupts his mirth to praise 'Amour sainct et vertueux'.[26] It seems, at first, that Montaigne examines the two extreme views as a means of clarifying his own ideas. While admitting the intellectual pleasure he derives from such a confrontation, and while explaining the advantages of testing one's own thoughts against extreme established views, Montaigne nevertheless does not, on this occasion, leave us with irresolution. This essay is not, as is often suggested, a mere non-committal game, for Montaigne clearly sides with Democritus whose peals of laughter stress the 'ridicule, risible, insignifiant' side of man. He warms to such a cynical view not because Democritus's reasoning is more convincing but because he himself is already persuaded. The opposing of the two philosophers is a means of giving us the evidence, exciting our interest and allowing us to choose[27]—although, in fact, it is difficult to resist the force of Montaigne's affirmations about man's miserable lot, especially as reinforced in later additions to the essay.

From shifting contexts and dialogue it is but a short step to a multivocal and many-angled technique with which Montaigne constantly contrives to keep our mental processes mobile. It must be stressed at once that a method of argument which keeps the mind constantly on the move was admirably suited to Montaigne's view both of man and of the universe. Every second brought a new thought, changed conditions, fresh experience. The 'branloire perenne', which Montaigne describes with such excitement in the opening paragraphs of *Du repentir* (III:2), attacks even the most apparently solid of substances: the pyramids, or the Caucasus. Its most devastating impact, however, as far as Montaigne is concerned, is upon man himself, whose nature is in a constant state of flux and whose ability to assess these changes is subject to the same mobility. So it is, that, to come at all close to knowledge or to an analysis of such protean matter, Montaigne is forced to consider himself from diverse angles: 'si je parle diversement de moy, c'est que je me regarde diversement' (II:1,319). His *Essais* are an attempt to move around all the available material: 'c'est un contrerolle de divers et muables accidens et d'imaginations irresoluës et, quand il y eschet, contraires: soit que je sois autre moymesme, soit que je saisisse les subjects par autres circonstances et considerations' (III: 2, 782). He expects the reader to follow this restless motion which highlights first one moment of experience and then another, and to appreciate the intellectual agility which brings together, as a kaleidoscope, multiple thoughts from a variety of planes. Some are brought into sharp focus, as with a microscope, and are studied with detailed attention; others are quickly drawn, and left to jostle with yet more of the ideas crowding Montaigne's pen.

His attempt to give a complete account of his observations is not confused, however much his own frequent mention of contradictions and diversity in his writings might suggest such an impression. The fact is that he wants to achieve a double objective: to disturb the reader's equanimity making him question many assumptions; and to convince the reader that consistency, constancy, and a view of the universe dependent upon similarities between man and the cosmos, is not truth. He must have realised that, in this way, he was running directly counter to the well-established view that man, the microcosm, was a perfect mirror of all things contained in the universe, the macrocosm. The opening sentences of his last essay *De l'experience* are very explicit on this point: 'La consequence que nous voulons tirer de la ressemblance des evenemens est mal seure, d'autant qu'ils sont tousjours dissemblables' (III: 13, 1041). Accuracy in perception depended for Montaigne on having the flexibility of mind to sustain not merely a *pro et contra* argument, but to juggle with many more, allowing them to clash together, if need be, in order to achieve a composite truth.[28]

He recognised that the natural tendencies of the human mind were such that a multiple and even devious approach to a subject was specially appropriate. While in another context he would deplore the mental process which either multiplied interpretations of ideas, or dissected words and thoughts into more and more minute fragments (II: 12), he also appreciated that such methods had distinct advantages in the realm of analysis. The sometimes grudging admiration he accords to Socrates's logical processes which concentrated on investigation, 'tousjours demandant, et esmouvant la dispute, jamais l'arrestant' (II: 12, 489), is proof of this. His criticism of Gentillet's attack on Machiavelli states both the advantages of the analytical power of the mind, but also warns that such a process is never ending; 'Il s'y trouveroit tousjours, à un tel argument, dequoy y fournir responses, dupliques, repliques, tripliques, quadrupliques, et cette infinie contexture de debats que notre chicane a alongé tant qu'elle a peu en faveur des procez' (ii: 17,638). In the context of law Montaigne's disapproval is undeniable. Yet, in the *Apologie* where one would expect Montaigne's comments to be even more disrespectful, and where exactly the same kind of description of the interpretative and cumulative nature of the human brain occurs, the tone in fact betrays approval, hope and confidence in the capacity of successive generations of minds to find the way to truth: 'en retastant et pétrissant cette nouvelle matiere la remuant et l'eschaufant, j'ouvre à celuy qui me suit quelque facilité pour en jouir plus à son ayse, et la luy rends plus souple et plus maniable' (ii: 12,543). Here, Montaigne can scarcely hide his excitement at the possibilities open to the human mind. It is precisely because he is convinced of the impossibility of arriving at the truth of a matter by approaching it from one direction that Montaigne has high hopes of success when a multi-angled approach is used: 'Nous ne pouvons nous asseurer de la maistresse cause; nous en entassons plusieurs, voir si par rencontre elle se trouvera en ce nombre' (iii: 6,876); or again, 'diversement traicter les matieres est aussi bien les traicter que conformement, et mieux: à sçavoir plus copieusement et utilement' (ii: 12,470). Greater penetration, greater complexity, as well as more profit, are the recompenses which he claims for this approach which is by no means limited to the essays written at the end of his career.[29]

If one considers Montaigne's examination of solitude (i: 39), the analytical power of this encircling method is evident. He is aware of the two traditional views of solitude which he uses as a means of defining the exact nature of his own views: that is to say, the retirement of monks from the hurly-burly of the world to seek for spiritual peace; or the solitary country life of the man of Letters such as that advocated by Cicero or Pliny. Montaigne approves of neither view. He dislikes the first since it withdraws from what is most interesting in human experience and he despises the second since it has not withdrawn from the world at all but rather aims at what is most to be despised—public acclaim.[30] In his criticisms, Montaigne interprets these two traditional views according to the needs of his case, presenting only one aspect of each tradition. They are convenient, rather stereotyped, counterparts against which he can make his own ideas seem more alive and more persuasive.

From the very beginning of the essay it is apparent that his own view of solitude is largely an emotional one. It is based partly on the urge to have nothing to do with the despicable methods of his contemporaries, anxious to climb the ladder to public favour and renown; and partly on the need to build up resistance against the loss of La Boëtie.

As the essay proceeds, it is also clear that Montaigne has no literal view of solitude—that is, his idea is turned directly against physical withdrawal from society, and concentrates on developing a mental state which allows him to observe the world at close quarters, to live in society with wife, children and social responsibilities, but to remain fundamentally untouched by its trivial preoccupations. He takes the two extremes of activity and inactivity—the man of war and the scholar 'tout pituiteux, chassieux et crasseux'—to show what he does not mean, before he affirms what he does think. The warrior and the scholar in no way belong to themselves, whereas he is convinced that 'la plus grande chose du monde, c'est de sçavoir estre à soy' (1:39, 236); and this is further defined by an extended discussion of the need to adapt one's inner being to circumstances so that they do not dominate one's inner life. The free activity of the mind is what counts, and this does not necessarily depend upon solitude, but rather on the ability to abstract oneself from irrelevancies, while using the world about one as a source of observation and inspiration: 'Nostre mal nous tient en l'ame . . . il la faut ramener et retirer en soy: c'est la vraie solitude' (1:39, 234). The liberty of the mind which Montaigne sought and advocated was dependent on, yet independent of, the society in which he lived; and only a circumlocutory means of argumentation could make the precise nature of this paradoxical feeling clear to the reader. Thus, an oblique approach provides, simultaneously, a means of discovery and a method of communication.

As an alternative to feeling his way around a problem by examining many unusual angles, Montaigne frequently had recourse to a multivocal technique, the force of which Erasmus had, as we have seen, more than adequately demonstrated in *The Praise of Folly*. Both writers use the technique to involve the reader: yet Montaigne's method seems to have a much more exploratory quality about it. Erasmus, despite a general air of ambiguity, gives the impression from the outset that he himself knows what he wanted to say. With Montaigne, on the other hand, the reader feels less that he is being persuaded of something, and much more that he is being allowed to participate in solving the problem under discussion. In *Que philosopher c'est apprendre à mourir* (1:20), for instance, Montaigne assembles a great mass of evidence in defence of his subject. He argues with paradoxes, affirmations, and proverbs, and finally, in an attempt to establish his case, he abandons the personalised use of the 'je' form which had dominated the earlier part of the essay. 'On' and 'nous' come to stand for 'Je', incorporating into the essay the supposed feelings of the person reading. This expression of a double consciousness is not only used by Montaigne as a means of integrating the reader into his work, it is also part of his effort to persuade himself of the insignificance of death. Since arguments from individual experience fail, Montaigne argues as a representative of all men. But he still finds his reasoning unconvincing; and he switches to the assumed voice of the critical reader (1:20,82), thus challenging his own stupidity and fear of death. Then he turns his mind to the contemplation of others who fulfil all the natural functions of life, careless of the possible imminence of death, and tries to imitate their carefree attitudes. Yet, his obsession with death does not leave him. After describing very realistically how death creeps upon him daily; after noting philosophically that his own demise is the source of life for others; even after admonishing himself with the folly and idiocy of worrying about the passage to peace, Montaigne is still not reconciled to the idea of dying. His arguments remain as unconvincing as those which he orchestrated on the subject of pain in *Que le goust des biens et des maux dépend en bonne partie de l'opinion que nous en avons* (1:14). However agile the intelligence which tries to come to terms with evidence of physical discomfort, he cannot escape, nor can he do much to reduce, the effects of pain or the thoughts of death. On this last topic he tries one final remedy. Adopting the voice of nature—which sometimes seems simply Good Mother Nature, at others the sound of destiny, or even the voice of God—he rehearses all the best traditional reasons for accepting the fact of death quietly, resignedly, and even thankfully. His elaborate arguments ring hollow when placed before the last paragraph of the essay which depicts the death-bed scene and brings us (and Montaigne) back to the grim details of dying, surrounded by one's wailing family and all the paraphernalia of sorrow; and they fall impotent before the last sentence with its heartfelt wish: 'Heureuse la mort qui oste le loisir aux apprests de tel equipage' (1:20,95). Here we have Montaigne trying to come to terms with his fear by every rhetorical means he knows, and not succeeding.

Because Montaigne fails to convince, does his elaborate argumentation then seem any more than a game? It is true that it is not always easy to distinguish when Montaigne is partly indulging his mental agility for the sheer pleasure of exercise, and when the game is serious. Montaigne himself would probably argue that it is for each individual reader to make up his own mind. He makes the problem more difficult himself when he describes both these activities by the same word: 'escrime'. He used it in the *Apologie* where he had similarly shown his capacity for speaking authentically in another voice, and where the

perspectives change so rapidly that at one moment Montaigne speaks as
a star, and at the next as a tiny bird (ii : 12,514). It is easy to miss the
contrapuntal force of such swiftly changing voices through admiration for
Montaigne's virtuoso performance, particularly so, since, in the *Apologie*
—although he is keen to make out the best case possible in an essay which
was written with a specific debunking purpose in mind—Montaigne
remains relatively detached: his own personal self is not intimately
involved in the argument.[31] In the essay we have just examined, it is
obvious that Montaigne *is* involved in a very different and much more
desperate way than in the *Apologie,* yet here he again uses the word
'escrime'. The link between the two essays seems to be in the curious
coincidence of an increasing complexity in method and an awareness of
a lack of conviction. In both essays Montaigne is conscious, in differing
degrees, that his reasoning is forced, and formalistic techniques of argument are the sign of a mind basically unsatisfied with its handling of a
problem. It is interesting, too, that in both these essays Montaigne takes
up the commonplaces which refer to life as theatre and to life as a game.[32]
He seems to be trying to say that when solutions to problems do not
occur immediately (or even after great effort) you must try other
means; vary your methods, increase your skill, multiply the angles of
approach and the number of voices you use: 'les plus belles ames sont
celles qui ont plus de varieté et de soupplesse' (iii : 3,796). You may
never succeed in convincing yourself or others. You may only succeed
in discovering that the 'souverain bien' is for ever outside your reach:
but it does exist (*D'un mot de Cæsar,* i : 53,296-7), and the nostalgic
search for it is a strengthening process.

It follows that one must not dismiss the idea of game in Montaigne
as something essentially frivolous, as an idle manipulating of the mind to
no purpose. Quoting from Horace, he reminds us in *Sur des vers de
Virgile* (iii : 5,855) that truth is often said in jest. He himself was quite
explicit on the value he attached to exercising the mind: it perfected
one's reasoning power (iii : 3,807) ; it clarified one's ideas (iii : 8,906) ;
and, far from being some easily acquired art, he insisted on its difficulty
(ii : 6,358). Montaigne's conception of game can seem oblique, and even
misleading, until one understands the degree of seriousness which
attaches to it. It suggests play, but leads, most often, to independent
reflexion.

*   *   *

While we are concerned more generally with Montaigne's oblique
methods of arousing the interest of his reader, a word must be said of his

ability to change the tone of an essay, and to make such changes carry the weight of his persuasion. In his discussion on varying the tone of one's speaking voice, he had noted the appropriateness of certain tones for certain thoughts: 'Il y a voix pour instruire, voix pour flater, ou pour tancer. Je veux que ma voix, non seulement arrive à luy, mais à l'avanture qu'elle le frape et qu'elle le perse' (III: 13, 1066). In addition, his *Essais* show that he linked force of impact with control of tone. Some essays begin on a light-hearted note like the opening sentence of *De l'incommodité de la grandeur* (III: 7): 'Puisque nous ne la pouvons aveindre, vengeons nous à en mesdire'. Such a beginning puts us into the frame of mind where we expect an entertaining, witty demolishing of aspirations to greatness. We are hardly prepared for 'la paillardise, dissolution, desloyauté, blasphèmes, cruauté, hérésie' (III: 7, 898) which hit us as sharply as the weapons of civil war upon which such immoral attitudes thrive. Such words make us reflect upon the nature and consequences of war, and they do so all the more effectively because we had not expected them.

Sometimes, differing tones are intertwined within the same passage:

> Voyons combien il a de tenue en ce bel equipage. Qu'il me face entendre par l'effort de son discours, sur quels fondemens il a basty ces grands avantages qu'il pense avoir sur les autres creatures. Qui luy a persuadé que ce branle admirable de la voute celeste, la lumiere eternelle de ces flambeaux roulans si fierement sur sa teste, les mouvemens espouvantables de cette mer infinie, soyent establis et se continuent tant de siecles pour sa commodité et pour son service? Est-il possible de rien imaginer si ridicule que cette miserable et chetive creature, qui n'est pas seulement maistresse de soy, exposée aux offences de toutes choses, se die maistresse et emperiere de l'univers, duquel il n'est pas en sa puissance de cognoistre la moindre partie, tant s'en faut de la commander? Et ce privilege qu'il s'atribue d'estre seul en ce grand bastiment, qui ay la suffisance d'en recognoistre la beauté et les pieces, seul qui en puisse rendre graces à l'architecte et tenir conte de la recepte et mise du monde, qui lui a seelé ce privilege? qu'il nous montre lettres de cette belle et grande charge. (II: 12, 427)

In this quotation from the *Apologie* Montaigne controls two very different tones: one ostensibly mounts in enthusiastic crescendo with the description of the 'voute celeste'; the other undermines the first with the irony latent in verbs like 'pense avoir', and 'persuadé', with the note of incredulity contained in the question, 'Est-il possible?', and with the superlative touch Montaigne has given to the very great and the very small. It is like a two-part invention which allows its two themes to weave in and out without losing their identity, but whose blending finally produces a new tone characteristic of neither theme in its single state. The final joke at man's expense, developed out of the word 'seelé', provides the demolishing touch, and succeeds in doing precisely what Montaigne has just said he was going to do in the *Apologie*: 'froisser et fouler aux pieds l'orgueil et humaine fierté; leur faire sentir l'inanité, la vanité et deneantise de l'homme; leur arracher des points les chetives armes de leur raison; leur faire baisser la teste et mordre la terre soubs l'autorité et reverance de la majesté divine' (II: 12,426). We do not lose sight of the majesty of creation, but at the same time we feel the stupidity of man's pretentions. This double response is maintained by a skill which intermingles the enthusiastic tones of man's pride with the deflating confidence of the critic. It must be admitted that, in this excessively long essay, Montaigne does not always control his tone as persuasively. Too frequently he abuses his role as the domineering critic as when he asks us, unprepared, to accept this description of ourselves: 'Oyez braver ce pauvre et calamiteux animal' (II: 12,468). The long example which I have analysed does nevertheless suggest that when he plays both roles at once—the critic and the criticised—his power of persuasion is considerable.

Montaigne studied reactions to words, changing tones, arguments, and even to jokes. He observed himself and others in discourse. He knew how to catch minds and emotions and set them in action. Nor did he ever underestimate the complexities of the responses he anticipated and aroused. To whatever lengths Montaigne is prepared to go to entice the reader into his work, he never forgets that there might still remain considerable resistance to his argument. The reader is both friend and adversary. In this chapter I have tried to show that when one considers the way he marshals arguments, builds his essays, and defines a concept, Montaigne reveals himself not only as a conscious artist aware of the range of literary and rhetorical techniques open to him, but also as a *moraliste* conscious of the complexities of the human mind and behaviour, and firm in the knowledge that these can only be analysed and communicated fully to the reader by methods as mobile as themselves. There is no better way of summing up the 'craftie and secrete methode' of Montaigne than by citing Peter Ramus' perfect manner of dissimulation, despite the fact that the passage refers to a rather limited definition of the 'craftie' method.

Si c'est homme cault et fin, il ne fault pas incontinent manifester noz pièces l'une après l'autre, mais changer, entremesler, frivoler, feindre le contraire, se reprendre, ne monstrer aucun semblant d'y penser, dire que c'est chose vulgaire et accoustumée, se haster, courroucer, débatre, procéder par grande hardiesse, et en fin finalle descouvrir et exécuter l'embusche tellement que l'adversaire estonné dye: 'A quelle fin tend cecy?'.[33]

4

PARADOXES

C'estoit un commandement paradoxe que nous faisoit anciennement ce Dieu à Delphes : Regardez dans vous, reconnoissez vous, tenez vous à vous ; vostre esprit et vostre volonté, qui se consomme ailleurs, rame- nez la en soy ; vous vous escoulez, vous vous respandez ; appilez vous, soutenez vous ; on vous trahit, on vous dissipe, on vous desrobe à vous. Voy tu pas que ce monde tient toutes ses veues contraintes au dedans et ses yeux ouverts à se contempler soy-mesme ? c'est tousjours va- nité pour toy, dedans et dehors, mais elle est moins estendue. Sauf toy, ô homme, disoit ce Dieu, chaque chose s'estudie la premiere et a, selon son besoin, des limites à ses travaux et desirs. Il n'en est une seule si vuide et necessiteuse que toy, qui embrasse l'univers : tu es le scrutateur sans connoissance, le magistrat sans jurisdiction et apres tout le badin de la farce. (III : 9, 979-80)

IN this interpretation of the Delphic oracle's advice to man, with which Montaigne ends his essay *De la vanité*, two aspects of man's condition are underlined : alone, among mortal creatures, man's natural tendency seems to be to strain outwards beyond the limits fixed by creation ; while his happiness resides in turning inwards upon himself in order to recognise the narrowness of those limits. Thus Life itself is presented as a paradox ; man's search for truth is fraught with seeming contradictions ; and his intellectual activity is seen as a teasing exercise which either leads straight to a knowledge of the universe which is useless, since it is founded upon the observations of the unqualified, or to an apprehension of man's limited capacity. An appropriate end indeed to a chapter on the theme of Vanity!

Traditionally, the paradox was defined as an essentially verbal

structure, a mere form of argument stating sentiments contrary to received opinion. Montaigne sometimes uses the paradox in this way; but,
more frequently, he extends its use, either building on its balanced, provocative character in order to affirm a truth, or, as in the example just
quoted from *De la vanité*, he introduces conceptual overtones making the
paradox embrace a view of life fraught with contradictions. In this way,
he comes closest to our modern view of paradox.

Now, on the face of it, paradoxes seem at some remove from the
frank talk that Montaigne had promised for his self-exposure to the
reader. But what straightforward talk could communicate, as effectively
as this last paragraph of *De la vanité*, the often simultaneous pull in opposite directions which Montaigne describes as the condition of man?
Placing two contrary urges in close opposition brings us nearer to the
truth of our situation. Paradoxical expression allows a clearer, sharper,
and more immediate grasp; it provides a means of coping with apparently
self-contradictory material.[1] In our examination of Montaigne's discussion of Virtue in the previous chapter, we noted how he reached his
definition of such abstract notions through the medium of their opposites.
Montaigne had observed in himself the power of argument through opposites—rather 'par fuite que par suite' (III: 8, 899); and he had noted
that 'les contradictions . . . m'esveillent seulement et m'excercent' (III:
8, 901). He also recognised the powerful attraction of what you don't
possess, of what is difficult to get, or of what you are about to lose.
Faith becomes deeper when under attack: so does desire (*On est puny
pour s'opiniastrer à une place sans raison*, I: 15, *passim*). It is not surprising,
therefore, when he tries, at one and the same time, to alert the reader and
to clarify the complexities of truth, that he should resort to a stylistic
device which he personally had found stimulating.[2]

Not only were paradoxes especially suitable for intractable material, they were also—in the sixteenth century—an extraordinarily popular
means of expression. The advantages of striking off one set of opinions
against another had been employed by writers Montaigne knew well,
such as Boiastuau in his *Théâtre du Monde* (though, it must be admitted,
Boiastuau is far more eloquent on man's misery than upon his dignity);
or by friends such as Pasquier or Jacques Peletier du Mans, with whom
Montaigne frequently conversed.[3] Pasquier, in his harangue against
Medicine (perhaps textually inspired by Montaigne), maintained
'vous trouverez n'y avoir rien de certain, que l'incertain en cest art', and
he rams home his point with two contradictory opinions: 'l'un des plus
solennels aphorismes d'Hippocrat est celuy: *Contraria contrariis curantur;*

et l'un des plus solemnels de Paracelse est: *Similia similibus curantur'*.[4]
This is a single instance taken from a grand medley of contrary opinions
juxtaposed, with which Pasquier regales Turnebus. All these men had
been taught this form of argument at school, for the composing of paradoxes was the ultimate exercise in mental gymnastics—the disjunctive,
'either/or' being replaced by 'this opinion and its opposite' viewed together.[5] Writers were proud when they succeeded in mastering this technique. Again we may quote Pasquier whose self-confidence is such that
he derides the achievements of the great Cicero in this field as: 'qui n'est
pas a mon jugement œuvre de trop grand merite'; and declares that he
will set forth modern paradoxes altogether more worthy than those in-
vented by the Ancients, which were not true paradoxes at all.[6] It would
be a vain task to list the numbers of writers who tried their hand at such
works before, during, and after the composition of Montaigne's *Essais*.[7]
Caspar Dornavius in 1619 collected together hundreds of such works in
his vast *Syllabus* which in itself provides a fairly eloquent guide to the
popularity of the paradox in the sixteenth century.[8]

It is true that Dornavius lumps together mock encomia, proverb,
paradox, and aphorism. Indeed it is difficult sometimes to distinguish
these various forms which have much in common:[9] they all provoke
reflexion and tend to be witty; they all state their content in a very extreme way using superlative expressions such as *tout, quiconque,* and
jamais, to generalise their wisdom; and, with the exception of the mock
encomia, they are usually pithy. In fact, the paradox, when given concentrated form, strangely acquires the assuring tone of the proverb. On the
other hand, it shares with the mock encomium the capacity to arouse
uncertainty about assumptions, and—disturbingly—to seem to say the
opposite of what one would expect. Yet, though their form is deceptive,
their aim is very far from dissembling the truth. Just as the most celebrated mock encomium of the sixteenth century—*The Praise of Folly*
— led men to Erasmus's truth through their own mental efforts, so
paradoxes served—in Donne's phrase—as similar 'alarums to truth'.[10]
Whatever their nationality—French, English or Italian—sixteenth and
seventeenth-century writers were agreed that the paradox, since it had
considerable clarifying properties, was a road to truth. Ralph Venning
was even persuaded that this method could be used for narrow moralising.
In his *Orthodoxes Paradoxes* he aimed to make 'Christ, and the mystery
of Godlinesse more perspicuously knowne to the world'.[11] How such a
process worked can be judged from the prefatory remarks given by
Henri Estienne to his translation of perhaps the most influential work of

paradoxes in the sixteenth century—the *Paradossi* of Ortensio Landi.[12] After stating the advantages of getting at the truth through a juxtaposition of contrary opinions, Estienne cites a knight and a lawyer as examples of the use to which the paradoxical method could be put. Not only does it have the clarifying properties in general which we have already mentioned, but it develops argumentative powers above the common sort, and an ability to define the exact nature of things. Also, and even more significantly if we think back to Montaigne's use of the extended paradox referred to at the beginning of this chapter, it provides a means of grappling with the most difficult material. Finally, it injects a pleasurable diversity into experience.

> Tout ainsi, Lecteur, que les choses contraires rapportees l'une a l'autre, donnent meilleure cognoissance de leur euidence & uertu: Aussi la uerité d'un propos ie trouue beaucoup plus clere, quand les raisons contraires & opposites luy sont de bien pres approchees: D'aduantage, qui ueult bien dresser un cheualier, il le fault exerciter en faicts d'armes moins uulgaires & communs, affin que les ruses ordinaires luy soyent de moindre peine puis apres. Au cas pareil, pour bien faire un aduocat, apres qu'il a longuement escouté au bareau, il luy fault donner a debattre des causes que les plus excercitez refusent a soustenir: pour a l'aduenir le rendre plus prompt & addroit aux comuns plaidoyers & procez ordinaires. A ceste cause ie t'ay offert en ce liuret le debat d'aucuns propos, que les anciens ont uoulu nommer Paradoxes: C'est a dire, contraires a l'opinion de la pluspart des hommes: affin que par le discours d'iceux, la uerité opposite t'en soit a l'aduenir plus clere & apparente: & aussi pour t'exerciter au debat des choses qui te contraignent a chercher diligemment & laborieusement raisons, preuues, authoritez, histoires & memoires fort diuerses & cachees. En quoy toutesfois ie ne uouldrois que tu fusses tant offensé, que pour mon dire ou conclusion, tu en croye autre chose que le commun. Mais te souuienne, que la diuersité des choses resiouit plus l'esprit des hommes que ne fait tousiours et continuellement uoir ce qui leur est commun & accoustumé.[13]

Estienne here is really developing more fully the sentiments of Cicero who in his second *Tusculan Disputation* explains why the paradox gives him so much pleasure: 'sans cela on ne sçauroit trouver autrement ce qui est veritable en chasque chose: mais aussi grande exercitation d'eloquence'.[14] The Stoics had indeed been strikingly addicted to this form of discourse, as Seneca makes clear in his Letters to Lucilius, and their appreciation seems to have been largely founded upon the latent moralising of the paradox as well as upon the beauty of its formulation.

There are, therefore, obvious reasons why a man like Montaigne would be attracted to the paradox since it combines intellectual and moral delights with a concern for aesthetic performance. It provided a more refined form of shock than Montaigne's brutal *entrée en matière* in *Sur des vers de Virgile* (III:5,825). Furthermore it involves a reader in the thinking process more fully than any device that we have so far examined. It was generally liked because it flattered intelligence, drawing forth the reader's admiration for the unexpected (the apparent opposite of the truth) and, from this wonder, stimulating further speculation.[15] Essentially the paradox is open-ended; it teases the mind by running counter to normal assumptions and expectations; and it rarely seems (on the surface at any rate) to solve anything, but rather invites the reader into the thought, so that he might carry its implications further and make up his mind for himself. A. E. Malloch has summed up its functions very aptly: 'The office of the paradoxes themselves is not to deceive, but by a show of deceit to force the reader to uncover the truth. The true nature of the paradox is revealed when the reader overturns it'.[16]

*   *   *

From our observations so far, it would seem that in the paradox Montaigne had a form which suited his purposes well. It put the reader in a central position and gave him the onus of interpretation, while allowing the writer considerable freedom to write elegantly and in a way that would dazzle and provoke attention. Indeed, the titles of many of the early essays have a slightly paradoxical flavour: *Que philosopher c'est apprendre à mourir* (1:20), *Le profit de l'un est dommage de l'autre* (1:22), *De fuir les voluptez au pris de la vie* (1:33), *Comme nous pleurons et rions d'une mesme chose* (1:38), and so on.[17] These are by no means as audacious as Landi's efforts—'Meglio è morire, che longamente campare'[18]—yet they do seem to have a similar effect, beckoning the reader, puzzling him a little, and encouraging him to read further. The teasing nature of the paradox no doubt attracted Montaigne from the first. It is highly likely that he knew Landi well since the French translation of the *Paradossi* ran through ten editions in the decade after its first publication in 1553. Furthermore, we know that he particularly appreciated the paradoxes of ancient writers. He used Cicero's *Paradoxes* to lend support to his argument (1:14,66); he borrowed most extensively from Seneca to give an air of authority to his own words (1:20,85); and he ended an essay—*Comme nostre esprit s'empesche soy-mesmes* (II : 14, 595)—on a double paradox taken from Pliny ('solum certum nihil esse certi, et homine nihil miserius aut superbius'), to provide a startling, and seemingly irrefutable, finish to his thoughts.

Montaigne's wish to surprise and open our ideas to a state of being which demands correction is frequently given extreme paradoxical and affirmative form, as in *De l'institution des enfants* (I : 26, 162) when he states 'on nous aprent à vivre quand la vie est passée'. Sometimes he will summarise pages of discussion with an assertion which again comes close to paradox, constantly teasing the mind. A typical example would be: 'Il nous faut abestir pour nous assagir, et nous esblouir pour nous guider' (II : 12, 472). Alternatively, he gives memorable affirmative expression to thoughts as in: 'la vertu n'advoue rien que ce qui se faict par elle et pour elle seule' (I : 37, 226). He acknowledges that there are times when he cannot resist bombarding his listeners with words or notions which he knows will make them gasp with astonishment or rejection. When he says: 'le plaisir est nostre but', and stresses the hold which 'la volupté' has over all of us, he adds: 'Il me plaist de leur battre leurs oreilles de ce mot qui leur est si fort à contre cœur' (I : 20, 80). It is not just a question of a little malicious enjoyment. By creating such resistance Montaigne makes us reflect for ourselves. He performs a similar act when he utters 'les choses les plus ignorées sont plus propres à estre deifiées' (II : 12, 497). As we consider the detail of the arguments and evidence provided by Montaigne we are forced to accept the truth of this paradoxical assertion, while the irony with which it is underscored reveals Montaigne's own strong disapproval that such facts contrary to Moral Truth should exist. These are fairly conventional uses of the paradox, which one could find in any contemporary of Montaigne. Frequently, however, he uses the paradox in a more personal, and perhaps more modern, way; this may first be illustrated from a study of his presentation of the traditional paradox: that 'Life is death and death is Life'.[19]

He gives extended discussion to this theme in two *Essais*—*Que philosopher c'est apprendre à mourir* (I : 20) and *Coustume de l'isle de Cea* (II : 3)—both inspired by, and freely translated from, Seneca's *Letters* and *Moral Works*. 'Il est incertain où la mort nous attende, attendons-la partout. La premeditation de la mort est premeditation de la liberté. Qui a apris à mourir, il a desapris à servir' (I : 20, 85).[20] This staccato series of perfectly balanced phrases, seemingly paradoxical, occurs at the end of a long passage in which Montaigne exhorts himself to come as close as possible to death—for that, he thought, was the only way by which fear of death might be mastered. The sentences quoted above had been preceded by a series of imperatives which though they had commanded had, seemingly, not convinced. The paradoxes appear to clinch the argument: to persuade where exhortation has failed. But somehow in this context they do not seem to carry conviction. It is not, I think, simply the fact that we know that these lines are taken directly from Seneca which undermines their persuasive force. It is, rather, that paradoxes are used at this point of the essay on exactly the same level as all the other methods of persuasion; and where these fail, so too does the paradox.[21]

Later in the essay, far from alleviating fear in the face of death, Montaigne's use of paradox seems almost to enhance it. The voice of Nature, in the process of urging man to depart from this life in the same way as he made his entry, stresses the naturalness of dying with: 'le premier jour de vostre naissance vous achemine à mourir comme à vivre'. This phrase in Montaigne's first version of the *Essais* is left undeveloped, though supported by two Latin quotations from respectable authorities —Seneca and Manlius. When he came to read his essays again in the months preceding his own death, Montaigne chose to multiply the paradoxes on life and death: 'Tout ce que vous vivez, vous desrobez à la vie; c'est à ses despens. Le continuel ouvrage de vostre vie c'est bastir la mort. Vous estes en la mort pendant que vous estes en vie. Car vous estes apres la mort quand vous n'estes plus en vie. Ou si vous aymez mieux ainsi, vous estes mort apres la vie; mais pendant la vie vous estes mourant, et la mort touche bien plus rudement le mourant que le mort, et plus vivement et plus essentiellement' (1:20,91).[22] The paradox which he first borrowed from Seneca no longer seems adequate to describe what he feels as he himself, after years of considerable (though intermittent) pain, faces his own death. His development seems to start off as mere play upon the paradox already cited. As his analysis spreads outwards, however, a totally different note appears. Meditation upon Life and Death is no longer something that can be contained by the jugglings of an agile mind. His thoughts have left a rather bitter taste in his mouth, and the sole purpose of Life is given as 'bastir la mort'. Here we are witnessing the emotion of a man who has suffered much, and whose strength of experience is such that it breaks through the series of paradoxes, which had hitherto seemed to control feeling, with the three forceful adverbs 'rudement', 'vivement', and 'plus essentiellement'.

This moment of bitterness, highlighted through paradoxical expression, should be set beside the welling confidence which marks *De*

l'experience (III : 13), where Seneca's phrase, 'tu meurs de ce que tu es vivant' (III : 13, 1070),[23] borrowed by Montaigne and used in a context
similar to that of his source, strikes another tone entirely. Placed at the
centre of his attack upon the doctor's inadequate arts, it throws a sudden,
unassailable air of confidence into the discussion. We cannot help but be
startled by its formulation; and the more we reflect upon its implications
the more the paradox acquires indisputable authority. Paradox becomes
as effective an attacking tool in *De la vanité* where 'Qui se faict mort
vivant est subject d'estre tenu pour vif mourant' (III : 9, 957) is the last
of a series of paradoxes used by Montaigne to argue against the view
which sees nothing good in Life. This is the final shot which carries conviction, not merely because the last of a series seems to contain the most
irony and thus seems most incontestable, but also because Montaigne
has tucked it in before 'J'en ay veu',

> Qui se faict mort vivant est subject d'estre tenu pour vif mourant. J'en
> ay veu prendre la chevre de ce qu'on leur trouvoit le visage frais et
> le pouls posé, contraindre leur ris par ce qu'il trahissoit leur guairison,
> et haïr la santé de ce qu'elle n'estoit pas regrettable.

The paradox and faithful eye-witness interact to produce the maximum
persuasive force.

*   *   *

   Montaigne quite early recognised the advantages of the paradox
as a means of argument. In *Coustume de l'isle de Cea* (II : 3), the following
example provides his point of departure for a discussion on suicide: 'on
demandoit aussi à Agis comment un homme pourroit vivre libre: Mesprisant, dict-il, le mourir' (II : 3, 330-331)—that is to say, possessing a
willingness, even an urgent desire to die. Further paradoxes direct the
development of his argument: 'Le vivre, c'est servir, si la liberté de
mourir en est à dire' (II : 3, 331-2). The analytical power of the paradox
is exploited to the full, as Montaigne places it in a specific or qualified
context: 'If the freedom to die is lacking, only then, is Life slavery';
and, later in the same paragraph, 'If Life is slavery, then it is worse than
death'. The conclusion implied by Montaigne (and only implied) is that
in such circumstances suicide becomes permissible. It would seem that
paradoxes have brought him neatly to the position of holding the same
permissive views on suicide as those extolled by many Stoics. But, a closer
look at this essay will reveal that, so far, paradoxes have simply served
to clear the ground, and they are later used as a means of combatting

the Stoic view. His first paradox involving 'mespris de la mort' is answered and turned on its head in the phrase: 'Et l'opinion que desdaigne nostre vie, elle est ridicule' (II:3,334). Since Life is all we have, to despise it, says Montaigne, is to despise death (in other words, to be willing to die). And this is both unnatural and presumptuous. The essay should be seen as an attempt first to clarify the arguments for and against suicide; and second, to bring the reader to the realisation that any serious thoughts upon suicide in real life are going beyond man's limits. Morally and naturally, he has no powers over Life or Death, and the words 'vanité' and 'contre nature' sound out strongly against the play of paradox. In this essay, paradoxes mirror each other, and sift out the truth which seems to emerge between them. On the same theme, in the *Apologie* (II:12,507), Montaigne translates Stobaeus as further evidence to show our inability to distinguish the true nature of Life and Death. Montaigne the aesthetician might say 'la mort la plus volontaire est la plus belle': but Montaigne the moralist certainly never entertained the idea seriously.

This manner of throwing fundamental concerns into relief is a particular virtue in Montaigne's use of the paradox. In *De la vanité* he writes on his own copy of the *Essais*: 'Ils disent, comme la vie n'est pas la meilleure pour estre longue, que la mort est la meilleure pour n'estre pas longue' (III:9,949). Now such a paradoxical statement is slipped in as an aside into Montaigne's deliberations on pain and death. It serves as a mirror to throw back light, not as something on which to ponder for itself, but to concentrate attention more precisely on what Montaigne is saying around the paradox. The paradoxical expression develops the idea of pain over the range of Life and Death, giving the measure of Montaigne's misery, as well as illustrating this 'miserable condition, comme est la nostre'.

The conventional paradox 'Life is Death', as used in the Christian tradition,[24] or borrowed from the Stoics' rich fund of examples on the same theme, has been largely transformed by Montaigne. It is no longer the summary of a stock attitude which is accepted with the sort of conviction which belongs to the proverb. It has lost most of its characteristics as a truism and becomes, more interestingly, either a stepping stone in an argument (as in Montaigne's discussion on suicide), or that which suddenly triggers off an intense realisation of a state of being —Montaigne's experience of pain.

One can gain a good idea of Montaigne's originality in using this form if one compares his own borrowings from Seneca with the translations into French of Seneca's letters, made by his brother-in law—the sieur de Pressac.[25] In the first instance, Pressac chooses to translate only those letters of Seneca which have to do either with death or with the onset of age and its accompanying pain: two themes so prominent in Montaigne that one is encouraged to think that the two men influenced each other. Pressac is very faithful in his rendering of the Latin. Paradoxes abound, often herded together to make an argument the more convincing: 'Nous mourons tous les jours. Car chasque jour nous racle quelque partie de la vie, et à mesure que nous croissons, la vie nous descroit . . . Et ce mesme iour, auquel nous vivons, nous le partageons avec la mort'. Their very abundance ensures that the final impression is an acutely intellectualised one. The man of mature experience seems left far behind, and we seem to be heeding the neat maxims of someone expert at coining them. It might well be that Latin, as a language, lends itself naturally to paradoxical formulations, while such frequent usage in French seems excessive. What is interesting, however, is that Pressac's careful rendering frequently removes all the sparkle from paradoxes since there are too many of them for that language; while the sense of proportion which Montaigne developed, and his knowledge that the paradox is a precious tool of persuasion, makes his own use less wholesale, more varied, and ultimately more convincing.

While sharing his contemporaries' enthusiasm for the paradox, Montaigne exploits its use in a diversity of contexts. 'J'honnore le plus ceux que j'honnore le moins' (1:40, 247) teases the reader's mind into play. The point—implying emptiness of praise—is not a significant one, but its formulation does prepare us for a quick understanding and appreciation of the second point which carries more weight: '[je]me presente moins à qui je me suis le plus donné' (1:40, 247). The play on similar constructions can seem not very far from gratuitous word play—the sort of wit which simply asks for a nod of approval as in the phrase Montaigne added to *Sur des vers de Virgile* (III:5, 869): 'l'insuffisance et la sottise est loüable en une action meslouable'. Such a comment can be refuted with difficulty. The shock initiated by the juxtaposition of 'insuffisance' and 'sottise' with 'loüable' is utterly undermined with the appearance of the word 'meslouable'. But such a let-down occurs infrequently in Montaigne's handling of the paradox. Mostly he is concerned to preserve the maximum sense of surprise, allowing the paradox to summarise a story or an argument, and to leave the reader's mind puzzling, and thus open to further thought. His late addition to a story (III:10, 986), 'ses pertes luy sont plus glorieuses que ses victoires, et son deüil que son triomphe', neatly rounds off a tale of the inadequate services of an enthusiastic servant to a prince, who is introduced as Montaigne's friend. The action of the paradox, however, encourages the reader to find instances of his own, while reflecting at the same time more generally on the nature of service to princes. 'Il n'est rien si dissociable et sociable que l'homme' startles because, logically, it would seem that man cannot have both qualities at once. It immediately demands to be set in a specific context, and Montaigne helps us on the way by adding 'l'un par son vice, l'autre par sa nature' (1:39, 233).

Sometimes the paradox itself initiates further reflexion by Montaigne on a subject. In *Du repentir* (III:2), his first thoughts on the virtues of moderation have ended on the assertion: 'Le pris de l'ame ne consiste pas à aller haut, mais ordonnéement' (p. 787). This idea was expanded later in a fairly long passage which begins: 'Sa grandeur ne s'exerce pas en la grandeur, c'est en la mediocrité'. A statement so couched in riddles has an almost mesmerising effect until, reflecting on the context in which Montaigne has placed the paradox, one remembers that the discussion has been concerned to denigrate public acclaim and throw into relief the advantages of the private self-absorption which Montaigne himself advocates. The moral value of the 'grandeur' usually attached to public fame is transferred to the domain of the individual's private life, and it is the paradox which gives crystallised expression to this transference. Not only does it add lustre to Montaigne's moral arguments, it also provides an important source of protection for Montaigne who is here challenging, at the very least, an orthodox social view of 'grandeur' and mediocrity. The word-play of the paradox hides the criticism implied beneath an ambiguity which is resolved only by the reader who wishes to take upon himself the burden of interpretation. Montaigne lights the way: one can choose to follow him, or not. He goes even further in his essay *De la gloire* (II:16), where he uses the paradox both as a means of giving moral encouragement and for delivering specific warning on the dangers of war. His comment is well prepared by many examples, and is given extra force by specific reference to the contemporary Civil Wars of France. And his twin aim is summed up in the statement: 'les moins esclattantes occasions sont les plus dangereuses' (p. 606).

An ability to distinguish the literal and metaphorical planes, on which Montaigne might often be using the same term, is fundamental to a proper appreciation of the paradox, the long-term influence of which depends on its defining power. When, for instance, Montaigne persuades

his reader of the difficulties of kingship, he uses the literal plane of measurement to throw into relief the moral overtones of omnipotence: 'con-
cevez l'homme accompaigné d'omnipotence, vous l'abismez' (III:8,897).
The writer who can draw nice distinctions, such as 'Ce n'est pas macheure
[tache], c'est plustost une teinture universelle qui me tache' (III:2,791),
can also rivet attention with paradoxes, where success depends upon a
similar fine sense of words: 'La jurisdiction ne se donne point en faveur
du juridiciant, c'est en faveur du juridicié' (III:6,881). A reader is not
only dazzled by the unexpected, or overwhelmed with admiration at the
word-play; such sensations encourage other reactions; he is invited to
analyse the paradox, to search out its implications, and, indeed, to invent
paradoxes of his own. Nor are the repercussions limited to an examination of the context and implications of a phrase. Since such an analysis
can only be achieved through the closest attention to form, the reader's
response is necessarily geared to stylistic considerations. Anticipating
such reactions, Montaigne can also employ the paradox for purposes of
irony, as when he makes fun of the hypocrisy he detects in woman's
relationship to her mate—'la vie est pleine de combustion; le trespas,
d'amour et de courtoisie' (II:35,722); or he can replace it by a proverb,
as at the end of *Sur des vers de Virgile* when, anticipating the angry
comment of his female readers, he seeks to save himself from their wrath
—'Le fourgon se moque de la poele'.

*   *   *

Irony, implying the opposite of what it says, is a natural ground
for paradox, just as Montaigne's conception of the complexities of Life
seems most perfectly expressed through paradoxes. Change/stability,
diversity/unity, and spontaneity/control are all major themes in Montaigne. These opposites are not seen as alternative views. Rather, they
complement each other; or they might simply express a view of Life
seen from a particular angle or in a specific context; or, on the other
hand, they may be used by Montaigne as two extreme points between
which he can travel in his search for the truth.[26] Paradox can juxtapose
extreme polarities: youth and age linked by the necessity of moderation
(III:5,818); or appearance and frank exposure joggled together so that
we might learn to distinguish the true nature of each (III:5,823-4). Such
juxtaposition often produces a curiously purifying effect on the opposites
brought together so abruptly. Truth and falsehood, in the following example, seem to have a clear-cut solidity of meaning: 'Qui est desloyal
envers la verité l'est aussi envers le mensonge' (II:17,631). Montaigne

felt the need to explain this somewhat paradoxical generalisation, and, in a later addition to the *Essais*, adds examples for elucidation. The quality of constancy, in *De la constance*, (1:12), has more associations with flexibility than with the craggy characteristics customarily associated with this virtue: it is shown as a state of mind, and an ability to control the effects of disturbance. Already in this early essay, Montaigne is anticipating some of his most startling discoveries—the solid movement of the Caucasus or Pyramids: 'La constance mesme n'est autre chose qu'un branle plus languissant' (III:2, 782). The moral world inside us, the physical world we apprehend, and the moral world again—Montaigne moves with ease from one to the other. He is fascinated and astonished, attracted and repelled, charmed and puzzled. The paradox embraces the multiplicity of his reactions and goes some way to satisfying man's need to explain what he sees. This form is inherent in Montaigne's view of what he sees around him, and it furnishes the most accurate, as well as the most stirring, means of communicating to others how he feels when he confronts the universe.

*   *   *

A paradox which had enjoyed great currency, especially since the time of Nicholas of Cusa and beyond, was that concerning wisdom and ignorance.[27] From what we have already observed from Montaigne's response to paradoxes in general, it is easy to understand why this particular set of extremes should hold considerable fascination for him. In the first place, it provided an infinite fund of matter for word play: 'sagesse', in the *Essais*, is termed (sometimes apparently indiscriminately) 'ignorance, sottise, inanité, vanité, insipience' and so on The following passage from the *Apologie*—'nostre veillée est plus endormie que le dormir; notre sagesse, moins sage que la folie; nos songes vallent mieux que noz discours' (II:12,551)—is a good example of the ease with which Montaigne, at the end of his life, accumulated phrases of paradoxical flavour, linking them by a neat control of 'plus', 'moins' and 'mieux'. At first glance their balanced structure has a rather frivolous touch. Mere coining of words from some spontaneous machine, we might say. But a closer look reveals that the movement from 'plus' to 'moins' and 'mieux' is not haphazard: from a kind of quantitative assessment of waking and wisdom, Montaigne moves to an evaluative statement about Life. The affirmative ring which often accompanies the paradox is very much in evidence here, and it is made more obtrusive by the cumulative syntax.[28] Usually the reader has an opportunity to overturn the assertion, but the construction, 'plus', 'moins', 'mieux', discourages such a course.

Before we examine in more detail the function in Montaigne's *Essais* of this particular paradox, it must be pointed out that his use of the dichotomy 'sagesse/folie' is sometimes prejudiced. He moves between interpreting 'sagesse' as wisdom and interpreting it as mere erudition: and his scholars are always vain, crabbed, arrogant and stuffed with useless learning which turns them into those caricatures of wise men, whom we call fools. His argument is rarely tempered with the moderation he so often advocates. Scholars are either modest or they are not; and they are mostly not, since they belong in Montaigne's eyes to that class of professionals with which he feared to be associated. In this way, paradox becomes a tool of satire which he will exploit against scholars and doctors alike, using this form in an opposite manner to that of Erasmus. Montaigne does not envisage, for example, that there can be wisdom in madness. Committed to serious criticism of these two professions, he ignores the protective advantages employed by the earlier humanist. His topsy-turvy world moves in one direction only, making fools out of the experts.

But let us turn to some of the more fundamental uses of the paradox, wisdom/ignorance, in the *Essais*. Straining outwards, while happiness lies within, was but one of the contradictory pulls which made up man's existence, according to Montaigne. 'Nostre vie est partie en folie, partie en prudence' (III:5,866). It is not that Montaigne does not perceive any nuances between these two extremes of existence, but rather that he feels that man's natural tendencies veer dramatically towards one extreme or the other. Philosophies similarly incline towards two dramatically opposed interpretations of Life, placing significance either on pride and knowledge, or, alternatively, on the lack of it: 'Les uns tiennent en l'ignorance cette mesme extremité que les autres tiennent en la science' (III:11,1013). As one might expect, these extremes, in Montaigne's view, are not static. For him, wisdom and ignorance are elastic concepts. Both have similar needs since both lend themselves to excess: 'la sagesse a ses excés, et n'a pas moins besoin de moderation que la folic' (III:5, 818). On a cosmic scale, the distance between divine wisdom and human ignorance is, of course, infinite. But, in the realm of the terrestrial, human wisdom is at no great distance from human folly. Montaigne cites with relish the story of Gallus Vibius whose study of madness rendered him insane. 'De quoy se faict la plus subtile folie, que de la plus subtile sagesse?', he asks mischievously in the *Apologie* where, as is well known, he takes particular delight in joining wisdom and folly hand in hand.[29]

The paradox provides an amusing caution to the reader!

In the long and persistent discussions devoted to these topics in the *Essais*, it becomes clear that Montaigne is using these two polarities in order to get at some clearer conception of moral excellence. Neither wisdom nor ignorance in a pure state is of any use to someone attempting to develop a personal code which can be effective in the constantly changing political situations of the sixteenth century. Knowledge is as frequently inept in specific moments of behaviour as ignorance (II:12, 467), and this is no better illustrated than by the 'maistre ès arts' whose proud expertise never raises him above the lowest ground (III:8,904-5). Indeed, knowledge is more often a handicap than an advantage: its subtleties, more often than not, refine pleasure out of existence (I:30,198). It should not, of course, be assumed that its counterpart—ignorance— fares any better at Montaigne's hands. Although he declares 'J'oy journellement dire à des sots des mots non sots' (III:8,915-6), Montaigne really despises the unthinking stupidities of the countryfolk whose simplicity he so often extols for the sole purpose of deflating the presumptions of the learned. Only through a synthesis of these two extreme positions can Montaigne come close to the moral code he searches for. The philosophy he advocates most fervently is that which acknowledges that the greatest wisdom has a recognition of ignorance as its end—the kind of ignorance 'pour laquelle concevoir il n'y a pas moins de science que pour concevoir la science' (III:11,1008). Only a wise man can admit the limits of his knowledge. We have come round full circle to the problems posed by the Delphic oracle at the beginning of this chapter. But Montaigne has, in part, found the solution to that particular tangle. 'Look into yourself', he seems to say, 'find out your own limits, resist the pull of outside affairs; and if you cannot do this, then so arrange your life that such affairs build up your capacities. Observe, take in the sound words uttered unconsciously by fools, learn from other people's habits, test your mind against Life's diversities as well as its adversities'. That is the mortal wisdom which Montaigne advocates in his paradoxical *De la vanité* (III:9), where the notion that all human activity, wisdom, and experience, are vain, acts as the structural pivot of the essay (p. 967). The mental anguish he endured during the civil wars made him long for some respite, and persuaded him more forcibly than ever of the need to build up an inner resistance. Each individual is responsible for the present state of decay: 'la corruption du siecle se faict par la contribution particulière de chacun de nous' (III:9,923), Montaigne states categorically; and only a careful examination by the individual of his inner self, and a sustained education of that self, can go some way to combatting the civil disorders.

These last suggestions of Montaigne are tentative. He does not know that his proposals will really solve anything: 'il semble que ce soit la saison des choses vaines quand les dommageables nous pressent' (III: 9,923). His writings are 'vaines'; but this word has a double meaning. Vanity, it is true, is the natural condition for human beings when viewed through God's eyes: 'et vanité toute la sagesse', Montaigne reminds us with a quotation from the psalms (III:9,967). On the humble, human level, vanity is more frequently synonymous with wisdom, as the whole tenor of the essay *De la vanité* has tried to show. What Montaigne is certain about, at least, is that general reflexions on States, and philosophical precepts out of specific contexts, are useless. Like so many of his contemporaries Montaigne would have liked to thrust upon men the importance of God by emphasising the littleness of man: 'nostre sagesse n'est que folie devant Dieu' (II: 12,427).[30] He knows that the straightforward tactics of other moralists have led straight to the slogans of war, and he reserves the right to moralise, but in a much more subtle way. Here is my wisdom, he declares, but it's vain and useless compared to that which God offered you. Remember that He chose to manifest His greatness through the humblest of his creatures to make known wisdom through others' ignorance (II: 12,479). It is against this background that one must judge Montaigne's statements on the vanity of human wisdom. Pasquier could start a letter to his friend M. de Seurin: 'vous ne recevrez de moy, sur le commencement et milieu de cette mienne lettre, que bouffonerie: et toutes fois bouffonerie qui porte quant et soy une philosophie, et contemplation generale de la vanité de ce monde'.[31] So, in the same way, Montaigne, equally enthusiastically, could advocate a way of life which takes account of all the contradictions of existence; and which can (as the occasion warrants) blend contraries, oppose them, use them to define each other, and even render them interchangeable. There is something essentially paradoxical not only in Montaigne's perception of Life, but even about the moral attitudes he proposes in order to live the best Life.

Whatever one might think about Montaigne's moral position, it is impossible not to concede a certain admiration for the man who walks the tight ropes between wisdom, folly, and ignorance, with such confidence and so positively. He knew himself that wonder and astonishment were half-way to persuasion; that they predisposed a reader to accept propositions because he could not resist the invitation to enquire further.

In his paradoxes, the element 'surprise' is always contained within the limits of plausibility, even though this might receive extravagant expression. Although the traditional function of the paradox was to present the opposite of truth in a startling way, Montaigne never goes as far as Landi. He never proposes something so obviously impossible as 'Che M. Tullio fusse non solo ignorante di Filosofia, della quale tanto temerariamente si vanta, ma ancha de Retorica, di Cosmografia, et dell' Istoria'.[32] Such a paradox falls back upon its inventor and puts him in a ridiculous light: although there is still that intriguing desire to see just how Landi could sustain proofs for such a proposition. Any writer of paradoxes knew that the attraction of this form came primarily from its strangeness, its enigmatic quality, and its extraordinary charm. Indeed, the natural human cult of the extraordinary provides the best ground for the propagation of paradoxical expressions, and Montaigne noted more than once his own, and others', attractions towards the rare: 'Estrangeté donne credit', he stated in *Qu'il faut sobrement se mesler de juger des ordonnances divines* (1:32,213). The rare is memorable, he affirmed in *De la force de l'imagination* (1:21, 104).[33] The world of nature is turned into some 'poésie énigmatique—comme peut estre qui diroit une peinture voilée et tenebreuse, entreluisant d'une infinie varieté de faux jours à exercer nos conjectures' (II:12,518). He derides those who succumb to the invitation of looking further through those false, enticing windows; while, at the same time, he recognises the magnetic power of the unexplained.[34] Similarly, he despises those who yield to the wonders of magic, giving to 'singeries' 'poids et reverence' (1:21,99), yet he acknowledges their power of seduction. Montaigne himself, conscious that such yielding is the surest sign of mental weakness (1:54, 298), knows that he does not escape the appeal of the unusual, whether it be an extraordinary act—such as the exploits of Caesar or Alexander —or the 'beauty' of a suicide. Both these happenings remain outside Montaigne's real experience, yet they still possess the power to fascinate him intellectually.

As Montaigne reflects upon such matters, he realises first that, on close examination, things which had seemed extraordinary are far from being so; and that, in fact, the mind can frequently find many such instances: 'J'ay trouvé . . . que nous avions pris pour un exercice malaisé et d'un rare subject ce qui ne l'est aucunement; et qu'apres que nostre invention a esté eschaufée, elle descouvre un nombre infiny de pareils examples' (1:54,300). His second discovery was that people— seeking to interest, influence, or gain some hold over other people—

did not record their day to day experience; but, instead, resorted to prognostications which have currency 'de ce qu'elles sont rares, incroiables
et prodigieuses' (*Des prognostications*, I:11,44).

We have seen how Montaigne caught the attention of readers
through tactics no less prodigious. In his final essay, *De l'experience*
(III:13), he determined to adjust his reader's sights and reveals what
was, in his opinion, the really extraordinary content of a man's existence. And this, too, he accomplished by paradoxical means, demonstrating that the apparently ordinary is more often the truly extraordinary.
Others make their impact by searching for the most startling, uncommon
event: Montaigne makes his by emphasising the most unexpected, common aspects of man. In *De la ressemblance des enfans aux peres* (II:37,741),
Montaigne had already noted: 'parmy les choses que nous voyons ordinairement, il y a des estrangetés si incomprehensibles qu'elles surpassent toute la difficulté des miracles'. In this essay, he explored the
remarkable passage of tiny characteristics from father to son, and mar-
velled at the imperceptible and complex ways illnesses are stored, grow,
and flourish. These were natural secrets which defied the attentions of
even the best doctors, and which seemed ordinary because they were
natural, but which, because they remained unfathomable, deserved more
properly to be considered as 'miraculous'. In a similar way, for all his
humble presentation of self, his excuses, and his apologies, Montaigne
knows that his self-exposure is extraordinary. The idea must have come
to him fairly early, for in *De l'aage* (I:57,312) he remarks on the way in
which people accord admiration to the wrong things. To die suddenly is
commonly regarded as an unnatural event, though, given the natural
state of man, living at a time of civil war, 'mourir de vieillesse, c'est une
mort rare, singuliere et extraordinaire'—and yet, this has conventionally been termed 'natural'. There is no more convincing way of rubbing
your reader's nose in riches he refuses to recognise, than by building
upon this knowledge of his blindness, using his cult of the extraordinary,
and pinpointing the distinctions which separate the ordinary from the
unusual. This was the work of *De l'experience* (III:13),

> D'autant qu'à mon advis, des plus ordinaires choses et les plus
> communes et cogneuës, si nous sçavions trouver leur jour, se peuvent
> former les plus grands miracles de nature et les plus merveilleux
> exemples, notamment sur le subject des actions humaines.
>
> (III:13, 1059)

Montaigne recognised, at the end of his life, that the ideals which he admired from the past, the human feats which astonished the mind by their audacity, were tools of measurement and analysis, not monuments to be emulated by all. He does not devalue the extraordinary; but, while acknowledging that certain 'âmes venerables' perform acts that are memorable but impossible of imitation, he allows what is commonly termed the 'rare' to pass into ordinary acts of life. He uses the extra-ordinary to throw light on the riches of man's day to day existence. Our admiration for the difficult, for that which resists our efforts, is diminished when placed beside 'la forme de vivre plus usitée et commune' (p. 1084). To this last Montaigne accords his most glowing praise—the ordinary is 'la plus belle', 'saine', 'légitime', 'noble', 'naturelle'. 'C'est une absolue perfection, et comme divine, de sçavoyr jouyr loiallement de son estre' (III: 12, 1096–7). Humble man, fully aware of his limitations, enjoying the wisdom which recognises ignorance, acquires all the attributes of the divine. Montaigne can go no further than his claim of absolute perfection for such wise ignorance.

5

AFFIRMATION IN THE 'ESSAIS'

'WHY, but essays are but men's school themes pieced together', so
Florio informs us in the address to the Reader which prefaced his
translation of the *Essais* in 1603.[1] 'School themes' were the commonplaces, topics, or (more narrowly) the *sententiae*, which provided the
subject matter for a Renaissance student's discourse. If such a student
were to follow Erasmus's instructions for learning—and his work, the
De Ratione studendi, summarised much contemporary and subsequent
practice[2]—he would cram his notebook full of worthy notions, carefully
selected from the works of esteemed writers such as Cato or Seneca.
The *Distichs* of the former, and the *Sayings* of the latter, were his handbooks. Their pithy words of wisdom furnished him with a code of
behaviour suitable for every occasion, a moral response for every
moment of experience, and a summary of virtuous conduct for every
stage of a man's life.[3] For a student in the sixteenth century such works
seemed to contain all the knowledge necessary for leading a good life.
It was little wonder, therefore, that emblem books, moral handbooks,
and the like, multiplied at this time, and they were written by eminent
students: lawyers such as Alciati or Camerarius, would-be poets like
Corrozet, or theologians such as Théodore de Bèze.[4] These works
constituted their sum of knowledge, recorded for the use of others, and
always open to addition. The more succinct the phrase containing their
moral truth, the easier it rested in the memory, and the more persuasive
force it possessed. The brevity so frequently demanded by the aesthetic
theorists was closely allied to the communication of moral truths. Jean
Des Caurres in his Epistle to his *Oeuvres morales* sums up sixteenth-
century attitudes on this subject:

Les escrivains ne se doivent pas seulement contenter d'une simple narration des choses, ains parmy elles entremesler quelques belles sentences, à fin que ceux qui lisent leurs oeuvres puissent facilement apprendre quelques bons enseignemens, qui sont le vray fruict de l'histoire.[5]

In spite of Montaigne's repeated efforts to decry his schooldays, and his insistence that, as the *Essais* developed, he borrowed little—and nothing which he did not make his own—his method of argumentation reveals that habits of writing which he learned at school remained with him throughout his life. In addition, as a law student, he would have studied the *loci communes* set out by Gribaldus and other famous teachers: for all professions at this time depended on the ability to speak well—whether you were lawyer, politician, or doctor.[6] Speaking well depended on the ability to argue, and to persuade; and these, in turn, were dependent upon skill in elaborating set themes, and startling your listener from time to time with moral truths—or *Sententiae*—which he could store in his memory or enter in his notebook collection of striking ideas. Erasmus's *Adages* is simply one example of the development of such themes and of the use of proverbs; and his comments on the virtues of the proverb are relevant here. Consider, for example, the opening sentences to *Festina lente*: 'The interest of the idea and the wit of the allusion are enhanced by such complete neatness and brevity, necessary in my mind to proverbs, which should be as clear cut gems; it adds immensely to their charm'.[7] A glance at the early *Essais* of Montaigne shows that he set himself similar topics for study. The title to the slightest *Que l'intention juge nos actions* (1:7) is one of the moral truisms encountered everywhere in contemporary handbooks, as is *La fortune se rencontre souvent au train de la raison* (1:34), or *Toutes choses ont leur saison* (11:28). One begins to see the attraction that affirmation might well have had for Montaigne. These titles are so general that they, in fact, affirm nothing. They are open-ended, and susceptible to any idiosyncratic interpretation. They impose no specific moral angle. Their reader is not immediately dictated to, but is rather encouraged to think further and to fill out the general implications with detail—along the lines, perhaps, suggested by Montaigne.

It has already been noted that Montaigne became ever more confident as the bulk of his writings grew. This confidence is matched by a moral tone which dominates the essays more and more, and which becomes increasingly assertive. 'C' additions to the *Essais* underline this

tendency, since Montaigne frequently inserts a pungent phrase giving an
air of 'not to be refuted' to some thought which was much more tentative
in an earlier version. In the first version of *De l'institution des enfants*
(1:26), his discussion of the need for a student to ponder deeply the
thoughts of authoritative writers, to understand them thoroughly, and to
make them his own, reads: 'Qu'on luy propose cette diversité de jugemens : il choisira s'il peut, sinon il en demeurera en doubte'. This advice
simply proposes. An altogether different note is struck by the later
addition, 'Il n'y a que les fols certains et resolus' (1:26, 150). There is no
opportunity now to discuss the point as a possibility, for Montaigne has
clinched the argument; and, just in case you might want to protest, he
adds a series of aphorisms all pounding home the same point: 'Qui suit un
autre, il ne suit rien. Il ne trouve rien, voire il ne cerche rien . . . qu'il sache
qu'il sçait, au moins' (p. 150), and, 'sçavoir par coeur n'est pas sçavoir'.[8]
Montaigne, some twenty years older, destroys the original exploratory,
discovering tone, and replaces it by insistence and a feeling of intense
emotional commitment—his student is to be forced to 'rester en doute'.

I am not trying, through these examples, simply to establish that
Montaigne became increasingly assertive. I also wish to make the point
that there are many different types of affirmation in the *Essais*. The type
which brings Montaigne closest to his contemporaries—that is, the use
of aphorisms merely to establish a point—is probably the least interesting. Other types he derived from a close study of ancient Stoic writers—
Seneca, Cicero, Plutarch, and Marcus Aurelius, for example—modifying
their practice and moulding it to suit his own specific needs. The personal
twist which Montaigne often gave to moral aphorisms, and the air of
spontaneity with which he introduced them, are attested by his friend
Pasquier who precedes a list of eighteen such sayings[9] by summarising
his impression of the *Essais* in this way:

> Mais, sur tout, son Livre est un vray seminaire de belles et notables
> sentences, dont les unes sont de son estre ; et les autres transplantées
> si heureusement, et d'une telle naifveté dans son fond, qu'il est
> malaisé de les juger pour autre, que siennes.[10]

It seems obvious that Montaigne did not lose his schoolboy habit of
elaborating themes and using *sententiae*; but I hope to demonstrate
further that he extended their possibilities for two main reasons which
seem inter-connected: his own personal need for self-expression; and his
desire to have a moral effect upon readers who lived in 'un siècle si gasté'.

*   *   *

In his discussion of the weaknesses of language both as a form of communication and as a vehicle for philosophical speculation, Montaigne makes the point that French 'est tout formé de propositions affirmatives' (*Apologie*, II: 12, 508), and that man's processes of argumentation move similarly from one statement of opinion to another. Later in *De l'art de conferer* (III: 8, 915) he observes that general statements about man are meaningless, 'ne disent rien'. Yet, he himself, though conscious of the inadequacies in man's mental equipment, is subject to the same limitations as other men. Awareness does not necessarily cure the natural habit of affirmation. There is the further complication for Montaigne: that his reader would most likely share sixteenth-century writers' conviction that moral assertions, briefly stated, were both ornaments and consecrated truths; and that, as such, they carried maximum power of persuasion. His own approach, as far as affirmation is concerned, seems to try to take account of these contradictory elements. He uses *sententiae* as topics for discussion which, on the surface at least, impose nothing upon the reader. The generality of many of these statements ensures an element of agreement. Many of them are proverbial in quality, when— as in the opening of *De la force de l'imagination*, ' "Fortis imaginatio generat casum" disent les clercs'—they reassure the reader. They provide a common ground for discussion so that the author's elaboration of such points is heeded with interest and sympathy. The familiarity thus created suggests that no great demands are going to be made; and, furthermore, the reader feels free to 'stir and toss' (in Bacon's phrase) the matter for himself. General statements, in spite of their affirmative ring, by their very generality are all-embracing; and, while appearing to sum up a situation, they serve to provoke further thought.

Montaigne's use of affirmations as different facets of the same problem often gives a restless impression to his writing. In *Que nostre desir s'accroit par la malaisance* (II: 15), for instance, the affirmative ring of the title is supported by further affirmations in the text of the essay: 'La difficulté donne pris aux choses', and 'Nostre appetit mesprise et outrepasse ce qui luy est en main, pour courir apres ce qu'il n'a pas' (p. 597).[11] They mark the main stages in Montaigne's thought; but, it will be noticed, all these statements are variations on the same theme, providing the reader with stepping stones in an argument otherwise rendered difficult by a maze of anecdotes and images.

The feeling of participating in an exploration is, therefore, very strong; and, of course, the more one is involved in the process of discovery the more one may be inclined to agree with Montaigne's conclusions. His demonstration of the nature and force of custom, for instance, is built upon a clear pattern of assertions. The first of these is introduced by the unlikely tale of the woman who, through habit and affection, continued to carry a calf around with her even when it was fully grown. Montaigne declares that, in the context of habit, he is not only prepared to believe the story, but to approve its invention: 'car c'est à la verité une violente et traistresse maistresse d'escole que la coutume' (1:23, 106). From habits acquired in childhood Montaigne passes to a consideration of habits of the mind, and introduces the subject of religious conviction. In the first version of the essay, the religious theme is merely touched upon, and Montaigne goes on to develop ideas about customs consecrated by the law. Much later in his life he returned to the question of religion in this essay with the affirmation: 'Les miracles sont selon l'ignorance en quoy nous sommes de la nature, non selon l'estre de la nature' (p. 110). And, at the same time, he underlined the moral content of his examples and anecdotes with another assertion: 'Les loix de la conscience, que nous disons naistre de nature, naissent de la coustume'. The pattern of argument is clarified by such additions which, furthermore, give more force to his main points. As he accumulates similar assertions throughout this essay, a sense of inevitability seems to creep over his thought pushing him naturally and inexorably towards the resounding conclusion: 'c'est la regle des regles, et generale loy des loix, que chacun observe celles du lieu où il est' (p. 117). What seemed to begin as a critical exploration into the nature and force of custom ends on an acceptance and reinforcing of its power. You can make your own arguments, arrive at your own conclusions, but, if you accept the specific context in which Montaigne places his arguments, it is difficult to refute his train of thought. Throughout the essay are reminders of the political and religious situation which gave rise to such thoughts: squabbles over miracles, and the desire to change the laws of the land or the dogma of the Church. Montaigne's demonstration seems much less an objective appraisal than an attempt to persuade men to stick to the *status quo*.

Montaigne does not always proceed in company with the reader in such matters. On the question of the all-powerful force of opinion, he starts by making a statement with which he knows few people will disagree—and, just in case they might be tempted to do so, he cites the ancient authority of Greece as his source: 'Les hommes (dit une sentence Grecque ancienne) sont tourmentez par les opinions qu'ils ont des choses, non par les choses mesmes' (1:14, 49). He then speculates on the practical applicability of such a realisation. Perhaps man's miserable lot might be improved, if only he could learn from this knowledge? By 1588, Montaigne was in no doubt as to the terrible limits of man's endeavour in this sphere: 'L'opinion est une puissante partie, hardie, et sans mesure' (p. 61). Repetition gives added strength to his comment; and the evidence he provides to give substance to such an assertion (made even more explicit in 'C' additions) consists not merely of anecdotes taken from the history of Rome, but also of references to 'nostre Religion'. In this instance, it seems to me that he gives the reader no chance to weigh the evidence for himself, so emphatic and emotionally charged are his assertions.

The use of affirmation to call attention to the argument of an essay is as characteristic of the last *Essais* as of the first. *De la phisionomie* (III: 12) is studded with assertions which both demand notice and elucidation. 'Nostre monde n'est formé qu'à l'ostentation' (p. 1014), provides the topic for discussion, and Montaigne's subsequent affirmations are variations upon this same theme. The affirmations show quite clearly the multi-angled way in which Montaigne attacks a problem. He approaches it first on a tantalising and provocative note: 'Nous sommes chacun plus riche que nous ne pensons' (p. 1015); he then proceeds to elaborate it: 'Toute cette nostre suffisance, qui est au delà de la naturelle, est à peu pres vaine et superflue' (p. 1016). As Montaigne examines the deceptive power of appearances, he is led to the discovery that almost all men's perceptions are deficient; and, furthermore, that the arts which people interpret so frequently as their principal source for pride are only impressive on the surface. Particular circumstances highlight this latent inefficiency, and render the claims men make for themselves even more questionable. War, for instance, the 'monstrueuse guerre', produces conditions in which 'Nostre medecine porte infection' (p. 1018), and where 'la longue souffrance engendre la coustume, la coustume le consentement et l'imitation' (p. 1019). Later in the essay, knowledge itself is shown to be equally light-weight: 'La plus part des instructions de la science à nous encourager ont plus de montre que de force, et plus d'ornement que de fruict' (p. 1026). However, there is a morsel of comfort to be gained from this state of affairs: the appearances of death, and all the fearful premonitions which men attach thereto, are more disturbing than the experience of death itself. (p. 1028). After an extended discussion of this theme, Montaigne's thoughts return to the point on which his considerations began, reiterating (with another affirmation) the force of impact appearances can have on the minds of men: 'C'est une foible garantie que la mine' (p. 1036). When he came to re-read his work, contemporary religious affairs thrust ever more sharply into his mind, and provided further evidence on the strength of appearances, bringing, in the passage which follows, affirmation and emotion into close contact: 'Ruineuse instruction à toute police, et bien plus dommageable qu'ingenieuse et subtile, qui persuade aux peuples la religieuse creance suffire, seule et sans les moeurs, à contenter la justice divine. L'usage nous faict veoir une distinction enorme entre la devotion et la conscience' (p. 1037). A superficial show of devotion is at an enormous distance from true religious feeling. Social upheaval serves to expose the inadequacies of human resources.

The dependence on affirmations to throw into relief the main elements of his thought, is, to my mind, primarily responsible for Montaigne's 'hopping style'—as critics have called it. The 'hops' Montaigne makes from one stage of thought to another only seem 'hops' because the affirmations stand out so prominently from the rest of his prose; and because Montaigne, as we have seen, suggests this impression by his ostentatious, but superficial, 'Revenons à nostre sujet'. Affirmations used as steps in an argument, coupled with a deliberate disorientating technique, keep the reader on the alert, and help preserve the impression of spontaneity which Montaigne so prized. Together, they destroy the effect of authoritarianism which usually comes about through frequent assertion; because the very number of affirmations allows us to pause, consider for ourselves, agree or reject the proposition before passing on to the next stopping place.

From the discussion so far it is obvious that the defining power of affirmation is considerable. In *De l'ineqalité qui est entre nous* (1:42), Montaigne starts by affirming, in the most general way, the singularity of each man: 'qu'il y a plus de distance de tel à tel homme qu'il n'y a de tel homme à telle beste' (1:42, 250). Indeed, his propositions throughout the essay are so vague and imprecise that the problem of individuality, with which he begins, seems to disappear altogether as Montaigne, assuming common moral denominators for all men—'C'est le joüir, non le posseder, qui nous rend heureux' (p. 254), for example—demonstrates that all men are the same, except for kings who are worse off than most. A similar combination of assertiveness and exhortation is present in his analysis of cruelty: 'Le tuer est bon pour éviter l'offence à venir, non pour venger celle qui est faicte' (ii:27, 673). Inevitably the attention is aroused, and the reader's emotions might well rise against the objective coolness of such a statement.

There are many examples where Montaigne similarly challenges the reader: 'Rien ne presse un estat que l'innovation' (III:9,935), asks to be refuted, and one is encouraged to measure one's own evidence to the contrary against the findings of Montaigne. While recognising the truth of the assertion 'La mort se mesle et confond par tout à nostre vie' (III:12, 1082), one wants to rebel against the unrelieved bluntness of the statement. Montaigne could possibly be thinking of Seneca's comments on the persuasive force of blunt maxims such as 'Know thyself':

> Such maxims need no special pleader—they go straight to the emotions . . . Virtue is aroused by a touch, a shock. Moreover, there are certain things which, though in the mind, yet are not ready to hand but begin to function easily as soon as they are put into words.[12]

Montaigne exhibits a similar knowledge of the workings of the human mind and its responses to words. It is impossible to pass over a phrase such as: 'La convoitise n'a rien si propre que d'estre ingrate' (III:6,882) for its almost paradoxical formulation imposes thought.

* * *

Conscious that affirmation was alien to his relative view of human activity, Montaigne employs this form of discourse so that he can then undermine its assertive force, ironically noting: 'Il ne faut pas croire à chacun, dict le precepte, par ce que chacun peut dire toutes choses' (II: 12,554). In this way, commonly-held assumptions are used for ironic, or sometimes sarcastic reflexion, since, according to their context, they may carry within themselves assertive power or gross and inaccurate overstatement. In *De l'art de conferer* (III:8,922), after making his thoughts on the subject of communication quite clear through a series of affirmed opinions and examples, he characteristically uses an affirmation —'tous jugemens en gros sont laches et imparfaicts'—to spell out the looseness, the incompleteness, and the weaknesses of all such affirmative opinions. The assertion which opens *Que l'intention juge nos actions* (I:7, 32) is carefully qualified by a 'dict-on', before being demolished. In the same way, starting from the assertion that national customs limit man's endeavour (*Des coustumes anciennes*, I:49), he himself sweeps aside the force of such habit 'afin qu'ayant en l'imagination cette continuelle variation des choses humaines, nous en ayons le jugement plus esclaircy et plus ferme'. Sarcasm is very frequently built into the affirmation to show its falseness. On the other hand, sarcasm sometimes reinforces the force of an assertion. There are many such instances in the *Apologie*; and they occur in equal abundance when Montaigne mounts one of his favourite hobby-horses: 'L'ignorance pure et remise toute en autruy estoit bien plus salutaire et plus sçavante que n'est cette science verbale et vaine, nourrice de presomption et de temerité' (*Des prieres*, 1:56, 306). In this last example, Montaigne has prepared his conclusions by a set of emotionally loaded adjectives—'execrable', 'tres odieuse', 'fantastique', 'fascheuse', 'temeraire', 'vicieuse', and so on—which serve to denigrate the pretentions of the knowledgeable, so that the bitterness of his sarcasm in the assertion might strike all the more acutely.

Within the great mass of general declarations in the *Essais*, by far the largest number are protests concerning man's imperfections and weaknesses. Montaigne's assertions frequently have this negative quality about them: 'Nostre propre et peculiere condition est autant ridicule que risible' (*De Democritus et Heraclitus*, 1:50,292). They declare that the dominant pattern of the world is the non-existence of pattern; and that its characteristic features are change, instability, and immense variety. Nothing in the world or in human experience exists in a state of purity and completeness; pleasure is contaminated by pain: yet acute pleasure is difficult to distinguish from pain; anticipation enhances enjoyment: yet possession frequently destroys it. Man's desires constantly outstrip his capacity to control even the insignificant details of his life: 'Nous embrassons tout, mais nous n'étreignons que du vent' (*Des cannibales*, 1:31,200). His powers of judgement are prey to a multitude of deviating influences. His mind fragments, exaggerates, and distorts: he dwells on details which obscure a general view; he utters universals which ignore complexities; and he avoids present exigences by anticipating future happenings, or by recalling the past: 'Nous pensons tousjours ailleurs' (*De la diversion*, III:4,812). The most worthy feature of man is his recognition of his own ignorance and weakness; and his best plan is to dominate his natural tendencies, as far as this is possible (though his abilities in this sphere are severely limited), and render himself supple and flexible, so that even if he cannot control 'la vie [qui] est un mouvement inegal, irregulier et multiforme' (III:3,796), at least he remains conscious of his lack of control, and more able to adjust his reactions according to the flow of happenings.

The similarities between this assertive record of instability and the one left by Marcus Aurelius, in the handbook of guide-lines he wrote for himself, are I think, worth noting. He, too, had affirmed 'the inconstancie and variableness of human judgment',[13] developing the idea later:

For both the substancies themselves, (wee see) as a flood, are in a continuall fluxe; and all actions in a perpetuall change; and the causes themselves, subject to a thousand alterations, neither is there anything almost, that may ever be said to bee now settled, and constant.[14]

He, too, had insisted that 'the effect of true Philosophie is, unaffected simplicity and modestie',[15] that 'the true joye of man, is to doe that, which properly belongs unto a man',[16] and, finally, that the study of man and of the self, and a revealing of that self to others, is his most important occupation.[17] From affirmations about the ever-shifting nature of man and the world in which he lives, he had passed to moral assertions on the best way of meditating that state, of controlling it, and of acting upon it. It is, I believe, possible that Marcus Aurelius's handbook provided Montaigne with a much richer source of inspiration than is usually realised. Of course, it is unlikely that he was solely responsible for Montaigne's views; but his contribution seems to have been considerable, particularly in turning the Frenchman's mind towards moral solutions based on self-study.[18]

*   *   *

Naturally, any discussion of affirmation demands some consideration of moral preoccupations. The extent of Montaigne's dogmatism requires that we should look further not only at his moral intentions (as far as we can judge them) but also at what he is asserting. He hastens to assert that his intention is to impose upon no one. He obliges no one to be impressed by his thoughts, 'comme chascun fait', he states unconditionally at the beginning of *Du jeune Caton* (1:37,225). His thoughts are incomplete, irresolute, and tentative, he stresses at the beginning of *Des prieres* (1:56,302); and he adds that he has no desire to thrust his ideas down peoples' throats. He is not concerned 'pour establir la verité, mais pour la chercher'. It is presumptuous, he claims, to assume that since, generally speaking, all men look alike, it necessarily follows that they have the same thinking capacity, the same moral characteristics, the same gifts, or the same urges (III:2). Yet, in spite of these defensive affirmations, some essays were explicitly written at the behest of certain individuals who demanded instruction. *L'Apologie de R. Sebond* (II:12), possibly composed for Marguerite de Valois, is one instance—and Montaigne's main tool for such special pleading is affirmation used to satirise and denigrate man. Other examples are *De l'institution des enfants* (1:26), written for Diane de Foix, Contesse de Gurson; and *De l'Affection des peres aux enfans* (II:8), composed for Madame d'Estissac. There is, moreover, plenty of other evidence to suggest that, although Montaigne persistently declared that he did not want to teach, he was possessed of some very clear-cut moral opinions which he put forward as forcibly as he knew how. One has only to look at the strong moral terms abounding on every page of the *Essais*. There are, for example, the emotive, almost exaggerated, words he uses to describe telling lies: it is 'un maudit vice', knowledge of which arouses 'horreur' and makes one think of 'crimes'. Or, there are the endless lists of derogatory words carrying Montaigne's disapproval: for man's vain thoughts of death, 'fol', and 'ridicule' (1:20); or for pretentions to knowledge described as 'sottise' and 'fatras' (1:25, 135, 143). On this subject (as on many others)— despite his emphasis on the need to explore, to test ideas against the evidence, and to resist the affirmative tendencies in man's make-up— Montaigne has made up his mind in advance, and the larger part of some essays is given over to *proving* what he already thinks. The *Essais* are littered with Montaigne's egotisms: 'je veux', 'je ne veux pas', 'je hais'; which he alternates with 'il faut', or 'on doit', often accompanied by urgent imperatives and direct appeals to the reader. Or, to take two examples from Book 1: there are his assertive claims in *De Democritus et Heraclitus* (1:50, 289), which move from the more tentative 'il me semble' to 'à mon humeur' and 'je ne pense point'; while the same extreme personalisation occurs in *De l'aage* (1:57, 311–3), with 'je ne puis recevoir', 'Quant à moy', 'j'estime', 'je tiens pour certain que', and 'je me plains'. We perhaps do not always notice how dogmatic Montaigne can be, because we like to feel that we share many of his humanitarian views, such as his blunt condemnation of torture (II:5, 348–9), or his emotional descriptions of the moral effects of war—the 'inhumanité sur tout et desloyauté' (III:9, 934); and because we realise that Montaigne's strong moral convictions are natural to his impulsive character.

When we look back upon writers of the sixteenth century, all so preoccupied not only with the debating of moral issues, but with the affirming of 'right causes', it is tempting to see Montaigne in a singular, isolated light. His remarks on the vanity and impossibility of arriving at fixed conclusions about human beings appear so sane and so enlightened, that we all but miss the arrogant tone in which they are couched: 'il m'a semblé souvent que les bons autheurs mesmes ont tort de s'opiniastrer à former de nous une constante et solide contexture. Ils choisissent un air universel, et suyvant cette image, vont rengeant et interpretant toutes les actions d'un personnage, et, s'ils ne les peuvent assez tordre, les vont renvoyant à la dissimulation' (*De l'inconstance de nos actions*, II:1,

315). Montaigne—who loved antithesis, and declared that his mind and actions frequently and deliberately ran counter to the usual established patterns—himself, on numerous occasions, maintained that, while others were concerned to build and educate men, he was content merely to describe human activities: 'Les autres forment l'homme, moy je le récite' (III:2,782). They—the moralists of classical times or of his own—did one thing, he does another: not, he claims, because he wants to be different, but because he believes that moral absolutes, human laws, and codes of behaviour, only exist in so far as they can be applied to specific moments of experience.

Nevertheless, despite his desire to operate differently from his contemporaries, Montaigne does dogmatise. Even if he is reluctant to offer positive advice for his fellow men, he is never slow in showing his disapproval of human acts when they deserve it. If he will not show man how to behave, he is often ready to tell him what he should not do; and, usually, he lards his comments liberally with sarcasm, as in the following example where he castigates man for his perversity:

> Tu ne crains point d'offencer ses loix universelles et indubitables, et te piques aux tiennes, partisanes et fantastiques; et d'autant plus qu'elles sont particulieres, incertaines et plus contredictes, d'autant plus tu fais là ton effort. (III:5,858)

Montaigne never fails to respond with adverse comment to the many manifestations of man's vanity. Sometimes, as in the *Apologie* (II:12), his exposure of the countless contradictions and inadequacies of man's attempts to explain the supernatural is made with a kind of glee and with a certain detachment. Speculation is acceptable just as long as it makes no claim to alter man's habits; when it impinges on the everyday, causes war, torture and death, then Montaigne's strong resistance becomes coupled with the most outspoken dogmatism.

The best instance of this passionate response is found in *Des boyteux* (III:11) where the notion of deformity is used to qualify the operation of thinking rather than any physical state. The essay opens, characteristically, with a statement describing human reasoning power as 'un instrument libre et vague' which, by its very nature, ignores the facts in front of it in order to concentrate on distant and intangible speculation. The affirmation—'Nostre discours est capable d'estoffer cent autres mondes et d'en trouver les principes et la contexture (III:11,1004)—is only the first of a series of such sarcastic statements setting the stage for the main matter of this essay: Montaigne's rigorous and heartfelt denunciation of the art of judging and condemning witches. Before he actually raises the detailed question of witches, however, Montaigne is concerned to establish a general point: that statements involving general testimony are so impossible that they must be rejected out of hand. He therefore draws a picture of human reason weakened by the difficulties of distinguishing the true from the false ('La verité et le mensonge ont leurs visages conformes, le port, le goust et les alleures pareilles: nous les regardons de mesme oeil' p. 1004); undermined by its need to embroider the simplest fact, and to tell a good story; and, above all, rendered suspect by each man's urge to persuade the crowd of the rightness of his opinions. This is the common pattern of human mental activity; and within this pattern, Montaigne highlights two extremes—the uncertain judgement of the crowd so easily swayed, and the arrogant pride of judges fearful of admitting their ignorance and in a hurry to condemn their victims.[19] As he describes these two 'difformities' his tone grows more affirmative and more emotionally charged: 'il y a du malheur d'en estre là que la meilleure touche de la verité ce soit la multitude des croians, en une presse où les fols surpassent de tant les sages en nombre' (p. 1005). This gullibility of the crowd provides the main support for 'l'impudence de ceux qui font profession de sçavoir, et de leur outrecuidance démesurée' (p. 1013). General stupidity, and, in particular, the stupidity of magistrates are responsible for the cruel fate of 'pauvres diables' who frequently suffer death whether they have been caught out on a prank, or are jailed for impersonation. When he thinks about stupidity, Montaigne can hardly contain his indignation; but when such stupidity is the source of judgements involving the health, and even the lives, of other people then his indignation explodes in fiercest sarcasm. Specific examples of torture or death, personal experience of examining known so-called witches,[20] and a familiarity with witchcraft literature,[21] combine to give Montaigne's affirmations great power; and he uses this knowledge (well charged with irony) to confound the reasoning of Jean Bodin, the most eloquent defender of witch trials in France: 'Je vois bien qu'on se courrouce, et me deffend on d'en doubter, sur peine d'injures execrables. Nouvelle façon de persuader. Pour Dieu mercy, ma creance ne se manie pas à coups de poing' (p. 1008). His own style warms and sharpens to match the tone of his famous adversary: 'A tuer les gens, il faut une clarté lumineuse et nette' (p. 1009); and later, 'C'est mettre ses conjectures à bien haut pris que d'en faire cuire un homme tout vif' (p. 1010). Between these two phrases we have the crux of Montaigne's thought: conjecture is not reasoning, and in any case, even man's power of reason is defective: 'Il n'est rien si souple et erratique que nostre entendement' (p. 1012). In contrast to Bodin, Montaigne has his anger under control, and his comments are carefully kept in perspective. An exposition of mental frailty is cogently set forth through detailed discussion of some of the most appalling excesses the human mind has managed to perpetrate. Montaigne's case is unanswerable; and, even someone who does not share the sane views developed in *Des boyteux*, would find it difficult to resist being persuaded by a man who, in this same essay, side by side with the fervent affirmations directed against all witch-hunters, also wrote, 'J'ayme ces mots, qui amollissent et moderent la temerité de nos propositions, A l'avanture, Aucunement, Quelque, On dict, Je pense et semblables' (p. 1007).

In *Du repentir* two similar, diametrically opposed attitudes coincide. It is in this essay, where Montaigne asserts that he is content to describe the minute to minute happenings of his own life, while others waste their time attempting to erect moral absolutes which are available to all men in all circumstances, that he provides us with some of his most positive moral affirmations. By setting side by side, antithetically, those features which are common to all men and those which define individuality, the latter stand out as most significant and worthy of analysis. Montaigne works from the general to the particular before finally presenting adages of his own which, whatever he intended, have the ring of absolutes: 'J'ay mes loix et ma court pour juger de moy' (III:2,785), 'Le pris de l'ame ne consiste pas à aller haut, mais ordonnéement' (III:2,787), or, later in the essay, 'A mon advis c'est le vivre heureusement, non, comme disoit Antisthenes, le mourir heureusement, qui faict l'humaine felicité' (III:2,794). In the same essay, immediately after stating 'Je n'enseigne poinct, je raconte', Montaigne sets down, affirmatively, judgements upon man's response to vice and virtue with which no one would quarrel, and which could well serve as useful and unambiguous yardsticks in any moral discussion: 'Il n'est vice veritablement vice qui n'offence, ct qu'un jugement entier n'accuse . . . Il n'est pareillement bonté qui ne resjouysse une nature bien née' (III:2,784). The insistent nature of the statements is to be noted, together with the profound sense of responsibility which emerges from *Du repentir*. Montaigne usually employs superlative forms of expression when he puts forward his belief in order, moderation, the power of judgement, the richness of life, the virtues of living naturally, the usefulness of knowledge properly handled, or the preservation of one's individuality.

*　　*　　*

If we study in more detail the way in which Montaigne manages
the transitions from general affirmations, which have a proverbial quality
with which no one would disagree, to ego-centred statements—the eloquent 'I' comments—we shall gain a clearer idea of the nature of what
I have called Montaigne's dogmatism, and perhaps have some inkling
of the reasons for it. Frequently, Montaigne qualifies his general aphorisms by a parenthetical 'à mon gré', 'à mon advis', or 'selon moy'. Out
of context this might easily be interpreted as a means of toning down
the impact of an affirmation: as if personalisation made it more tentative
and less all-absorbing. Examination of specific examples, however, reveals that Montaigne often increases the assertive power of these statements by this inclusion of himself.

> L'heur et le mal'heur sont à mon gré deux souveraines puissances.
> C'est imprudence d'estimer que l'humaine prudence puisse remplir le
> rolle de la fortune. Et vaine est l'entreprise de celuy qui presume
> d'embrasser et causes et consequences, et mener par la main le progrez
> de son faict: vaine sur tout aux deliberations guerrieres.
>
> (*De l'art de conferer*, III:8,912)

Here, it is not simply a question of mouthing accepted generalities which
pass familiarly through our minds like water off a duck's back. Montaigne
is emotionally aroused, consciously accepting responsibility for these
statements, and wilfully allowing his heated response to war to come to
the fore. The original affirmation, together with the idea of war, spark
off thoughts about the extent to which his own mental activity is controlled by the haphazard, and his eloquence becomes yet more emphatic
with the insistent: 'Je dis plus . . . ma volonté et mon discours se re-
mue . . . Ma raison a des impulsions'. Correspondingly, in *Du repentir*,
by skilfully juxtaposing the general and the personal, Montaigne achieves
considerable power of persuasion:

> il n'est personne, s'il s'escoute, qui ne descouvre en soy une forme
> sienne, une forme maistresse, qui luicte contre l'institution, et contre
> la tempeste des passions qui luy sont contraires. De moy, je ne me sens
> guere agiter par secousse, je me trouve quasi tousjours en ma place.
> (III:2,789)

Perhaps there are those who have no need for Montaigne's personal
application of the extreme statement made here, in order to turn in upon
themselves and meditate upon its implications. There must be many, also,
who gratefully learn from Montaigne's method of listening to himself,

and are encouraged by his personal analyses to perform in a like manner.

The fact that men have common characteristics, which do not cancel out any individual qualities they may possess, allows Montaigne to move freely between the general and the particular, without arousing criticism. Indeed on the contrary, the general comments please especially when they confirm other's experience; and the particular comments intrigue. So Montaigne seems to gain advantage whichever line he takes. 'I' provides irrefutable proof to support shaky or audacious generalisations, such as Montaigne's assertion that one must either submit entirely to the dogma of the Church or not do so at all (*C'est folie de rapporter le vray et le faux à nostre suffisance*, I: 27, 177–8). The formula 'j'ay veu' is equally powerful when Montaigne wants to substantiate 'Noz yeux ne voient rien en derrière' (III: 8, 908). Most often, however, (and in a way more revealing) Montaigne utilises affirmations to justify his own discoveries, to condone his behaviour or natural tendencies, or to confirm his personal feelings. A strong sense of moral commitment emerges from these justifications. His wish to keep out of public affairs as far as possible, in order to follow his natural tendencies and to preserve an inner tranquillity, makes him diminish the value of renown, dwell upon *De l'incommodité de la grandeur* (III: 7, 894–5), and assert that we make too much of reputation.[22] His own experience of the civil wars makes him express most intensely his hatred for any change of government, 'C'est vice et folie'; and this extreme opinion is buttressed by the general assertion: 'Non par opinion mais en verité, l'excellente et meilleure police est à chacune nation celle soubs laquelle elle s'est maintenuë' (III: 9, 934). His method of diversion, which he offers as a means of coping with difficulty, is justified not only by his own experience which found 'Tousjours la variation soulage, dissout et dissipe', but more especially by reference to Nature herself who 'procède ainsi par le benefice de l'inconstance' (III: 4, 813). The general and the particular work in harmony, supporting each other, and preserving Montaigne's individual experience; while constant appeals to more universal states always allow for general moral interpretation to be made.

That Montaigne was very concerned to justify his self-portrayal is clear from his frequent recourse to general statements which bolster up what he is doing. In *Sur des vers de Virgile* (III: 5) he explains why he was recounting the detail of his love-life to the reader. First, he suggests that, once started on the road of self-revelation, he has some kind of moral obligation to ensure that his self-exposure is complete: 'Je dois au publiq universellement mon portrait' (p. 866). This sense of duty is explained by Montaigne as following naturally upon his observation of man's condition generally: 'Nostre vie est partie en folie, partie en prudence. Qui n'en escrit que reveremment et regulièrement, il en laisse en arriere plus de la moitié' (p. 866–7). Montaigne, it seems, has made up his mind to explore himself in every corner, and general perceptions about man's state merely give extra cogency and authority to what he is already doing.

This is particularly evident in an early passage in *De la praesomption* (ii : 17) where, to explain his personal response to ill-fortune, he shifts his statements on to a general ground:

> Aux evenemens je me porte virilement; en la conduicte puerillement. L' horreur de la cheute me donne plus de fiebvre que le coup. Le jeu ne vaut pas la chandelle. L'avaritieux a plus mauvais conte de sa passion que n'a le pauvre, et le jaloux que le cocu. Et y a moins de mal souvent à perdre sa vigne qu'à la plaider. La plus basse marche est la plus ferme. C'est le siege de la constance. (ii : 17,628)

Anticipation of unhappy events, and thinking about misfortune, he finds intolerable; and he justifies such an apparently weak personal reaction by a series of general statements. These start with a proverb suggesting some kind of general approval for his attitude, and this impression is enhanced by the addition of a set of typical examples which experience cannot refute. The argument then becomes more abstract, and even more affirmative, so that these two resounding sentences, 'La plus basse marche est la plus ferme. C'est le siege de la constance', not only seem to underline general assent to Montaigne's response, they also give to his personal attitude an unmistakeable ring of moral rectitude. Near apologies for himself thus become transformed into moral truths for others to follow.

On other occasions Montaigne uses criticism of general affairs to highlight the value of self-study. In this way he employs criticism of diversity in French law (iii : 13, 1049), or of contemporary historians (ii : 10, 397–8), as a sort of backcloth to his own presentation of himself and his method. He will fasten our eyes on general faults, and dwell upon them in detail, in such a way that we are immediately ready to accept as valuable and noteworthy anything which he sets up in opposition to them. Thus his discussion of the inadequacies of his native laws is abruptly terminated by the assertions, 'Je m'estudie plus qu'autre subject. C'est ma metaphysique, c'est ma phisique' (iii : 13, 1050), which impinge upon our minds not only because they are expressed in such a startling way, but also because Montaigne has prepared us to accept any alternative to the stultifying, multiplying nature of the law.

Another technique in the early essays is that of highlighting the specific by showing it in silhouette against the general. In *De l'institution des enfants* (1:26), for instance, he criticises the punishment of pupils in schools in a general way, but allows his admiration for his own school—and particularly his teachers, Muret, Buchanan, and Gouvea—to emerge very specifically.

Many of Montaigne's most valuable discoveries about himself are made when he places his own person either in direct opposition to affirmations upon a general state of being, or when he mirrors them. The opening sentences of *Du repentir* (III:2) show how Montaigne prepares for such paralleling. 'Le monde n'est qu'une branloire perenne . . . La constance mesme n'est autre chose qu'un branle plus languissant. Je ne puis asseurer mon object' (III:2,782). There were plenty of people in the sixteenth century who had stressed the ever-changing nature of the world, discussed its mobility, and listed its diversities—Agrippa and Louis le Roy are but two famous representatives.[23] Montaigne's originality lies in the fact that he sets *himself* within a general pattern of shifting horizons, and that his observations of constant movement in the universe suggested to him the idea of exploring similar mobility within himself. The general reveals Montaigne the individual to himself. And once the idea is launched, Montaigne develops the implications with mounting enthusiasm:

> Je ne puis asseurer mon object. Il va trouble et chancelant, d'une yvresse naturelle. Je le prens en ce point, comme il est, en l'instant que je m'amuse à luy. Je ne peints pas l'estre. Je peints le passage: non un passage d'aage en autre, ou comme dit le peuple, de sept en sept ans, mais de jour en jour, de minute en minute. (p. 782)

Studying his own experience against a general background, Montaigne discovers a method of defining his own nature. And yet, the recording of a constant flow of movement, the writing down of fleeting perceptions and of spontaneous reactions, is a difficult if not impossible task. Montaigne's discovery of this method revealed fundamental truths about man's mobile state which had not been so sharply set in focus before; but how was he, with words on a page, to give accurate formulation to a constantly shifting mass of material?

It is interesting to note that—although Montaigne has unquestionably mastered the art of describing man's variability—when he himself tries to analyse his own responses, he has recourse once again to an alternating method, moving from general to particular affirmations and observations, and offering present responses to a past often recalled (and thereby distorted) with nostalgia. In *De la vanité* (III:9,960), he sets in opposition the two assertions: 'La decrepitude est qualité solitaire. Je suis sociable jusques à excez'. It seems that he really needs some general notion against which he can measure his own individuality. Already, as early as the first version of *Du jeune Caton* (1:37,225)— thought by Villey to have been composed in 1572—the opening sentence to the essay separates Montaigne from the common run of man: 'Je n'ay point cette erreur commune de juger d'un autre selon que je suis'. For such confidence in his own singularity, Montaigne apologised less and less. As the *Essais* grew, and especially by the time he came to write *De mesnager sa volonté* (III:10) in the years 1586–7, one may talk in terms of Montaigne literally parading his individuality in public. 'Men behave in this way, I am different', he discovers, as he analyses the temptations of public life. The essay began with the lines 'Au pris du commun des hommes, peu de choses me touchent' (p. 980). It continues with a series of affirmations, 'Les hommes se donnent à louage . . . Leur esprit cache son repos en branle' (p. 981), against which Montaigne defines his own natural tendencies: 'Je prens une complexion toute diverse' (p. 982). Alongside the element of pride contained in these oppositions, there is an anxiety lest his portrait of himself should not be properly understood, or accurately seen. He wants to make sure that we perceive his uniqueness: so he takes the general with which we are familiar, in order to reveal the particular. 'Distinguish precisely' is what he urges, and what he tries to do.

As his confidence in his ability to project an accurate image of himself upon the pages of the *Essais* grows, he ventures the possibility: 'Publiant et accusant mes imperfections, quelqu'un apprendra de les craindre' (III:8,899). In this way Montaigne gives his own person the status which he had accorded to general affirmations. Montaigne, with his 'estre universel', becomes the yardstick against which we can define and measure our own personalities. His conviction is such that a tone of earnestness enters his work as he argues his case for living life to the full at the end of *Du repentir* (III:2), or in *Coustume de l'isle de Cea* (II: 3,334). Life—'c'est nostre estre, c'est nostre tout'. He no longer feels the need to excuse his assertions, for 'estre à soy', to have an 'arrière boutique toute nostre' (1:39,235), stand out as necessities he does not have to defend. They are valuable possessions permitting him to assert with authority and eloquence: 'Nostre grand et glorieux chef d'oeuvre c'est vivre à propos' (III: 13, 1088).

The study of affirmation in the *Essais* has unravelled some of the problems in Montaigne's modes of argument. Intellectually speaking, he distrusted assertions, though he found them useful as signposts in argument, or as generally accepted notions which needed to be questioned. On an emotional plane, he felt impelled to tell others about his passionate convictions regarding religious strife, witchcraft, and war. And what he had to say on these topics was frequently voiced through affirmation. Futhermore, an increasingly assertive tone informed the reader of the inner strength he had found in meditating upon himself. Exhortations on self-study stand out against general statements on man's condition.

Montaigne had, no doubt, pondered deeply the wise words of his mentor Seneca:

> Advice is not teaching; it merely engages the attention and rouses us, and concentrates the memory, and keeps it from losing grip. We miss much that is set before our very eyes. Advice is in fact a sort of exhortation. The mind often tries not to notice even that which lies before our eyes: we must therefore force upon it the knowledge of things that are perfectly well known.[24]

Through affirmation Montaigne had managed to achieve that feat of opening his readers' eyes to much they had hitherto not seen. Before he could expect to be heard, he had first to undermine entrenched opinions.

6

HISTORICAL AND CULTURAL
ANALOGIES

THE physical, moral, and intellectual distress which the Wars of Religion brought into being is an important concern in the *Essais*. Montaigne's general view of man is inevitably coloured by his experience of civil war. Man's stupidity, his imbecile pride in the sort of intellectual achievements which splintered the Reformed Church into a multitude of warring sects, as well as his overweening ambition which gave birth to movements like the Catholic League, are spelt out in the *Apologie de Raimond Sebond* (II : 12) : but this essay is by no means an isolated moment in the general body of Montaigne's work. Phrases such as 'dans un siècle si gasté', 'ce siècle malade', and 'en un temps si corrompu', are continually used to remind the reader of the specific historical context in which Montaigne is writing and thinking.

Montaigne's most thorough-going disapproval of war and its consequences occurs in Book III and in later additions to the earlier books ; and when he writes of war his language becomes more violent ; and expressions such as 'nouvelle desbauche', 'horreur', 'mal', 'dangereux', 'horribles corruptions', and 'inique' occur more frequently. After the death of Monsieur and the formation of the League (1584/5) the fighting, hitherto principally confined to sporadic outbursts of discontent in certain largely protestant localities,[1] spread rapidly to reach the disastrous proportions of general lawlessness and total disregard for even the most elementary moral principles. This change in the nature of the war coincides with the writing of Book III. It is not surprising, therefore, that in later additions to the *Essais* Montaigne makes his strong feelings on religious wars clear by, for instance, multiplying references to religion. In *Que le goust des biens et des maux dépend en bonne partie de l'opinion que*

nous en avons (1:14), they are added to demonstrate the destructive force
of opinion: and they tend, more and more, to serve as the climax of an
essay. *C'est folie de rapporter le vray et le faux à nostre suffisance* (1:27)
affords a good instance of a technique which moves from general points
on man's weaknesses and presumption, through a series of fairly unimportant facts illustrating the argument, on to religion itself as *the*
example which clinches the matter once and for all. And this movement,
which throws religion into great relief, is underlined and strengthened
by later additions to the essay. A somewhat similar effect is achieved in
De la coustume et de ne changer aisément une loy receüe (1:23), where the
first version of the essay is merely argued by references to laws, whereas
in the final version the miraculous elements in religion stand to the fore.
Montaigne was quite clear in his mind that 'il ne faut pas mesler Dieu en
nos actions', and this conviction became sharper as he observed men's
behaviour in civil war, and watched their religious beliefs being transformed into some kind of pathological and exclusive obstinacy: 'fascheuse
maladie, de se croire si fort, qu'on se persuade qu'il ne se puisse croire au
contraire' (*Des prieres*, 1:56, 305).

    While on the one hand Montaigne would concede that war (like
other forms of adversity) could inspire men to great moral and physical
efforts; on the other, he was overwhelmed by its bad moral consequences. War was no longer the *Commentaries* of Caesar or the military
manoeuvres extolled in other history books; it represented bitter personal experience of one of the most extreme forms of human folly. Montaigne was appalled at the way in which ambitious and unscrupulous men
used war for private gain and as an excuse for every kind of brutality
(*De l'utile et de l'honneste*, III: 1, 771 & 780). To Montaigne civil war was
the worst kind of strife not only because it brought him closest to the
ravages of war and offered a permanent threat to his security, but also
because it upturned all moral values, and made solutions impossible by
the very fact of carrying within itself self-perpetuating seeds of destruction: 'Monstrueuse guerre . . . Elle vient guarir la scdition et en est
pleine, veut chastier la desobeyssance et en montre l'exemple; et, em-
ployée à la deffence des loix, faict sa part de rebellion à l'encontre des
siennes propres' (*De la phisionomie*, III:12, 1018). The impotence Montaigne felt when faced by such calamities, he could only express either in
highly emotional terms or through sympathetic descriptions of the victims. His overwhelming disgust comes clearly through in the following
example, where his horizons seem boxed in by an unrelieved view of
moral turpitude, where he seems mentally stunned, and where his courage

is severely undermined by the extent of the wickedness he observes in every corner of the world:

> Je vois, non une action, ou trois, ou cent, mais des moeurs en usage commun et reçeu si monstrueuses en inhumanité sur tout et desloyauté, qui est pour moy la pire espece des vices, que je n'ay point le courage de les concevoir sans horreur; et les admire quasi autant que je les desteste. (*De la vanité*, III:9,933–4)

The French Wars of Religion had, Montaigne thought, changed man's view of virtue and vice. The ability to recognise the values taught for centuries by the Church or advocated by the ancient writers, and which the Humanists had admired and tried to imitate, had disappeared.[2] Now, Montaigne points out, man's scale of punishment starts with killing (*Couardise mere de la cruauté*, II:27,672): for this is a merciful end, when roasting the soles of the feet, blowing off the fingers of the hands, or forcing 'les yeux sanglants hors de la teste à force d'avoir le front serré d'une grosse corde' (II:32,702), were commonplace tricks of human perversity, and often performed not, as one might think, to extort information, but for the sheer pleasure of inflicting pain and watching the agony. The intense emotion Montaigne felt about such incidents is made abundantly clear by the crudity of the details he records. One particular instance of suffering which he knew about personally, recounted in an almost clinical way, is perhaps even more moving than the elaborate metaphors and accumulation of loaded adjectives and expletives used by d'Aubigné in *Les Tragiques* (Books I and V) to produce similar effects:

> J'en ay veu un, laissé pour mort tout nud dans un fossé, ayant le col tout meurtry et enflé d'un licol qui y pendoit encore, avec lequel on l'avoit tirassé toute la nuict à la queuë d'un cheval, le corps percé en cent lieux à coups de dague, qu'on luy avoit donné non pas pour le tuer, mais pour luy faire de la douleur et de la crainte; qui avoit souffert tout cela, et jusques à y avoir perdu parolle et sentiment, resolu, à ce qu'il me dict, de mourir plustost de mille morts (comme de vray, quand à sa souffrance, il en avoit passé une toute entiere) avant que rien promettre; et si estoit un des plus riches laboureurs de toute la contrée. Combien en a l'on veu se laisser patiemment brusler et rotir pour des opinions empruntées d'autruy, ignorées et inconnues! (*Defence de Seneque et de Plutarque*, II:32,702)

As we sit comfortably in our armchairs, at some considerable distance from the incident, we are stirred by such a story where Montaigne's only concession to persuasion is the reflective generalised comment with which it ends. Would Montaigne's contemporaries, for whom violence, pain, suffering, and immorality had become everyday events, respond in the same way. Their minds had grown accustomed to accepting, as normal happenings, outrageous deeds which had not only to be endured, but also condoned. Montaigne could hardly hope to arouse them by recounting something which happened many times a day. It seems then that, in the incident just quoted, he was doing little more than relieve his own pent-up emotions, while making clear his own position and his desire to cling to sanity in a season of chaos.

The moral consequences of civil war and entrenched opinions moved Montaigne so profoundly that he could not rest content as the mere observer of human disaster which he pretended to be in a passage added to *De la phisionomie*: 'puis que je ne la puis retarder, suis content d'estre destiné à y assister et m'en instruire' (III:12, 1023). As we have seen, his thoughts were often preoccupied with war and the moral issues which it raised, and this suggests more than an idle, or merely intellectual interest. Nevertheless, how could he entice his fellow men out of their unseeing fog of habit, and encourage them to feel the horror of what was happening around them; how could he enlighten them in such a way that they would want to search seriously and conscientiously for solutions? He knew their responses were dulled. He also knew that the natural activity of the human mind tended to lead men into self-deception (I:4,25), and that words themselves had proved dangerous incitements to war. In the *Apologie* Montaigne had examined closely the inadequacies of language—'cette folle fierté de langage'. He had shown how it multiplied religious disputes: 'combien de querelles et bien importantes a produit au monde le doubte du sens de cette syllabe HOC!' (II: 12, 508).[3] And he demonstrated just how vulnerable words are, and how open to misinterpretation, deliberate or otherwise: 'en la parole la plus nette, pure et parfaicte qui puisse estre, combien de fauceté et de mensonge a lon fait naistre' (II: 12, 569). One could no longer trust that what was said was truthful; and it was natural to assume that people hid their real thoughts. Impartiality had ceased to exist. Words no longer enlightened, but puzzled. They were dismissed as false and worthless, or condemned as distorted and exaggerated. Montaigne had plenty of evidence from contemporary political pamphleteers to prove his points, had he wished to use it. And the last thing he wanted was that his own efforts should be confused with their prejudice-ridden and uncritical 'miliasse de petits livrets' (II: 32, 699)—such as the *Reveille-matin* or *Le Tocsain* of the extremist protestant supporters.[4] He realised that such comment on public affairs not only distorted the facts, but was also a very dangerous procedure: 'en ce temps, qu'il ne se peut parler du monde que dangereusement ou faucement' (III : 3, 788–9). In these circumstances what could Montaigne do? He rarely engaged in dispute over doctrinal points. When he did choose to plunge into verbal combat, his remarks are mostly satirical, as in his challenge to the protestants on the subject of predestination in *De la vertu* (II : 29, 687); or when he arrogantly, and almost derisively, dismissed their point of view,—or when, after more than adequately demonstrating the feebleness of the human senses, he ironically adds;

> Que ceux qui nous ont voulu bastir, ces années passées, un exercice de religion si contemplatif et immateriel, ne s'estonnent point s'il s'en trouve qui pensent qu'elle fut eschapée et fondue entre leurs doigts, si elle ne tenoit parmy nous comme marque, tiltre et instrument de division et de part, plus que par soy-mesmes. (III : 8, 909)

Such ridicule might convince the converted, but it would hardly persuade either Montaigne's opponents or his sympathisers to desist from war.

$$* \qquad * \qquad *$$

Despite the difficulties which I have just outlined, there were several ways open to someone as ingenious as Montaigne to awaken men's minds to the atrocities they witnessed so blindly. Three writers, contemporary with Montaigne, and equally disturbed by the deplorable state of affairs in France and anxious to change them, may help illustrate other approaches to the problem, which came close to the method finally adopted by Montaigne. They are Louis le Roy, Philippe Canaye, and Henri Estienne, and a consideration of their works also provides a background against which the many politically orientated *Essais* may be set.

The major part of Louis le Roy's writings, whether translations and commentaries upon ancient texts or exhortatory pamphlets, was concerned to analyse the political situation of his day, and to alert men to the need for preserving the monarchy intact 'sans chercher mutations pernicieuses'. Some works, such as his series of booklets published in the 1560s, are direct appeals to the public; others adopt a more oblique approach, such as his commentaries on the *Politics* of Aristotle which (according to Villey) exercised some considerable influence over the political thinking of Montaigne.[5] This influence, it seems to me, is difficult to evaluate in two men who shared the same attitudes: in the face of civil war, both maintained a thoroughly conservative position, and supported the monarchy while admiring the stability of the Venetian republic (like so many sixteenth-century political writers); and both shared the fervent wish to end civil strife in France.[6] For our purposes, the most interesting part of Le Roy's work occurs in his comments on Aristotle's fifth book 'On Revolutions', where suddenly the translator breaks away from the merely informative pattern of comment employed in earlier books, and addresses the reader directly. He explains that he proposes to spend much more time on an exploration of those seditions in other states brought about for religious and political reasons. Indeed, he intends, in unprecedented fashion, to expand upon the original remarks of Aristotle, not only analysing the seditious factions in Rome, but also detailing more modern civil calamities in Italy and England: 'a celle fin que les François instruits des autres, delaissent toute division: exerceans plustost les armes contre les estrangiers, qu'à leur ruine mutuelle'.[7] The commentaries to this book end on an emotionally charged appeal to all French men to live in harmony. Le Roy simply refers men's minds to other calamities in order that they may cure their own.

Philippe Canaye, seigneur de Fresne, in his adaptations of Aristotle, is much more ambitious and more intelligent than Le Roy. In 1589[8] he published a work entitled *L'Organe c'est à dire l'Instrument de Discours* —a commentary on Aristotle's *Logic*—where he tries to tackle the problem already posed by Montaigne concerning the difficulties, in such a depraved century, of using words to persuade. In his preface to the reader, Canaye claims that the reason why political and religious debate is so disastrous is precisely because people refuse to argue reasonably, calmly, and with logic. He laments, 'Que si les Conciles, colloques et disputes tenues cy devant sur le faict de la Religion n'ont pas esté propres pour guerir nostre furieux mal de l'opinion, que diray-je de nos violences plus que barbares, par lesquelles nous nous entremordons et deschirons comme bestes farouches, au lieu de discourir ensemble comme les raisonnables'.[9] He hopes in his work to evolve a method of analysis which may be used to solve the dire problems confronting the state of France. After examining the different parts of Logic, Canaye demonstrates how this art may be used effectively, by setting himself a series of problems to be argued from opposing angles. Prominent among these is one concerning civil war: 'A sçavoir si la guerre civile est un bon moyen pour reünir l'Estat en une seule saincte religion Catholique ou non'.[10] Over fifty pages of folio, he outlines the arguments for and against, but—assuming by this time that his readers have been thoroughly grounded in the art of reasoning well—he leaves his conclusion open-ended so that each reader may supply his own assessment of the demonstration. It is obvious from this work that Canaye thinks that everything can be said and put in order; and that, once ordered, the argument is perfect.[11] He even arrogantly asserts that anyone who says otherwise is ignorant of 'des principes'. And he ends his elaborate demonstration, just as Le Roy had done (and as most writers in this rhetorical tradition usually did), on an ardent prayer to God:

> Or ie prie Dieu pere des lumieres et de toute verité, d'allumer au coeur de tous bons Chrestiens un tel desir de congnoistre le vray, et le pouvoir separer du faux, qu'au lieu de tant d'heresies et perverses opinions qui desmembrent l'union de l'Eglise, au lieu de tant d'opiniastres contentions, qui offusquent la pure verité de la doctrine celeste, nous puissions desormais recongnoistre et confesser nos erreurs par une vraye repentance, et nous reünir par une vraye foy et charité fraternelle à l'obeissance de la parolle eternelle de nostre Dieu.[12]

In his work—*L'Introduction ou traité de la Conformité des merveilles anciennes avec les modernes ou traité préparatif à l'Apologie pour Hérodote*—published fourteen times between 1566 and 1607,[13] Henri Estienne expounded the protective advantages of another method of persuasion. It was indirect but effective. As a militant protestant, always vulnerable to physical attack whenever he visited Paris, he clothed the sharpest of his criticisms of modern excesses, and his indignation at the immoral consequences of war, in an elaborate series of parallelisms. In his preface, while defending his exploration of the extraordinary in Herodotus, he pretends to be marking the differences which separated those ancient times from his own. But his purpose, in fact, as exposed in his title, is to make their similarities manifest to all: 'Si entre peuples voisins et qui sont du même temps, les façons de faire sont si discordantes, nous ne devons pas trouver incroyable la différence entre nous et ceux dont parte Hérodote, étant si éloignés de nous non seulement de distance de lieu, mais aussi de temps'.[14] The use of distance in time or place to illuminate the present and the immediate has a long tradition and almost every Renaissance historian would subscribe to Livy's expressed intention of withdrawing from present calamities, and by turning his mind to the history of the past throw light on the problems of the present.[15] The researches of scholars like Atkinson reveal a veritable legion of writers in the fifteenth or sixteenth centuries who followed suit, among whom can be quoted Machiavelli, Bodin, Montchrestien, Viret, Pasquier,

Belleforest, Guillaume Postel, and—last but not least—Michel de Montaigne.[16] For, although the latter would, no doubt, have appreciated the techniques employed by Le Roy and Canaye, and although, as we shall see, much in his own approach may be compared to theirs, his main means of enlightening his fellow men on religious and political matters was the comparative method, or historical analogies, a technique most favoured by his contemporaries.[17]

*   *   *

However, as usual, it will be seen that Montaigne is not content to adopt such a method without refining it. He would not have been impressed, for example, by the simple contrast employed by Pasquier who, in his discussion of the new lands just discovered, merely assumed a simple black and white distinction between the crude habits of the 'Sauvages' and the civilised customs of Europeans. 'Et neantmoins vrayement neufves, si vous parangonnez les moeurs brusques de leurs peuples, avec la civilité des nostres'.[18] Montaigne uses the newly discovered lands, the Roman state of the past, the customs of the Turks, or figures from Greek and Latin literature in a manner suggesting that he has profited far more from a writer such as Estienne who questioned the 'strangeness' of distant events: 'quant aux moeurs et diverses complexions et façons de faire de divers pays descrites par Herodote, ie trouve estrange qu'elles soyent trouvees si estranges qu'on ne les puisse croire'.[19] A study of History shows that there is a strong continuity in human affairs. Even elements from the past or from distant lands which seem novel, strange, extraordinary, or indeed, barbarous have their modern counterparts; but these are not always recognised by the people who witness them.

In *Des mauvais moyens employez à bonne fin* (II:23) Montaigne takes a very complicated route to arrive at this same conclusion. At one moment he seems to have ascended Mount Olympus, and, from those great heights, surveys the swirling movement of the Universe, which he compares to the mutability of States. He seems very detached as he develops this comparison; tracing the movements of tribes, from the Franks 'partis du fons de l'Alemagne' to the colonising methods of the Romans, until references to 'cette emotion chaleureuse qui est parmy nous' reveals that his preoccupation is more precise. He studies the movements of the heavens and of the past in an attempt to see possible means of diverting 'ces humeurs peccantes qui dominent pour cette heure nostre corps' (II:23,664). The tenor of the essay acquires a more narrowly satirical flavour as Montaigne descends from the Olympian heights to start a discussion upon the means used by the Romans to educate 'le peuple à la vaillance et au mespris des dangiers et de la mort' (ii:23, 664). He describes graphically the enthusiasm, and almost barbaric encouragement, of the spectators as they goaded all-too-willing gladiators on to death. He dwells on their fight, their wounds, their courage, and on the angry or ecstatic response of the crowd; and he records the identity both of the gladiators and of the spectators. Then he adds, without further comment, at the very end of the essay: 'ce que je trouverois fort estrange et incroyable si nous n'estions accoustumez de voir tous les jours en nos guerres plusieurs miliasses d'hommes estrangiers, engageant pour de l'argent leur sang et leur vie à des querelles où ils n'ont aucun interest' (ii:23,666). His opinion is contained in the ironic force of the adjectives 'fort estrange et incroyable': gladiators have long since ceased to exist, but the incredible brutality and cruelty of their combats persist in the grim acts of the *lansquenets*. When looked at closely, the parallel is hardly exact in number or in intention, yet there is a sufficient relationship for the reader to accept the analogy, and to think along the critical lines suggested by it.

Into the past, Montaigne injects a considerable amount of idealism. Rome at its peak, 'Libre, juste et florissante' (iii:9,975), is the mirror which sends back the rosiest coloured pictures of man at his highest and most virtuous point of development. Looking at himself amidst the ravages of civil war, Montaigne admits 'me trouvant inutile à ce siècle, je me rejecte à cet autre'. Disappointment, frustration, and wishful thinking—a complex of emotional responses, in fact—all play their part in making up Montaigne's composite picture of the past. It is the disasters of the present which encourage him to see all things beautiful and good in other periods of time. Rome and the myth of the Golden Age come ever closer together in his mind, as he dwells on the first six centuries of the Roman State. So Montaigne, the acute observer of human activity and staunch supporter of recording the truth of what he sees, dresses up the facts of the past as a kind of compensation for the present.

He was by no means the only Frenchman in the sixteenth century haunted by the myth of the Golden Age.[20] Virgil's *Fourth Eclogue* especially had, throughout the Renaissance, provided both a refuge for the solitary man wishing to withdraw from the hurly-burly of warfare and collapsing states, and a source of inspiration for statesmen who hoped to emulate the calm tranquillity and peaceful prosperity predicted there. The myth acquired an extra dimension after the discovery of new, luxurious worlds across the seas; and Montaigne's vision of the New World

—where considerations of money were unknown, where the corruption of civilisation was scarcely experienced, where wars were fought only for self-defence, and where laws were natural and uncontaminated by the ingenuity of Europeans—could be matched by countless other visions sketched in the voyage literature of the time. What is interesting for us, however, is not that Montaigne's view of European corruption and primitive virtue had been anticipated more than fifty years before he wrote *Des cannibales* (1:31)[21] but that Montaigne takes the trouble to adopt a well-known parallelism, and to elaborate its implications with care.

Towards the beginning of his essay *Des cannibales*, Montaigne sets forth a description of the civil and moral state of these new nations, which seems to call in question every aspect of European civilisation. Their virtues are, significantly, exact opposites to European vices: and they surpass in excellence anything that Plato was able to conjure up as the perfect State in his *Republic*. The perfection outshines 'toutes les peintures de quoy la poësie a embelly l'age doré':

> C'est une nation, diroy je à Platon, en laquelle il n'y a aucune espese de trafique; nulle cognoissance de lettres; nulle science de nombres; nul nom de magistrat, ny de superiorité politique; nul usage de service, de richesse ou de pauvreté; nuls contrats; nulles successions; nuls partages; nulles occupations qu'oysives; nul respect de parenté que commun; nuls vestemens; nulle agriculture; nul metal; nul usage de vin ou de bled. Les paroles mesmes qui signifient le mensonge, la trahison, la dissimulation, l'avarice, l'envie, la detraction, le pardon, inouies. (1:31,204)

Furthermore, this new Eden of delights enjoys the choicest gifts of Nature; abundant food, temperate climate, and absence of disease. Montaigne then embarks upon an account of the natives' living conditions, their prophets, their religion, their wars, and their customs. He contrasts the inhabitants of the New World with those of the Old: and always to the advantage of the former. Their virtues shame our vices. He praises their beauty and their poetry; he applauds their scale of values which puts the strongest at the head of the state; and gives his blessing to their ability to 'sçavoir heureusement jouyr de leur condition et s'en contenter' (p. 209). The boost which Montaigne gives to their poetry is especially revealing of his real intentions to make their civilisation seem perfect whatever the cost. Their war songs are compared to the work of Anacreon; and the sound of their language is described as sweet and agreeable 'retirant aux terminaisons Grecques'. In the sixteenth century it would have been difficult to utter a greater compliment.[22]

Nonetheless, Montaigne has tried to forestall criticism of, or astonishment at, the romanticised picture he paints so enthusiastically. First, he insists on the veracity of the information he imparts. He accumulated it, he tells us, from someone who spent a long time with him, who had twelve years experience of these lands, and who, morevoer, 'estoit homme simple et grossier, qui est une condition propre à rendre veritable tesmoignage' (p. 202). And then, he focuses the reader's attention upon the varied meanings of the word 'barbare'. 'Barbarous', 'incredible', 'strange', 'beyond our experience', are all possible interpretations, and, he assumes, the ones most likely to occur to his reader. But Montaigne insists that such a reaction is misguided: and his elaborate attempt to familiarise us with the conditions of life in these new lands tries to prove this point. He has, however, another purpose in presenting, apparently so uncritically, his vision of a state more perfect than that depicted by poets in their descriptions of the Golden Age. It seems that Montaigne is, in fact, trying in some way to compete with poets on their own ground. He, too, seeks to get at his reader's emotions. He is trying to communicate the feel of a state which is undilutedly beautiful and good. The 'esprit primesautier' of Montaigne naturally responded with enthusiasm to the novel discoveries man had made across the sea: but the excitement he conveys is not, I feel, meant to be registered merely as a spontaneous reaction. Such enthusiasm might well inspire in his reader a desire to change everything in his own life running counter to this experience of the good so flowingly described.

It is significant that many of the elements which Montaigne pours into his picture of an ideal society, are not those we would expect to find there. His insistence on how the natives dealt with prophets for example; his long disquisitions on war; his extensive description of the courage of their prisoners—these can only be explained in the light of Montaigne's own remark that 'il y a une merveilleuse distance entre leur forme et la nostre' (p. 211). These elements—priests, war, prisoners and their limits of endurance— lie at the heart of Montaigne's preoccupations with the morals of his time. These are uppermost in his experience and in his criticism of the present. Only a detailed discussion of these anomalies can show his fellow men that their interpretation of the word 'barbare' as 'barbarous' should more properly be used to describe their own present actions. Men would not believe him if he called them savage to their faces. They had to be made to understand what the true nature of savagery was; and, to do this, Montaigne resorted to this system of analogy.

Prophets, in these new lands, lead a solitary life. When they do come down from the mountains into the village, and foretell the future, it is at the risk of their lives. If what they predict happens, they are safe; if not, they are cut to pieces. Thus, there is no encouragement for the ranks of the priesthood to increase themselves! The wisest among these countrymen give their counsel every evening: encouraging all to be brave and to respect their wives. Montaigne's natives rarely wage war, except in self-defence, or to test their courage. And it is interesting to note that, throughout his discussion of the causes and means of making war, Montaigne is most concerned with the natives' response as human beings to such situations of stress. He expands on the manner in which they deal with prisoners, and how the latter behave in captivity. He seems to exaggerate their courage, and their defiance of the enemy to the point of suicide. For a modern reader, he might seem to dwell too insistently on such gruesome details as the eating of dead prisoners (an extreme form of vengeance); but this is merely to make his comparative point, that the actions of their Portuguese invaders were worse, and that those of his contemporary Frenchmen were more reprehensible still. Montaigne accepts the argument that eating a man is 'une horreur barbaresque', thus consciously damaging the Utopian atmosphere he had created at the beginning of his essay. Nevertheless, this admission is made in order to stress one of the main preoccupations of the essay: to open men's eyes to the true nature of the barbarous deeds which they themselves commit. While we justly condemn the atrocities of others, how is it that we are blind to those we ourselves perpetrate? And, just in case any reader might wonder what Montaigne is getting at, he spells out his meaning by citing his own experience:

> Je pense qu'il y a plus de barbarie à manger un homme vivant qu'à le manger mort, à deschirer, par tourmens et par geénes, un corps encore plein de sentiment, le faire rostir par le menu, le faire mordre et meurtrir aux chiens et aux pourceaux (comme nous l'avons, non seulement leu, mais veu de fresche memoire, non entre des ennemis anciens, mais entre des voisins et concitoyens, et qui pis est, sous pretexte de pieté et de religion), que de le rostir et manger apres qu'il est trespassé. (pp. 207–8)

The power and insistence of the parenthesis leaves no corner clear into which an ashamed reader might withdraw in order to escape the cruel truth of the facts displayed before him. In the previous essay (*De la moderation*, I:30,199–200), Montaigne had castigated his natives by describing the alacrity and the resolution with which they sacrificed themselves to their Gods. In *Des cannibales*, he keeps their Gods in a distant place, and only allows the French gratification of theirs 'par nostre massacre et homicide' to come through.

The crowning indignity which Montaigne makes his reader suffer is to allow one of those 'barbarous' natives the luxury of passing judgement on the French nation. The native expresses surprise at the sight of puny Charles IX commanding his attendant retinue of strong armed men; and he registers astonishment at the enormous discrepancy between the magnificent nobles and the starving, scraggy specimens who knock at their doors. Before anyone can sweep away the implications with a laughing reminder of the primitive incompetence of the critic, Montaigne himself ends the essay on the following quip: 'Tout cela ne va pas trop mal: mais quoy, ils ne portent point de haut de chauses' (p. 213), showing that he realises that the reader will try to protect himself. He wants to prevent the qualities of his judge being undermined, while incidentally, preserving himself from any attack by the authorities he criticises. In this essay, at least, he leaves the reader little choice but to concur with his point of view.

In *Des cannibales*, the shrewd political observer and the acute analyst of human behaviour stood aside to allow Montaigne the polemicist to thrust home his views. Arguments were consistently weighted on the side of the primitive and the natural, and loaded against the civilised. The former enjoyed such descriptions as 'vive, vigoureuse, utile'; and its 'pureté', 'beauté' and 'richesse' were cruelly juxtaposed to the 'vice', 'goust corrompu', 'nature abastardie', and the feelings, 'alterez' and 'détournez', of the latter. Such an uneven balancing was extended in other essays: in the *Apologie* (II:12,471), for instance, where the Brazilians' tranquillity and serenity are contrasted with the 'passion . . . et occupation tendue ou desplaisante' of Europeans. And on the subject of law Montaigne invariably maintains the same kind of parallelism to the detriment of his countrymen. American natives 'passoyent leur vie en une admirable simplicité et ignorance, sans lettres, sans loy, sans roy, sans religion quelconque' (II:12,471), while Europe groans under the strains which stem from jurisprudence, 'generatrice d'altercation et division'. (III:13,1043)

*　　*　　*

There are other *Essais* in which Montaigne's ability to create Utopian worlds, either from the past or from the distant present, are used to make even more specific criticism of his contemporaries in Europe. It is one thing to make a fairly general attack upon the inhumanity of unnamed individuals: it is quite another to criticise the personal habits of monarchs, especially when you wish to remain relatively undisturbed in your tower at Montaigne. In *Des coches* (III:6) Montaigne widens his frame of reference to include both Rome and the New World. The essay starts with a sort of apology for leaving the strict realm of verifiable fact, and for delving into a world imagined by his own skill, justifying this move with the reminder that 'les grands autheurs, escrivant des causes, ne se servent pas seulement de celles qu'ils estiment estre vraies, mais de celles encores qu'ils ne croient pas, pourveu qu'elles ayent quelque invention et beauté. Ils disent assez veritablement et utilement, s'ils disent ingenieusement' (III:6,876). The essay then moves, as Etiemble has admirably shown,[23] from a discussion of modes of transport, to the ancient *chars de triomphe* on which victorious conquerors rode through the streets of Rome to be acclaimed by the populace. Their triumph was clearly deserved. But then Montaigne jumps to the present—pretending to do so spontaneously and in an offhand fashion as though the matter were of no importance—'L'estrangeté de ces inventions me met en teste cett'autre fantaisie: que c'est une espece de pusillanimité aux monarques, et un tesmoignage de ne sentir point assez ce qu'ils sont, de travailler à se faire valloir et paroistre par despences excessives' (III:6,879). Henri III is not mentioned. But no contemporary, reading this phrase in 1588, would have any difficulty in recognising the royal features either behind this remark, or behind this other criticism: 'Les subjects d'un prince excessif en dons se rendent excessifs en demandes' (p. 882). Lestoile's *Journal*, and Lucinge's letters written at the court of that monarch, both give an extraordinary amount of space to complaints about his monetary excesses—but neither, even though they knew themselves to be protected by the fact that their work would only come to light after Henri's death, went so far as to attribute the cause to the king's pusillanimity, as did Montaigne.[24]

As the essay proceeds, Montaigne's eloquence encompasses the architectural ingenuity of the Roman spectacle, whose fertile inventors lavished untold riches for the entertainment of the people. But his enthusiasm is abruptly cut short as he contemplates the diminished inventiveness of his own time, only capable of producing weapons for the destruction of the people. Worse still, power to destroy has contaminated the innocence, and reduced the potential, of those newly discovered lands across the Atlantic. Montaigne's mind lingers nostalgically on the vision of a nation, conjured up by blending the best of the virtues of ancient Greece and Rome with the innate virtues and vitality of the New World. His wishful thinking builds up an idyllic place 'meslant non seulement à la culture des terres et ornement des villes les arts de deçà, en tant qu'elles y eussent esté necessaires, mais aussi les vertus Grecques et Romaines aux originelles du pays!' (p. 888). Equally suddenly this vision is shattered by a precise account of the atrocities perpetrated by Europeans against the natural virtue and innate intelligence of the inhabitants of Peru, Brazil, and Mexico—and all for the greed of gold. Montaigne creates a vision of delights so that he may tantalisingly destroy it as soon as we are caught by its beauty; while, at the same time, he communicates some idea of his sense of shame at what we have lost. By such sudden transitions he seeks to shock his reader into appreciating the real value of gold and of man's ingenuity. The best civilisations of the Old World and the New used precious metals extravagantly, but they used them positively for the pleasure of the greatest number; their towns and palaces are huge in proportions, fine in conception, and lasting in materials. 'What can Europeans offer to counterbalance such achievements?', Montaigne leaves the reader to ask. Weapons of war, and kings who selfishly and greedily dissipate the wealth extorted from their starving peoples, are the answers Montaigne provides, and the partiality of his evidence is the best guide to his satirical intentions.[25]

On the whole, however, Montaigne is sympathetic to kings. Their task is a difficult one, exposed as they are to easy honours, to the exploitation of their weaknesses, and to the skill of corrupt courtiers[26] (*De l'incommodité de la grandeur*, III : 7). Nevertheless, there were times when Montaigne felt the need to criticise and to offer precise comment. And on these occasions he had recourse to analogies which (one would have thought) offered no such protective cover as did the grandeurs of the past or of the New World. His disapproval of Henri III's poltroonery in moments of crisis, his criticism of the king's soft and effeminate ways and reluctance to lead his troops into battle, could scarcely be more sharply stated than in the essay *Contre la faineantise* (II : 21), where the boldness and vigorous actions of the Turks are extolled as a lesson worthy of imitation. Elsewhere he observes that the discipline of the Turkish soldiery 'a beaucoup de differences et d'avantages sur la nostre' (III : 12, 1019). Most astonishing of all Montaigne's analogies, however, is that between Henri III and Julian the Apostate—a marriage of minds and actions which reveals the superiority of Julian, and for which Montaigne was severely criticised in Rome. Montaigne did nothing to reduce the shocking nature of the comparison: indeed, later additions merely served to make it sharper. How dare he compare the God-given King of France, anointed with the sacred oils, to the Roman Emperor whose first action on gaining supreme power was to abjure Christianity, and even to discourage its growth, by issuing edicts of toleration and withdrawing all Christian text books from the schools? Historically the comparison could well have been suggested by the Peace of Monsieur in May 1576, which had given freedom of conscience to the protestants—and the title of Montaigne's essay is, in fact, *De la liberté de conscience* (II: 19,650). But there is another point which justifies Julian's superiority over Henri III: Julian had achieved toleration without bloodshed. Montaigne insists on this point: 'Il estoit . . . ennemy de la Chrestienté, mais sans toucher au sang' (p. 652). Julian was so virtuous himself that 'il n'est aucune sorte de vertu de quoy il n'ait laissé de tres notables exemples' (p. 651). He was also just, personally taking the trouble to hear the case for both sides. Above all, Montaigne suggests, he abjured Christianity not only because he had been born with feelings against that religion, but also because he had experience 'par la cruauté d'aucuns Chrestiens qu'il n'y a point de beste au monde tant à craindre à l'homme que l'homme' (p. 654).[27] Montaigne further took care to make explicit the fcat that all Julian's deeds were thought out a long time ahead, and that they were deliberately performed, whereas the French king's motives for such an action were altogether more questionable: 'si croy mieux, pour l'honneur de la devotion de nos rois, c'est que, n'ayans peu ce qu'ils vouloient, ils ont fait semblant de vouloir ce qu'ils pouvoient'.[28]

*   *   *

So far, our discussion of analogies in Montaigne has tended to stress the more destructive use he made of them; although, of course, the comparative technique always implies a model solution. However, Montaigne did make more positive use of parallels, and the lessons which he gained from History go far beyond the generalities echoed in the works of his contemporaries, and enabling him to know himself more intimately. In order to understand his learning process more fully, we must first ask a question: since Montaigne was so obviously concerned about public affairs, what kind of contribution did he think each individual should make in an attempt to retrieve the disastrous political situation? Public disaster inevitably turns men's minds in upon themselves to study the extent of their own responsibility. Fundamentally, Montaigne has a practical turn of mind, and he has only imitated the ideal conceptions of Plato for a practical purpose, acknowledging that 'toutes ces descriptions de police, feintes par art, se trouvent ridicules et ineptes à mettre en practique' (iii:9,934). Morally he was convinced that every man who had the ability ought to play a role in public affairs, since each man was, he felt, partly responsible for the general confusion now reigning in France: 'la corruption du siècle se faict par la contribution particuliere de chacun de nous' (iii:9,923). Montaigne also knew, however, that public life and private morality were incompatible. He himself had tried to apply his private moral code to public affairs, and he had found its values 'ineptes et dangereuses' (iii:9,970). Fascinated by this incompatibility, Montaigne filled many pages of the *Essais* with considerations on public and private commitment. In fact, the attempt to grapple with this problem is one of the main recurrent themes of the third book of the *Essais*. Montaigne studied the nature of public life, its demands, and its limitations. He analysed what happens to a man's mind and behaviour when he has to answer to a commander or to a monarch. How far can a man go in immorality for the sake of public good? How far, indeed, was the present political situation in France retrievable? To these questions, Montaigne gives different answers at different times. Like most of his conservative contemporaries, such as Louis le Roy, Montaigne attributed enormous importance to the maintaining of laws and institutions as they are: at a time of civil war 'conserver' is both an emotional reaction and a practical response (iii: 10, 1001–2). This leads him, through the analogy of an 'enfant monstrueux', to suggest toleration as a solution for the present divisions in France: 'Ce double corps et ces membres divers, se rapportans à une seule teste, pourroient bien fournir de favorable prognostique au Roy de maintenir sous l'union de ses loix ces pars et pieces diverses de nostre estat' (ii: 30, 691). At moments of the greatest depression, finding no satisfactory explanation of the causes for such turmoil, and virtually convinced that there are no viable public solutions, Montaigne resorts to private ones. Adopting his favourite technique of diversion, he argues the case for running away from the strife; that is to escape from the war mentally and physically, by undertaking long voyages. (*De la vanité*). It is not that he is afraid of the dangers of war, though he does effectively describe each man's vulnerability as standing on the precipice of disaster (iii: 12, 1023): but he despairs of being able to do anything positive to stop the downward swing of his country's fortunes. His writing in *De la vanité* (iii:9) is conditioned by the strong, personal need for consolation which he felt when faced with the realisation that he did not belong to his century in so far as he could not conform to, or even condone, its immoral demands of 'meschamment faire'. The ills of France could not be cured by superficial changes. The situation required a general 'amendement de condition' (p. 937). The preservation of the State was beyond man's control. It is with justifications such as these that Montaigne tries to explain his understandable desire to get away from it all.

On the other hand, he could not get away. Public affairs not only fascinated him as a student of human nature, they imposed themselves upon him in such a way that he could not escape. If each man was responsible for the lamentable confusion which ranged through France then it was each man's responsibility to look into himself to search for explanations of causes as well as to discover solutions. Montaigne's distress in *De la vanité* seems also to express irritation that he himself lacked the greatness of spirit to sacrifice that precious 'arrière boutique à soi', which he stubbornly wanted to preserve intact and uncontaminated by the corrupting influences of public life; and whose preservation gave him considerable pleasure when writing *Du repentir*, 'ce n'est pas un leger plaisir, de se sentir preservé de la contagion d'un siècle si gasté' (III:2, 784). He sways, undecided, first in one direction and then in another. At the moment of writing *De la vanité* he seems to have despaired of being able to keep his private and public selves separate—a course he had believed in and advocated strongly in *De la solitude* (I:39,235), and was to put forward again in *De mesnager sa volonté* (III:10,980). He had argued with pride that his honesty 'est un peu bien dissonant à nos formes' in *De l'utile et de l'honneste* (III:1,772). In *De la vanité*, however, a much more intense emotional response to civil strife momentarily seems to make him regret the obstinacy with which he clings to this basic virtue. In *De l'utile et de l'honneste* a phrase such as 'le bien public requiert qu'on trahisse et qu'on mente et qu'on massacre' (III:1,768), had seemed filled with a satire meant to arouse the reader's protest; by the time Montaigne came to write *De la vanité* the phrase had acquired an irrefutable stoutness of fact.[29]

There was, however, another way of looking at this almost instinctive temporary withdrawal from the public arena. Already, in the first version of *Que nostre desir s'accroit par la malaisance* (II:15,598–9), Montaigne had argued that religious contention and civil strife had at least one virtue. Paradoxically, they were a source of moral rectitude, since they roused virtuous men from the idleness and sleep into which tranquillity had plunged them. The strength of mind and rectitude of such men could serve as the best defence against the consequences of war. Opposition strengthens the virtuous, and even those who are less admirable. Montaigne turns in upon himself to develop the power to handle public affairs competently; for the proper exercise of civil power lies in separating private ambitions from public good. The more one strengthens the ability of the individual, the greater and more effective use can be made of him in general affairs. Montaigne argues this position at length in *De mesnager sa volonté* (III: 10), which serves as an answer to the desperate tones of *De la vanité*. Much of his insistence on his own singularity seems to stem from the desire to persuade men to build up their inner resources before hiring themselves out to public service: 'les hommes se donnent à louage . . . Je prens une complexion toute diverse' (III: 10,981). The nourishing of mental energy, and the sharpening of moral vigour, were essential to a man wishing to become that ideal of civilised society, that 'homme meslé', who combined flexibility of mind with virtue, and was thus ready to tackle any eventuality. By maintaining emotional aloofness from public affairs, Montaigne hoped to make himself capable of controlling them expertly; 'Celuy qui n'y employe que son jugement et son adresse, il y procede plus gayement: il feinct, il ploye, il differe tout à son aise, selon le besoing des occasions' (III: 10,985). The inner privacy he had guarded so jealously, and that very distance which he cultivated so ardently, were intended to allow Montaigne to attain in public affairs the almost stoic impassibility which brought sound, and impartial judgement: 'Aus presens brouillis de cet estat, mon interest ne m'a fait mesconnoistre ny les qualitez louables en nos adversaires, ny celles qui sont reprochables en ceux que j'ay suivy' (III: 10,989).

To achieve this penetration of judgement and this confidence in his own ability, Montaigne had subjected himself to a long apprenticeship in learning about himself. An important method of discovery had been in the use of parallelisms—matching, contrasting, and refining himself against models from the past. In a general way, he was doing nothing more than what his contemporaries had done. They had used their inborn idealistic view of the past in an attempt to improve the present. In the *Essais*, however, Montaigne gives the impression that they used figures from the past to flatter aspects of the present.[30] Kings of France, great nobles, poets, and artists, applauded each other by multiplying comparisons with past heroes. Religious factions fought each other with references to the greatest figures of evil they could find in the Greek and Roman, or in the Church's literary tradition. But Montaigne would not accept their indiscriminate compliments, nor would he admire their injudicious analogies: the government of Charles IX could not reasonably be compared to that of Nero, nor could the Cardinal de Lorraine be properly matched with Seneca (*Defence de Seneque et de Plutarque*. ii: 32, 699). As usual, Montaigne required that the analogies be at once more detailed and more complex.

* * *

His greatest inspiration for the pursuit of such parallels was, without doubt, Plutarch whose *Lives* and *Moral Works* had taught him how much could be learned about man's mind and behaviour by comparing the thoughts and actions of great men.[31] So far, we have been more concerned in Montaigne with those analogies which extolled the past to expose, in general terms, the ills of the present. Now I wish to turn to 'ces riches ames du passé' which Montaigne used to build up the resources of the individual that he might withstand adversity. While recognising that modern souls were unworthy and unable to appreciate, or to appropriate, the riches of the past, Montaigne nevertheless urges his reader to ponder the deeds of great Greek and Roman figures: 'presentez vous tousjours en l'imagination Caton, Phocion et Aristide . . . et establissez-les contrerolleurs de toutes vos intentions' (i: 39, 242). This course Montaigne proposes, in *De la solitude*, as the most fitting way of learning to know yourself. It's no good withdrawing into yourself unless you are ready to profit from it: 'retirez vous en vous, mais preparez vous premierement de vous y recevoir' (i: 39, 242). This preparation could be perfected by using figures of the past to establish criteria and to measure self-knowledge. By taking their virtues and studying your own response, and by analysing what is possible to follow and what is not, you grow to understand the nature of virtue and to enjoy its possession; you learn to recognise the limits of your own possibilities, and, by this process, 'vous contenter de vous mesmes' (i: 39, 242). Such is Montaigne's advice in the closing paragraphs of his essay on Solitude. In other essays Montaigne himself shows us this process at work.

He uses analogies, with Pliny and Cicero, for example, to define the kind of life he wants to lead. Their version of solitude is too public for his taste, and he examines it in order to establish the nature of his own withdrawal from the public arena (i: 39). Great minds from the past help him to delimit what he can do. Socrates' attitude to death, for instance, is admirable because it stresses the naturalness of the event; yet Montaigne knows that his own emotional frame can never attain such

equanimity (III : 4). The Stoics' quietness of mind, he studies and emulates
as far as he can; and it is his analysis of their several virtues—their control of emotions, particularly—and the measuring of them against his
own, which shows him how far he would like to go, and just how far he
can go (*De mesnager sa volonté*, III : 10). There is nothing haphazard in
these analogies. Montaigne examines a figure such as Caesar, distinguishing his actions, his nature, and his good luck, before passing judgement on his achievements, and reminding would-be emulators that similar
effects are not necessarily produced by similar actions. (II : 33).

Although Montaigne considered Cato the Younger as a model
whose virtues soared far above the virtuous possibilities of his contemporaries—'Ce personnage là fut veritablement un patron que nature
choisit pour montrer jusques où l'humaine vertu et fermeté pouvoit
attendre' (I : 37, 227)—he did not hesitate, in a later essay (III : 9, 969),
to use him in a comparison with himself in order to convey what he felt
about his own position in the world of the late sixteenth century, and
to communicate his disgust at the depraved state of his age. Cato's virtue
might be so unique that it is unattainable at any period of history; yet
man's response should not be a despairing acceptance of moral weakness, but rather a realisation that it is worth striving to be more like
Cato and less like the corrupt men of the sixteenth century. Montaigne,
through his parallelism with Cato, sets himself up as a lesser model. He
frequently sees himself as this kind of link between the present and the
past. In *De la præsomption* (II : 17), while admitting man's tendency to
overrate himself, he thrusts forward his own virtues of good conscience,
self-knowledge, and good judgement, as being better than the values of
honour and valiance which his contemporaries so prize. By placing such
comments as these in an essay entitled, *On Presumption*, 'je n'ay affaire
qu'à moy, je me considere sans cesse, je me contrerolle, je me gouste
. . . moy je me roulle en moy mesme' (II : 17, 641), Montaigne shows
that, though he is a pygmy compared to the great minds of the Ancient
World, he emerges as a colossus in his contemporary setting, and he does
this in spite of his efforts to tone down his growing confidence and satisfaction in his unique self-absorption.

Increasingly the figure of Socrates is used by Montaigne as a
means of justifying his own discoveries, and of giving strength to his own
philosophical position. His preoccupation with self, and the fortifying of
one's own inner resources, are underlined with remarks such as: 'de
quoy traitte Socrates plus largement que de soy ?' (II : 6, 359). His conviction that man should cultivate all that is natural is argued by a simple

parallel with Socrates (III : 12, 1013) ; and the point is taken further, using the same means, when Montaigne demonstrates, at the beginning of *Du repentir* (III : 2, 787), that Socrates, by cultivating himself, created a worthier and a more versatile public servant than could all the deeds of Alexander. In the 'C' additions to the *Essais*, and in the third book generally, when Montaigne seeks some parallel figure to embody the wishes and thoughts he is trying to impart, it is Socrates who comes most readily to mind. He curtails more and more his initial hesitancies; and he narrows the gap separating Socrates from Montaigne until, for a reader of the later essays, it is difficult to distinguish between the ideal and its emulator.[32]

*   *   *

Analogies similar to those used by Montaigne may, of course, be found in a host of contemporary and antecedent authors. But it is not common to find someone who handles such models in so coherent a fashion. There is, however, one work—the *De Constantia* of Montaigne's friend and correspondent, Justus Lipsius—which compels attention, for it may well have inspired Montaigne's own attempts to come to terms with adversity.[33] And the parallels between the two authors are so close that, although a comparison between them may seem tangential to the principal theme of this chapter, I feel it worthwhile to attempt this not so much as a pendant to the discussion of analogies, but rather as an illuminating complement to the solution at which Montaigne arrived through his use of such analogies.

The *De Constantia* was first published in Latin by Christopher Plantin in 1584. Lipsius's main aim is stressed by the subtitle *Qui alloquium praecipuè continent in publicis malis*—which was significantly expanded by his English translator, John Stradling,[34] into 'and will serve for a singular consolation to all that are privately distressed, or afflicted, either in body or mind'. The work is presented in the form of a dialogue between Lipsius himself and his humanist friend Charles Langius, and it begins on a highly emotional note as Lipsius expresses to Langius his considerable distress and need for consolation. He has, he explains, just escaped from the rigours of the civil wars waged in his native Low Countries, and he seeks peace and comfort so that he might continue his studies. The context then is the same as that of the *Essais*. If anything, however, the desire for personal consolation is greater in Lipsius, since the plight of his native land at first colours entirely his view of the world, until Langius points out the selfish narrowness of his vision: 'Beholde if warre be among the Ethiopians or Indians, it moveth thee not: (thou art out of danger) if it be in Belgica, thou weepest, cryest out, rubbest thy forehead, and smitest thy thigh'.[35] Thus, alerted by his philosopher friend, Lipsius joins with Montaigne in the view that their feelings are not limited to personal or national sorrow; they are (like Socrates, whom they both quote) men of the world, speaking for all men. And as if to prove this last point, Lipsius devotes many pages towards the end of his book to the desolations, the slaughters, and the massacres perpetrated throughout the world—but most especially by the Spaniards.

Lipsius's reasoning in the *De Constantia* follows a pattern similar to that given by Montaigne in *De la vanité*. First of all, he goes to almost outrageous lengths in his attempt to justify calamity. He tries to prove that God causes ills; that they are necessary; and, moreover, that they 'be neither grievous, nor straunge'.[36] He then contends that the end of calamities 'tendeth alwaies to good', and that 'adversitie doth confirm and strengthen us'.[37] Finally, he points to the extent of the disasters in the world, thereby trying to diminish the significance of the local trouble in Belgium: 'by this communication or participation of miseries, lighten thine owne'.[38] Many of these arguments are ingenious, but hardly convincing, even for Lipsius himself, and his thoughts turn (just as Montaigne's did) to another source of consolation.

The only source of strength to emerge from the *De Constantia* is that determined by the individual himself. Forced by circumstances to turn in upon itself, our mind 'must be so confirmed and conformed, that we may be at rest in troubles, and have peace even in the midst of warre'.[39] For Lipsius, the 'conforming' of the mind depends upon an analysis of the real nature of one's responses to a situation, and on the cultivation of the stoic virtues: moderation of the affections, and constancy. This last quality is, of course, the one to which he gives most prominence, defining its elements and frequently thrusting it upon the reader's mind: 'Imprint Constancie in thy mind amid this casuall and inconstant variableness of all things'.[40] He shows that the only sane response in adversity is to remember your condition as man: 'Like as they which rode gloriouslie in triumph, had a servaunt behinde their backs, who in the middes of all their triumphant idolitie, cryed out oftentimes, "Thou art a man", so let this be ever as a prompter by thy side, that these things are humane, or appertaining to men'.[41] As in Montaigne, it is the individual who sits at the centre of responsibility, and at the heart of any solution to the problems they both shared. Lipsius is not concerned in the *De Constantia* to work out at all precisely what an honest man ought to do in civil war:

he reserves this task for the last of his *Politicorum Libri Sex* (1589).[42] But it is clear that, however emotional his spontaneous response to a situation of strife, he does not condone escape, any more than Montaigne did—except perhaps at moments of greatest depression. His suggestion that it is the individual's mind which must be strengthened, his offering of moderate passions and constancy, seem strangely familiar echoes of Montaigne's analysis of an analogous situation. They also reveal that Montaigne's personal philosophy comes remarkably close to Stoicism.[43]

7

CONTEXTS

EXPLORATION of Montaigne's oblique methods of persuasion has revealed the importance of contexts in the *Essais*. Indeed, the realisation that Montaigne's major notions—his view of man, his religious convictions, the power of reason, and the 'style soldatesque', for example —find their complete definition in a synthesis built from observing these notions at play in diverse contexts, is as essential as paying attention to the precise purpose animating a particular essay. In this chapter I have a two-fold purpose: I hope to demonstrate Montaigne's concern to study man's behaviour in specific contexts, his emphasis on the virtue of careful distinctions, and on the need to be aware of different levels of argument; and I also hope to show that Montaigne does not always write 'craftiely'.

Although modern criticism of Montaigne's work is beginning to note the importance of studying his thought in context—by analysing his use of key concepts such as nature, 'jugement', imagination, or death —the main concentration has been concerned with chronology.[1] Undoubtedly, Villey's huge thesis gave the impetus to the kind of study which partitioned off Montaigne's thinking into clear-cut moral categories, usually divided according to the three principal stages of composition of the *Essais*. But, while it is true to say that Montaigne's interests broadened in the course of time, and that his literary skill became perfected, I would be reluctant to argue that the moral development of a man already mature when he began to write the *Essais* followed a similar, evolving pattern.[2] Such an argument would suggest that Montaigne had not thought about man in general, or himself in particular, before making his decision to retire at the age of thirty-eight. And, such a suggestion, in its turn, would be difficult to sustain when one recalls that a large part of those years had been devoted to a career as a magistrate, where the judging of human behaviour was a constant duty. It is a suggestion, also, which assumes that a human being develops in a fairly consistent and coherent way. It takes little note of the fragmented nature of experience put into high relief by Montaigne; and it ignores the fact that any writer may adopt a multitude of guises in order to make his points. Montaigne, after all, often provides us with obvious means of identifying the specific purpose animating an essay. It might be a shift in tone, or an over-use of an element of syntax; he might collect disparate elements and treat them as though they were on the same plane. Or he might employ odd juxtapositions; or derisively pile up diminutives and demonstrative adjectives. In my opinion, attention to the detail of precise contexts has not yet been precise enough.

Let us start with the sustained argument in *De l'inconstance de nos actions* (II : 1) where Montaigne tries to sketch in a picture of the many contradictions which make up his own personality:

> Je donne à mon ame tantost un visage, tantost un autre, selon le costé où je la couche. Si je parle diversement de moy, c'est que je me regarde diversement. Toutes les contrarietez s'y trouvent selon quelque tour et en quelque façon. Honteux, insolent; chaste, luxurieux; bavard, taciturne; laborieux, delicat; ingenieux, hebeté; chagrin, debonaire; menteur, veritable; sçavant, ignorant, et liberal et avare, et prodigue, tout cela, je le vois en moy aucunement, selon que je me vire. (II : 1, 319)

This perplexing intricacy of thought, motive, and action, Montaigne tries to control through a style whose qualities can match the slightest change of mood. His words suggest that the process is a frequently confusing one; but it is, above all, a conscious activity, which demands an ability to distinguish a context, a mood, a set of conditions, or the level on which a discourse is being conducted. He emphasises these facts later in this same essay when he writes: 'Je n'ay rien à dire de moy, entierement, simplement, et solidement, sans confusion et sans meslange, ny en un mot. DISTINGO est le plus universel membre de ma Logique' (II : 1,319). Here then, we are shown a man looking at, and discovering himself, in our presence; and, as he gazes into the mirror of changing events and moods, he demonstrates a method of analysing human behaviour, which, precisely because it accepts the difficulties of such an inquiry, goes much further than the more static systems used by many of Montaigne's contemporaries. It is important to realise that Montaigne is not

being perverse when he writes about contradictions and confusion; he is
not attempting merely to bewilder the reader in order to demonstrate
some superior gift of mental manoeuvrability. The amount of space he
devotes in the *Essais* to these problems, and his insistent tone, argue
a sincere belief in the need to evolve new ways of coming to grips with
the overpowering complexities present in any attempt to make judgements upon life. This method does not depend simply on an ability to
see: 'Il n'importe pas seulement qu'on voye la chose, mais comment on
la voye' (1:14,68).

His insistence on the relative nature of human activity, and his
view that it is useless to judge behaviour from the distant standpoint of
moral values can be made clear by specific examples. Suicide, he argues,
cannot automatically be explained as an act of despair (ii:3), since moral
values change according to time and circumstance. In *De la vanité* he
takes this last point further, proving that 'l'innocence civile se mesure
selon les lieux et saisons' (iii:9,972). At times of civil war, the useless
—that is to say, the inactive—becomes a thing worthy of praise (iii:
9,923), while in *De l'utile et de l'honneste* (iii:1) the useful (the active)
should not necessarily be confused with the honest or the honorable. Nor,
Montaigne claims, should it be assumed that good advice in one context
will prove equally sound in another (1:24). Or again, he shows how
man's observations can be transformed by a simple alteration in the distance which separates him from the object he contemplates (iii:11,920).
Similarly, he holds that the pain he suffers can be intensified or lightened
by factors which have nothing to do with the source of the distress (1:
14,58). These are merely a few of the many instances in the *Essais*
where attention to context is needed to define the thought.

Montaigne used contexts to give us a fully-rounded view of a
problem. We know from the studies of Dow that Montaigne's conception of Nature was complex, and that his use of the term varied according
to the context.[3] We know that his notions of diversity depend upon
whether the context required him to stress the richness and variety of the
world, or to put into relief the bewildering mutability of things. And we
know that instability is decried in *De la praesomption* (ii:17,639),
whereas, at other moments, it is suggested as a source of exhilaration.
Obscurity in writing is condemned in the *Apologie* (ii:12,487) because,
there, Montaigne wants to demonstrate how it is used by *savants* to
hide the vanity of their art. Nevertheless, in many other places, he himself
uses the very same technique as a means of persuasion.

Montaigne's reliance on shifting contexts to communicate the

complicated nature of his thought, polishes the reader's power of judgement and increases his critical ability. Supposing that one wishes to
establish Montaigne's view of flexibility, for example, one would have to
take into account not only his assertion that the most supple minds are
the best (III: 3, 796), and that a man's most worthwhile task is to cultivate
resilience to changing events (I: 14), but also his bitter comment that
human beings are so flexible that they can accept anything (III: 5, 830).
The first position is argued when Montaigne is concerned that the individual should build up his own inner resources; the second emerges when
Montaigne looks at what has happened to traditional moral codes at a
time of civil strife. Flexibility is without virtue if it is found in the
chameleon shape of a courtier (*De la vanité*, III: 9, 964), but it acquires
admirable features as soon as Montaigne presents it as the only way a
man can come to terms with the constant shift of events in the outside
world (III: 9, 970).

In *Des coches* (III: 6), Montaigne demonstrates his ability to move
skilfully from one level of consideration to another, shifting from a distant
view of Roman spectacle to a cosmic view of the swirling sphere of the
world, and down to the feebleness of human knowledge: 'de cette mesme
image du monde qui coule pendant que nous y sommes, combien chetive
et racourcie est la cognoissance des plus curieux' (III: 6, 886). He acknowledges that most men frequently confuse planes and contexts; for the
most part they remain victims of received opinion, and, in addition, jum-
ble their thoughts without recognising that careful distinctions are necessary to reveal the true nature of things. Montaigne claims that he is
master of objectivity in a way in which they are not: 'je n'ay point cette
erreur commune de juger d'un autre selon que je suis' (I: 37, 225). He
can put himself into the mind of other individuals. He can equally well
leap out onto distant mountain tops from which his gaze reduces all men
—kings and peasants—to the same miserable state (II: 12, 454). Other
men confound knowledge of things with knowledge of causes, without
appreciating that the latter belong to God alone, while only the former
can be managed by human beings. Montaigne, of course, claims that he
himself makes no such confusion (III: 11, 1002–3). He will set handker-
chiefs and miracles together (I: 23, 109–10) to encourage his reader
to sift out a more exact meaning of 'étrange'. Define, distinguish, and
look closely from all angles, are his watchwords, and his method is to
give such mobility to perspectives that his reader has little option but
to do as he commands. A good instance may be taken from *Que philosopher
c'est apprendre à mourir* (I: 20), where he soars from his little world of

man, noting each elusive second as it ticks by—'A chaque minute il me semble que je m'eschape' (i : 20, 86)—to an apprehension of the enduring nature of the cosmos itself (i : 20, 90). From the intimate closeness of self, his thoughts have opened out to embrace the universe.

*　　*　　*

I have frequently alluded to the importance of the Religious Wars in Montaigne's thought and writing. In the last chapter I tried to show how far contemporary ills were in the forefront of his mind as he wrote his *Essais*, and I discussed one of the ways in which he grappled with the problems they posed. Here, I wish to argue more generally that Montaigne's experience of civil war and of religious controversy is primarily responsible for orientating his thought. His preoccupation with the weaknesses of law derives not only from his professional experience, but also from the blatant inadequacies of the legal system to deal with the civil confusion brought about by war (*De l'experience*, iii : 13, 1049). His discoveries about man's diversity, mutability, complexity of motive, and vacillating moral values, are made through close observation of human behaviour at precise moments of stress. It might be said that all this is obvious, and that once said it need not be repeated. Yet the fact that Montaigne reacts to the horror of contemporary events in a more positive way than many of his contemporaries however much they, too, deplored the topsy-turvy nature of the world is one worth stressing. Le Roy, for example, is frequently very eloquent on the subject : but this vehement reaction did not inspire him, as it did Montaigne, to seek solutions for the individual faced with such calamity. The *Essais* are Montaigne's answer to the violence, stupidity, pride, and self-interest, which accompany war. They also demonstrate that the conditions which a man might encounter in public affairs, differ very little, in their moral impact, from those brought about by war. Montaigne studies the precise nature of these moral demands, not so much in the hope that he might change the world, but that he might at least alert the individual and make him more conscious of the consequences of his undertakings.

Man must be forced to recognise his own limitations before he can achieve anything. And it is precisely the purpose of the *Apologie de R. Sebond* to grind human pride into dust; and Montaigne sets about this clearly defined task by systematically exposing the weaknesses of human reasoning power :

> Le moyen que je prens pour rabatre cette frenaisie et qui me semble
> le plus propre, c'est de froisser et fouler aux pieds l'orgueil et

humaine fierté; leur faire sentir l'inanité, la vanité et deneantise de
l'homme; leur arracher des points les chetives armes de leur raison,
leur faire baisser la teste et mordre la terre soubs l'authorité et reverance de la majesté divine. (ii : 12, 426)

The terms are strong, precise, and unequivocal. The attack is placed on
a general plane, so that any man can accept or reject these censures as he
thinks fit. Montaigne is set on a specific course in which every grain of
material, and every argument will be directed towards the same end.
The facts will be coloured by his intentions, and the arguments will be
shaped, twisted if necessary, to demonstrate his points. They might be
one-sided, and his themes might seem exaggerated, as in his long comparison of men and beasts where this well-worn topic is turned upside
down.[4] Readers of Montaigne—familiar with the conventional hierarchy
in which Christian and Platonic traditions had placed beasts, men, and
angels in an ascending scale—would be puzzled, and perhaps even outraged, by Montaigne's consistent belittling of man, and his upgrading of
animals. But the very space devoted to this theme suggests that it should
be judged rather as a means of demonstrating a view than as Montaigne's
considered opinion about the relative positions of men and beasts. In
other essays, written before and after the *Apologie*, Montaigne, in fact,
reverts to the traditional view on this topic and assumes man's superiority.
In *Que philosopher c'est apprendre à mourir* (i : 20, 84), and in *De l'inegalité
qui est parmy nous* (i : 42, 250), he attaches the customary sense of in-
feriority to the adjective 'bestial' and to the noun 'bête'. In *De l'affection
des peres aux enfans* (ii : 8, 366), *Couardise mere de la cruauté* (ii : 27, 671),
and in *De l'experience* (iii : 13, 1096), 'bestes' is no more than a term of
opprobrium used to castigate the moral disorders of contemporary
Frenchmen. Only in the *Apologie* are they presented as equal or superior
to man, and only then because such a reversal of an accepted convention
admirably suits the context of his essay. In the *Apologie*, man is removed
from the centre of significance in the world: but, in other essays, the
individual returns to his central position as Montaigne's principal preoccupation.

If we consider the contexts in which Montaigne decries man's
reasoning power it will be seen that they fall into two main categories:
the first occurs when Montaigne surveys the world from the standpoint
of God; the second, when contemporary religious or political matters
come to the forefront of his mind. In *De l'art de conferer*, he ironically
explains to the Protestants that they should not be surprised if their

followers are dissatisfied, since they have based their doctrine on the shifting sands of human imbecility (III : 8, 909). But it is more especially in the context of the Eternal that man is infinitely small. This point is rammed home not only in the *Apologie* but also in essays like *Des prieres* (I : 56, 311), where Montaigne enthusiastically remarks of divine law, 'il n'y a rien de si aisé, si doux et si favorable'. The generosity of the Divine seems almost beyond conception as Montaigne contemplates God taking unto himself human beings who are 'fautiers et détestables', and who can only be described in the biblical terms of 'vilains, ords et bourbeux'. Only God can make the generous gesture towards miserable humanity. Men who try to take the place of the divine are instantly labelled by Montaigne as arrogant and overweening; and their attempts to bridge the gap between the infinitely small (man) and the infinitely great (God) are nothing more than 'blasphemeuse appariation' (II : 12, 510). The essay *C'est folie de rapporter le vray et le faux à nostre suffisance* (I : 27) deals with this problem less emotionally; although Montaigne's terms—'sotte, folie, temeraire, absurde, bestise, hardiesse'—are very strong. There Montaigne argues from solid personal experience, inveighing against the incapacity of human judgement to discuss matters of religious doctrine, however small the points at issue. Men suffer from minds which are maimed, one-sided, prejudiced, and diseased: and the intellectual pretentions of theologians who try to tread the domain of the divine merely constitute one instance of such disability.

'C'est aux Chrestiens une occasion de croire, que de rencontrer une chose incroiable', writes Montaigne; 'Elle est d'autant plus selon raison, qu'elle est contre l'humaine raison' (II : 12, 478). Such phrases have frequently been hauled out of context to prove Montaigne's lack of belief. But, if they are replaced in the framework provided by Montaigne, it will be seen that they are a necessary part of his attack on human reason. Montaigne's anxiety, to make his own belief explicit and memorable, has given these phrases an especially paradoxical twist. They do stand out from the page. They are artistically satisfying. But the artist has not gone beyond the faithful adherent to Catholicism. Montaigne's convictions stand out in relief, to be measured against the everlasting defining niceties of the Protestants—but always, it must be remembered, within the context of debunking the rational pretentions of man. When he states, 'les choses les plus ignorées sont plus propres à estre deifiées' (II : 12, 497), his words are not ironical; he is not launching an attack upon one of the fundamental tenets of Christian religions; his context is not the twentieth century which has absorbed years of analytical probing into man's psychological needs for religious belief. His framework is that Faith is good, whereas a reasoning religion is dangerous, and he leans on a long Christian tradition which had emphasised the unknown, unknowable Godhead. His orthodoxy in this context should not be questioned; and it can only be doubted by those who refuse to accept the validity of Montaigne's declared standpoint: 'Nous ne pouvons digne-ment concevoir la grandeur de ces hautes et divines promesses . . . Il faut les imaginer inimaginables, indicibles et incomprehensibles' (II : 12, 499). The sixteenth-century Christian would nod in agreement at so felicitous a rendering of an important belief; the modern cynic merely applauds the artistry. Montaigne is working towards one of the climaxes of his long essay—the moment where he focusses his attack upon the central problem of the Protestant/Catholic doctrinal debate. His elaborate defence of Faith without Reason is opposed to the troublous consequences of wordy discussion: 'Combien de querelles et combien importantes a produit au monde le doubte du sens de cette syllabe HOC!' (II : 12, 508). Montaigne reveals quite clearly, at this point, where his main pre-occupations lie. They are not so much concerned with the desire to belittle man indiscriminately. The disparagement is directed at more specific political problems. And a little further along, in the same essay, he offers, the combination of moderation and abstinence as the only sensible remedy for the ingenious hair-splitting of the Prot-estants;

> Mais si quelqu'un de ces nouveaux docteurs entreprend de faire l'ingenieux en vostre presence, aux despens de son salut et du vostre : pour vous deffaire de cette dangereuse peste qui se repand tous les jours en vos cours, ce preservatif, à l'extreme necessité empeschera que la contagion de ce venin n'offencera ny vous ny vostre assistance. (II : 12, 542)

It would be wrong, however, to deduce from the *Essais* that Montaigne totally despises man. In the context of tangible, human experi-ence, 'de nos maladies la plus sauvage c'est mespriser nostre estre' (III : 13, 1091). His opinions on man are only apparently inconsistent; like his attitude towards man's rational faculty, they seem inconsistent be-cause they are complex.

Montaigne sets great store by reason and consciousness. 'Me considerer', the study by the self of the self in action and thought, became the most important thing in Montaigne's life. 'Je n'ay guere de mouve-ment qui se cache et desrobe à ma raison', he maintains in *Du repentir*

(III : 2, 790) ; while, in the previous essay, he had admitted his virtual addiction to the necessity of recognising the paramount importance of reason: 'car esclave, je ne le doibts estre que de la raison' (III : 1, 772). Passions assail him. They cannot be changed or diverted; and yet Montaigne claims: 'Mon jugement ne s'est pas trouvé infecté par eux' (II : 11, 407). On the contrary, his powers of discernment examine the nature of the passions, and thus give him an increased power of resistance. He extends his own experience to include similar judgements on human beings generally, and, because his conception of 'gloire' involves inner strength of mind, reason plays a most significant role (II : 16, 607). The consciousness which allows a man to anticipate physical pain has a double effect: it is possible that such preparation often suggests feelings of pain before the reality of pain is actually present; yet the thinking, conscious process does make control over pain easier (II : 37, 740).

    This degree of insistence on the advantages and power of reasoning is striking and may seem strange in a writer notorious as a devastating critic of the products of human rational faculties. Much better known is a phrase such as 'combien l'humaine raison est un instrument libre et vague'. But it must be remembered that this comment occurs in a context —*Des boyteux* (III : 11, 1003)—where Montaigne has deliberately set out to demonstrate the crippled nature of the human mind when it operates in spheres beyond its competence. He is less concerned to assert that man's reasoning power is hopelessly inadequate than to demonstrate that man wastes his power upon imagined, unproveable things, and turns away from facts which merit analysis. His line is precisely the same as it was in the *Apologie* where his attack upon reason was mainly directed against those who abused it—at those thinkers who indulged exclusively in speculation, and ignored the evidence staring them in the face.

    Of course, the human mind is susceptible to all kinds of pressures and conditions. Old age or ill health can severely impair the judgement (III : 5, 821 & III : 13, 1059). Habit, despite its many virtues in the context of health, frequently has a stultifying effect upon the activities of the mind (I : 23, 110 & III : 13, 1057). Appearances can produce equally confusing, and even erroneous effects, because our senses are often inadequate to seize the exact significance of a multitude of outward events (III : 8, 908). Extraordinary happenings, for example, tend to have an excessive impact on the mind; and we are, in consequence, apt to judge them badly (II : 2, 328). Fortune, above all, has authority over us, not only because she introduces a bewildering variety of events into our lives, but also because these events are nearly always impossible of prediction (I : 23,

121; I: 24, 127; & II: 4, 345). Man has two ways of combating her domina-
tion: either through extreme caution (I: 47); or, more effectively, by a
careful separation of acts and thoughts, and by concentrating attention
on the latter (II: 6, 358–9). Nevertheless, the factor which most disturbs
human mental activity is latent in the mind itself. Not only is it largely
circumscribed by common opinion, but it distorts truth by its own
subtlety: generalising without foundation from one small fact (I: 31,
203); exaggerating evidence (II: 6, 357–8); interpreting according to
desires rather than facts; and reasoning in circles without realising it
(II: 12, 585). Its natural tendency is to gain satisfaction from contempla-
ting future events, and, in this way, its operations are blinkered by looking forwards rather than backwards, outwards instead of inwards (III:
8, 908).

These inherent limiting factors of the human mind are clearly
recognised by Montaigne. Each element is subject to a specific examination, and detailed evidence is brought forward to demonstrate the validity
of Montaigne's contentions. However, when the author of the *Essais*
changes his perspective, it seems a different story. Excited by the value
of self-study, and made confident by the analysis of his own experience,
he speaks about the quality of his own reasoning power with an authority
suggesting that many of the factors hitherto thought to restrict the
activity of the mind have been overcome; and, in their place, he offers
a method of inspection all the more acute, since it refuses to ignore
potential weaknesses within itself.

It is in such a context that Montaigne's views on judgement must
be set. He does not change his opinion on man's reasoning power. But
he watches its working in many spheres, and under different conditions;
sometimes he focusses attention on a minute detail; and sometimes
he allows his thoughts to sweep around a general panorama. In each
case, his conclusions are slightly different, though the effect of his
meditations is cumulative. He discovers both the most and the least
valuable ways of using our mental apparatus.

A similar composite view emerges from an examination of the
contexts in which the 'humble crowd' is discussed. When he is intent on
smashing man's pride in the *Apologie* (II: 12, 479), one of his means of
doing this is to extol the virtues of ignorance as evidenced by the 'simples
et ignorans' witnesses God chose 'du vulgaire'. When he is trying to
disparage the value attached to honour in military performance (II: 16,
609), he draws attention, melodramatically, to the 'cinquante pauvres
pioniers qui luy ouvrent le pas et le couvrent de leurs corps pour cinq

sous de païe par jour'. And when he is concerned to stress the goodness and greatness of Nature, he paints a glowing picture of 'cette tourbe rustique d'hommes impolis' with their moral qualities of constancy, innocence, and tranquillity (III : 12, 1026). Even though, in this avowedly paradoxical essay, the natural wisdom of the humblest being contrasts with the learned ignorance propounded by the intellectual tradition which found its source in the teaching of Socrates, if we look independently at each of the cases I have just quoted the humble crowd may be recognised as a tool in Montaigne's argument, fashioned for the convenience of the point he is trying to make.

On other occasions, when he discusses their habits and their capacities, he is much less complimentary. Their intellectual ability is best described by the nouns 'bestise' and 'facilité' (I : 51, 293) ; and the most apt assessment of their nature is 'juge peu exacte, facile à piper, facile à contenter' (III : 7, 896). Their naturally poor judgement is made even weaker by the present conditions of civil war which encourage them to approve despicable acts, to judge according to superficial appearance (III : 8), and only to approve of that which improves their own particular cause (III : 10, 990–1). They ask no questions, and they are irretrievably susceptible to the power of everybody's rhetoric (II : 10, 394). Furthermore, the war conditions have laid bare their innate and horrible cruelty which inspires Montaigne's deepest indignation :

> ce qui fait voir tant de cruautez inouies aux guerres populaires, c'est que cette canaille de vulgaire s'aguerrit et se gendarme à s'ensanglanter jusques aux coudes et à deschiqueter un corps à ses pieds, n'ayant resentiment d'autre vaillance : . . . comme les chiens coüards, qui deschirent en la maison et mordent les peaux des bestes sauvages qu'ils n'ont osé attaquer aux champs. (II : 27, 672)

In the context of this black condemnation of the people, it is hardly surprising that Montaigne, who had already admitted his own impatience in the face of stupidity (III : 8, 905), should consider such animals unworthy of the sacred study of True Philosophy (I : 25, 140). In this early essay *Du pedantisme* (I : 25), in *De l'institution des enfants* (I : 26, 148), and much later in *De l'art de conferer* (III : 8, 910), Montaigne remains adamant that the creative art of thinking belongs to a highly select company. Only the limited few can save True Philosophy from the corruption which attacks her as soon as the many are allowed to dabble. Vulgarisation means profanation : of this Montaigne is convinced, and he is not merely thinking of translations of the Bible into the vulgar languages when he says it (I: 56, 306). Moreover, knowledge is a 'tres utile accessoire à une ame bien née, pernicieux à une autre ame et dommageable' (III: 8, 905). It is probable that by 'ame bien née' Montaigne is not merely describing the 'personnes élevées' in intellectual stature, with whom he was concerned in *De l'institution des enfants* (I: 26, 148). He is also making a social distinction in *De l'art de conferer* where, on the page before the passage just cited, he has referred to Plato in support of his exclusive view, pointing out that the Greek philosopher also 'prohibe cet exercice aux esprits ineptes et mal nays' (III: 8, 904). For all his sympathy for the plight of human beings in France at that time, and for all his agitated concern to produce conditions of thinking which might go some way to preparing for a better world, Montaigne was conscious that he spoke to an elite.

*　　*　　*

There are other subjects, however, over which Montaigne's conscious control seems much less secure. At certain moments, the need to distinguish carefully the precise context in which he is thinking seems overtaken by a stronger, emotional need which directs the argument. On a topic such as military affairs, which occurs frequently throughout his writing, Montaigne's view changes according to his mood and according to the context of discussion: so much so that it is impossible ultimately to reconcile the inconsistencies.

Like so many of his contemporaries, Montaigne was fascinated by anything to do with military activity. A great bulk of vernacular writing in the sixteenth century was concerned with memoirs of military exploits, and Montaigne seems to have known them all.[5] Monluc recorded his deeds as a soldier so that later generations might learn about the art of war. La Noue recorded his vast experience in many campaigns in his *Discours,* the content of which ranges from general reflexions on moral and political matters to technical discussions on military tactics. Works on stratagems, military manoeuvres, and the whole art of waging war, proliferated at this time, and Montaigne was an avid reader of them. Similarly, most accounts of the history of the period concentrate on military events: Machiavelli and Guicciardini, Froissart, Commynes, Bouchet and Gilles—all read and annotated by Montaigne—discussed military matters at length. Indeed, history in the sixteenth century was largely a question of listing wars, campaigns, sieges of towns, and the like. And Montaigne, who admitted that his favourite reading was history books, could scarcely escape from the fact and theory of war.

Even if we consider the ancient works he most favoured (particularly in the writing of the earliest essays), we note the Commentaries of Caesar, the Histories of Polybius and Livy, and the analyses of Suetonius and Tacitus, together with the considerations of Quintus Curtius, Laertius and Sallust. Plattard has argued, fairly convincingly, that Montaigne's first ideas concerning his own writing might well have been to produce some similar technical reflexions on his own time:[6] and titles such as *Si le chef d'une place assiegée doit sortir pour parlementer* (i:5), and *L'heure des parlemens dangereuse* (i:6), would confirm such a view.

There are also other reasons for Montaigne's preoccupation with military affairs. Though, as a magistrate, he was a member of a profession which settled most men socially in the upper reaches of the middle class, he was also a landowner, and was able to carry a sword, ride a horse, and perform most of the actions which distinguished the nobility from other social classes. While there is little concrete evidence that Montaigne was actively engaged in war on a professional basis, he clearly recognised that fighting was the most significant distinguishing mark of the true nobleman: 'la forme propre, et seule, et essencielle, de noblesse en France, c'est la vacation militaire' (*Des recompenses d'honneur*, ii:7, 363). It follows then that Montaigne's remarks on military matters must be considered in the light of a man who could intellectually appreciate technical points of strategy, but whose experience of them was probably severely limited. The man who had, as it were, just 'made it' socially, yearned for evidence in his countrymen of the martial virtues with which he was so familiar in his reading of Roman or Spartan campaigns. He reflects on the 'vertu simple et naive' of Caesar's soldiers, on their generosity, their skill, and their extraordinary fidelity (ii:34), contrasting these qualities with their absence in the 'vilains bourreaux soldats de ce temps' (ii:6); and his reflexions are filled with emotion and nostalgia. His notions of war are charged with enthusiasm and idealism, since they have been so consistently nourished by close reading of the glorious, but distant, events of the past. And yet, the acute observer of human behaviour cannot close his eyes to the atrocities committed by the soldiers of his own time.

In *De la phisionomie* (iii:12, 1024ff) the effects of war and plague stir his deep-rooted hatred of man's inhumanity to man. The impact of war, here, moves him so profoundly that he draws out to extreme length his descriptions of suffering, sparing us no details. The anguished tones seem all the more heartfelt in that they come after the biting satire of 'l'ambition, l'avarice, la cruauté, la vengeance n'ont point assez de propre et naturelle impetuosité; amorchons les et les attisons par le glorieux titre de justice et devotion' (III : 12, 1020). He responds to certain themes with such a degree of emotion that it is this rather than any rational argument which carries conviction for a modern reader.[7]

Similarly, in *Que le goust des biens et des maux dépend en bonne partie de l'opinion que nous en avons* (1 : 14, 56), Montaigne is arguing that the conditions of military life put all men—nobles and common soldiers alike—on the same level :

> s'il ne faut coucher sur la dure, soustenir armé de toutes pieces la chaleur du midy, se paistre d'un cheval et d'un asne, se voir detailler en pieces, et arracher une balle d'entre les os, se souffrir recoudre, cauterizer, et sonder, par où s'acquerra l'advantage que nous voulons avoir sur le vulgaire ?

Although his argument is clearly stated in these words, yet they carry other, stronger impressions : a sense of sturdy exhilaration in the midst of the fighting is balanced by an idea of the suffering to be endured when you are a military man. Montaigne's emotional response to the situation seems to make points about war which have far more power than his original aim which was simply to demonstrate that 'Death is a great leveller'.

More cool and with a greater awareness of the context is Montaigne's discussion of 'vaillance' and 'gloire'. He condemns the lack of true courage and virtue among his contemporaries and deplores their preoccupation with reputation and vainglory (*De ne communiquer sa gloire*, 1 : 41). As he gets more involved in the discussion, however, the newly recruited nobleman forgets himself; and his attention moves away, from praise of ancient military prowess, to reminders that astonishing military deeds are frequently the product of Fortune (II : 16, 605), and that the virtue which is really worthwhile has little to do with military performance at all (*Des recompenses d'honneur* II : 7 & *De la gloire* II : 16). In fact, the life of a soldier encourages people to think too exclusively in terms of honour and reputation, so that acts are performed, and severities are endured, beyond that which is reasonable (*De mesnager sa volonté*, III : 10, 997). Much more laudable, in Montaigne's view, is that the individual should seek to cultivate not the outward trappings of public renown but the inner assurance of good behaviour and right thinking—the 'asseurance de l'ame' as he calls it (II : 7, 362)—which far outweighs the shortlived congratulations offered to those whose public actions have been favoured by Fortune (*De la gloire*, II : 16). And, as soon as Montaigne assumes his 'moraliste' role, then the emotional response to Caesar's virtuous achievements disintegrates. The Roman general's efficiency and prowess are there when Montaigne remembers to look at them: but, on the whole, moral observations crowd out any such nostalgic recollections.

Other moments, other moods produced different responses. Montaigne, the avid reader of military books, and keen student of military exploits, could still stand back and revel in the clumsy antics of modern soldiery. In *Des armes des Parthes* (II:9), his sense of humour gets the better of him as he describes French soldiers who are never ready to fight because, only half-dressed, they hunt about for their innumerable pieces of armour which can scarely be traced on the field of battle where everybody's servants are running around with carriage loads of metal. Even when they are perfectly dressed for combat they are inept, and seem to be fighting more with their own accoutrements than with the enemy, so overcome are they by the weight of their armour—'plus chargez que couvers', as Montaigne aptly describes them. Then, when this derisive observer turns his imagination to the equipment of the future, he foresees how

> a présent que nos mosquetaires sont en credit, je croy que l'on trou-vera quelque invention de nous emmurer pour nous en garantir, et nous faire trainer à la guerre enfermez dans des bastions, comme ceux que les antiens faisoient porter à leur elephans. (II:9,385)

Montaigne has mischievously chosen the heaviest and clumsiest of animals; and his humour is further extended, later in the essay, when French soldiers are depicted as metal figures which have been given life:

> Horridibilis visu; credas simulachra moveri
> Ferrea, cognatóque viros spirare metallo.

On the other hand, Montaigne the merciless critic of the suffering, hardship and cruelty of war, could pen this strange effusive paragraph:

> Il n'est occupation plaisant comme la militaire: occupation et noble en execution (car la plus forte, genereuse et superbe de toutes les vertus est la vaillance) et noble en sa cause; il n'est point d'utilité ny plus juste, ny plus universelle que la protection du repos et grandeur de son pays. La compaignie de tant d'hommes vous plaist, nobles, jeunes, actifs, la veue ordinaire de tant de spectacles tragiques, la liberté de cette conversation sans art, et une façon de vie masle et sans ceremonie, la varieté de mille actions diverses, cette courageuse

harmonie de la musique guerriere que vous entretien et eschauffe et
les oreilles et l'ame, l'honneur de cet exercice, son aspreté mesme et
sa difficulté, que Platon estime si peu, qu'en sa republique il en faict
part aux femmes et aux enfans. Vous vous conviez aux rolles et hazards
particuliers selon que vous jugez de leur esclat et de leur importance,
soldat volontaire, et voyez quand la vie mesme y est excusablement
employé,

Pulchrumque mori succurrit in armis. (III: 13, 1075–6)

These sentiments seem to accord very ill with so much else that Montaigne wrote on war and its effects. Are they ironical? Are they a curious
lapse? Or should we regard them only in the context of *De l'experience*
(III: 13)? At a time when his thoughts turned frequently to death,
military life might have suggested itself to Montaigne both as an ideal
way of life, and especially, as a desirable means of death. The physical
pain, the vices which war brings in its wake, the false values, the cruelty
and the torture, all seem to be forgotten as Montaigne reflects on the
enspiriting qualities of military activities, and the grateful suddenness of
the death which is a soldier's reward.[8]

*   *   *

We remember Montaigne as the exponent of relativity, and as
the describer of flux, more readily than we remember other sixteenth-
century writers who dwelt upon the same themes,[9] both because he gives
a more complete account of these things, and, more particularly, because
that account is so startlingly vivid. These are the moments of the *Essais*
which remain in the mind, like good lines of poetry or certain musical
themes, and these are the moments where he seems to be writing at his
most spontaneous, and with the least degree of conscious 'craftiness'.
A good instance of such writing occurs in *De l'institution des enfants* (I:
26) where Montaigne employs highly figurative language to describe
his notion of True Philosophy, 'logée dans une belle plaine fertile et
florissante, d'où elle void bien souz soy toutes choses' (I: 26, 160). The
way to get to the pastures of philosophy is infinitely pleasurable 'par
des routtes ombrageuses, gazonnées et doux fleurantes, plaisamment et
d'une pante facile et polie, comme est celle des voutes celestes' (I: 26,
160–1). Montaigne multiplies adjectives, such as 'supreme, belle, trium-
fante, amoureuse, delicieuse, courageuse', to describe its virtuous effects.
He makes his tutor present to his pupil this True Philosophy as something sensuous bringing to mind love and the beauty of Bradamant or

Angelique: 'naive, active, genereuse'. We might well be with the
Poliphile of Colonna's *Hypnerotomachia*, treading the gorgeous pastures,
encountering the beautiful maidens, and admiring the splendours of
architectural monuments which belong to the land of Love and True
Philosophy. Montaigne's 'poësie sophistiquée', as he once called Philosophy, has a distinctly pastoral, even arcadian note.

An interesting concomitant to this kind of enthusiastic praise is an
equally vehement and intemperate attack on anything which seems to
disturb his idyllic picture of True Philosophy. In the same essay where
his vague picture of True Philosophy is made wonderfully desirable, he
turns the full blast of his satire upon schoolmasters who make a pupil's
life unbearable. As Porteau has shown, there is not much evidence to
suggest that the tortures Montaigne describes were the lot of every
schoolboy in the sixteenth century. The simple fact is that Montaigne
has got carried away by the case he has been putting forward. His
argument takes him beyond the realities, and he substitutes what ought
not to be for what is. What is astonishing is that such an acute critic of
style should have allowed to stand the exaggerated self-pitying tones of
'Combien leurs classes seroient plus decemment jonchées de fleurs et
de feuilles que de tronçons d'osier sanglants' (1:26, 165). But then, the
same man allowed his friendship for La Boëtie so to obscure his senses
that he described the latter, four years after his death, in terms similar
to those used by the disciples after the death of Christ—'ce n'est que
fumée, ce n'est qu'une nuit obscure et ennuyeuse. Depuis le jour que je
le perdy . . . je ne fay que trainer languissant' (1:28, 192).

Another instance where a similar lyrical enthusiasm colours Montaigne's thought, and frequently distorts his argument, is his praise of
everything that is natural. Whenever his thoughts turn to Mother
Nature, his language becomes eloquent, his sentences flow smoothly,
and his tone is full of warmth and admiration for 'cette grande image de
nostre mere nature en son entiere magesté' (1:26, 157). The natural
equals the good in every circumstance. It is healthy, just, and necessary.
It stands in direct opposition to art, artifice, and all man-made things,
and serves as a brake to the dangerous effects of these latter elements
(1:30, 198). 'Nature est un doux guide, mais non pas plus doux que
prudent et juste'. This statement, made towards the end of Montaigne's
last essay *De l'experience*, could equally represent his convictions in the
earliest essays: whether they were concerned with superficial topics such
as clothing (1:36), or more fundamental points such as natural man
as opposed to civilised man (1:31). In this context, Montaigne's

remarks upon law constitute, perhaps, the most telling example of his prejudice. The lawyer, one of those professionals whom he so frequently satirises, turns the language of law into an intolerable game of obscurity 'quoy qu'il die et escrive, ne trouve en cela aucune maniere de se declarer qui ne tombe en doubte et contradiction' (III: 13, 1043). On the other side, the laws given by Nature are invariably 'plus heureuses que ne sont celles que nous nous donnons' (III: 13, 1043). Now it is easy to demonstrate the idiocies of man-made laws, not only because they are so plentiful, but also because they are tangible facts, which can be handled. But the laws founded by Nature: what are they? Montaigne assumes that we know: and as proof to support his point of view he cites: 'Tesmoing la peinture de l'aage doré des poëtes' (III: 13, 1043). This is scientific evidence indeed! The golden age, described by poets, is a world where no professionals thrive; where judgements are made by a passer-by; or where a democratic crowd of naturally good citizens choose one among their number to sit in judgement in the market place upon the man who (incredibly, if one pushes Montaigne's point to its logical conclusion) has somehow escaped the good influences of Nature. Here Montaigne confuses the Natural with the primitive, and with the distant in time or space, just as he did in *Des cannibales* (I: 31).

There are other significant topics which similarly called forth from Montaigne extravagant responses: expressed in terms so extreme that his attitude might, more properly, be termed 'prejudice'. In the contexts of knowledge, rhetoric, art, and medicine, he can be relied upon to launch devastatingly eloquent attacks. Mention of any one of these four themes thrust him immediately into an antagonistic stance. At one time or another most sixteenth-century moralists inveighed against them: Lestoile never refers to 'maîtres ès arts' without adding the insulting adjective 'crottés'; Breslay gives a typical description of their verbal perversities when he writes of 'ces angoisseuses, épineuses et difficiles demonstrations, que égrafignent l'oreille et geinent la comprehensive des oyens';[10] Pasquier is equally hostile to the doctor's art: and Agrippa had included them in his long list of human activities to be ridiculed. Guazzo, La Primaudaye, Du Plessis Mornay, and others, all decried the arrogance of human curiosity for knowledge, and lamented its deleterious effects, particularly at times of civil strife.[11] The *Essais*, however, seem to go beyond these stock, traditional reactions to these themes, and develop—through the use of many different contexts—a more complete examination.

Knowledge is acceptable if properly used. But 'properly used' can be diversely, and not always rationally, interpreted by Montaigne. He is aware that the word 'cuyder' is Janus-like.[12] It may simply signify the act of thinking, but it also has the pejorative sense of pride—that is thought which has led to satisfaction and thence to arrogance, beyond which lies mental blindness: 'la peste de l'homme, c'est l'opinion de sçavoir' (II:12,467). In the majority of contexts Montaigne does, in fact, interpret thinking as knowledge which turns to pride. It is for this reason that he attacks doctors; and, while conceding the difficulties of their art, he succeeds in making out a good case against them (II:37 & III:12). On the subject of philosophers and teachers, however, his arguments are not so convincing. It is true that the case is, intrinsically, harder to argue. You can make people feel a blood-letting or an amputation; but it is not so easy to make an impression on their mental systems without, perhaps, exaggerating the evidence. The exponents of learning are nearly always presented as caricatures, and fit matter for comedy. *Du pedantisme* (I:25) opens with Montaigne's acknowledgement that the Italian comedy's laughter at the expense of pedants is entirely justified. This sets the tone of the essay in which Montaigne presents his own comedy trying to make his reader believe the most unlikely and outlandish stories by insisting, 'J'ay veu chez moy un mien amy' (I:25, 138), as though his personal assurance will support the improbabilities.

The study of Letters does not bring success. But does success and power bring goodness, as he assumes at the end of *Du pedantisme*? In every discussion of knowledge, Montaigne makes this basic assumption —which he never questions—that learning and goodness are natural opposites. For this reason he looks for faults and he prepares for moments when he can make such literary jokes as: 'le principal et plus fameux sçavoir de nos siecles, est-ce pas, sçavoir entendre les sçavans?' (III:13, 1046). Such criticism is unanswerable in rational terms. Montaigne has made his mind up in advance that knowledge means pedantry, that it signifies meaningless interpretations and commentaries, and that it implies a never-ending production of useless texts which grow larger with every edition. All this is, clearly, prejudice: and underlying it is Montaigne's distrust, and even hatred, of the professional. Parading of knowledge belonged to the social classes below the level of the nobility who considered it more proper to adopt an attitude of studied nonchalance.[13] Pretend to be an amateur; pretend not to be involved; do things elegantly not earnestly; that was the style of the nobility. This was the *sprezzatura* of Castiglione: and it was a style which Montaigne coveted, and which was, eventually, to lead to the notion of the 'honnête homme'. It is not surprising, therefore, that the learned man's language should be ridiculed as 'galimathias'; that logic and formal speaking should be castigated (III:8,904); and that Montaigne should select the most outrageous evidence to make his points about the rhetoric of poetry, poking fun at the 'fantastiques elevations Espagnoles et Petrarquistes' (III:10,391). It is in this context that one must place his comparison of Cicero's eloquence to so much empty wind (*Ibid.*, 393). And it is with noble aspirations in mind that he refers to the work of specialists as 'une façon de parler bouffie et bouillonnée de pointes ingenieuses à la verité, mais recherchées de loing et fantasques' (I:51,295), covering himself with a now very familiar blanket remark about the 'singulière ineptie de nostre siècle'.

*   *   *

In any attempt to assess the nature and value of his contribution to thought, these kinds of prejudice must be kept in mind. Nor must one assume, because a man is capable of the most penetrating examination into the flaws of others, that he is himself necessarily without inadequacies. There are chinks in Montaigne's armour. There are times, as I have suggested, when he seems unaware of deep-rooted responses, or of the actual angle from which he is arguing. Despite the great battle he waged in the *Apologie* against those who indulge in speculation to the extent of arguing from God's own point of view, we find, in that very same essay, Montaigne himself doing just that; 'la main de son gouvernement se preste à toutes choses de pareille teneur, mesme force et mesme ordre' (II:12,510). It is, of course, Montaigne's faith speaking here, as it is in another instance where he states 'de sa toute sagesse il ne peut rien que bon et commun et reglé' (II:30,691). Similarly, the diagnosing of a common fault in human kind does not eradicate that fault from the man who observed it. In many essays Montaigne stresses the wayward tendencies of the human mind, either anticipating future events, or turning back upon past events which can in no way be changed; and he urges his reader to concentrate upon the present. And yet, when those very same *Essais* are examined, it becomes clear that much of Montaigne's own writing is retrospective. *Sur des vers de Virgile* (III:5) must be seen in the context of an old man, aware of his age, looking nostalgically back upon the past; *De la vanité* (III:9) is a justification, in retrospect, of an attitude of mind already clearly established; and even in *Du repentir* (III:2), where he had most cogently argued the case for centering attention upon the present, there is a gap between theory and practice.

Throughout the *Essais* Montaigne is concerned with the relationship between the individual and his public duty, and with the problem of
reconciling the demands of the general situation with the desires of the
private person. His affirmation of personal integrity and individual value
is so heartfelt that he comes to the conclusion that only the detached and
honest man can hope to operate successfully and with impunity in the
public arena. Despite the frequency with which Montaigne discusses this
problem, his conclusion is never the result of logical argument. It is an
assumption. The 'honest man' looms so large in Montaigne's mind that
he completely obscures the reality and magnitude of the problems that
any individual encounters in public service.

Already, in *De la solitude* (i: 39, 236), his enthusiasm for the inner
solitude, which protects the self against the corroding effects of the outside world, gives us some idea of the lengths to which Montaigne is
prepared to go in order that he might preserve an area over which he can
exercise the maximum degree of personal control. He is not, however,
unaware of the difficulty of maintaining this position. Whereas, in some
essays, he had advocated truth and honesty in all spheres, in Book III
in particular, he realises that—in the precise political situation of giving
advice to a monarch, for instance—to tell the truth is often a question of
choosing the appropriate time (iii: 13, 1055). Furthermore, he recognises
that just as style and content must be adapted to the capacity of an
audience (iii: 9, 967–8), so codes of behaviour must be adjusted to varying situations. Public life is more arduous than private, and kings (contrary to all appearances) have a harder time of it than ordinary individuals
(i: 42). Once a man has accepted public office, he is caught up in 'les
mouvemens publics [qui] dependent plus de la conduicte de la fortune'
(iii: 8, 920)—that fickle, variable goddess who can only be controlled
by a flexibility as mutable as herself. Man is never his own master once
he has entered upon public service where individual values are so dominated by events that they have frequently to be sacrificed to the general
good. Yet, Montaigne himself is not prepared to sacrifice himself in
this way. He argued in *De l'utile et de l'honneste* (iii: 1) that public usefulness was not necessarily best achieved through private dishonesty,
even when this latter course seemed to impose itself. In any clash of
general and specific, public and private, Montaigne would consistently
choose the latter; and he pretends that, as a result, he is not a good public
servant. He takes a pride in this, and eloquently expatiates on the need
to evolve a neat system of double behaviour whereby the self remains
intact, unaffected by public position. In other words, the individual, in

Montaigne's mind, takes precedence over the public. The last lines of *De l'utile et de l'honneste* (III: 1, 781) make this clear: 'on argumente mal l'honnesteté et la beauté d'une action par son utilité, et conclud on mal d'estimer que chacun y soit obligé et qu'elle soit honneste à chacun, si elle est utile'. Montaigne's own sense of moral integrity is outraged at the thought that public necessity should undermine its values, not only with impunity, but even with approval in the sight of some. He wishes to keep the individual's moral code strictly separated from his public stance, and, thereby, uncontaminated. Public affairs stand to gain through being handled by someone who can remain objective: that is by someone like Montaigne who is content 'de m'en charger, non de les incorporer; de m'en soigner ouy, de m'en passionner nullement: j'y regarde, mais je ne les couve point' (III: 10, 981).

Nevertheless, in spite of Montaigne's attempt to preserve private integrity and effective public service within the same individual, his assumed willingness to partake in public affairs remains unconvincing. Nor has he really solved the problem for other individuals of similar high moral consciousness, who wish to follow a political career. What Montaigne is really advocating is a separation of the public sector from the private. He proposes a scale of priorities where individual needs are quite clearly set above more general concerns; and his use of the general public to define an individual code has resulted in an affirmation of the individual's value. Like most political commentators in the sixteenth century Montaigne does not fully face up to the basic problem of right and wrong in public life; though his arguments reveal not so much a writer afraid to develop this 'red-hot' theme, but one who was fundamentally committed to preserving the dignity of the individual and the value of his private code.

8

MONTAIGNE AND SOCRATES

I N *Des prognostications* (I : 11,45), Montaigne compares the inspiration which stirs within him, unbidden by his conscious mind, to Socrates's 'familiar' who, though more reliable and significant by reason of Socrates's greater virtue, came to visit in similar fashion.[1] This was by no means the first time that Montaigne compared himself to Plato's principal spokesman, nor was it to be the last; and it is the purpose of this final chapter to demonstrate that Montaigne knew and understood the work of Socrates, and particularly appreciated his method of teaching, while being able to distinguish Socrates the master, from Plato the pupil. Montaigne admired Socrates's character, his way of life, and the manner in which he faced death. The extent and depth of his knowledge of Socrates will be used, not so much to prove that the author of the *Essais* deliberately intended to model himself and his work upon that of his most revered philosopher from antiquity, but rather as a means of revealing all the more clearly Montaigne's own methods of analysis and teaching.[2] Socrates's oblique approaches to Truth have many affinities with Montaigne's 'craftie methode'.

For Montaigne, Socrates stood as a symbol of man's ability to range from greatness to littleness. He represented the summit of human wisdom because he recognised the limits of his own capacities. In this one person, Montaigne saw linked the extremes of wisdom and of ignorance which, in his *Essais*, he had tried to render through paradox; but, most of all, he saw a startling embodiment of the natural. Socrates was important as a man because he showed how to live 'l'humaine vie conformément à sa naturelle conditions' (III : 2,787)—that is to say, he was able to maintain the happy mean while demonstrating a richness and versatility of mind which set him far above princes, generals, and even philosophers. On the one hand, Montaigne insists upon the fact that Socrates is an ordinary man, as subject to fits of apoplexy as a porter; on the other, he sets him up as some inaccessible model whose constancy in the face of death is something beautiful, which we may admire but can never aspire to (ii:11,404). Socrates's calm acceptance of death remained a fascinating puzzle for Montaigne all his life. In *Que le goust des biens et des maux dépend en bonne partie de l'opinion que nous en avons* (i:14,51), he extols the happy tranquillity shown by Socrates during his last thirty days of life; and in a late addition to *De juger de la mort d'autruy* (ii:13,592), he continues to marvel at such serene indifference. At one moment, he tries to attribute this serenity to ordinary human motives, by suggesting that Socrates welcomed death as the best solution to the ravages which old age might wreak upon his marvellous mental faculties (iii:2,795); at another, he states reverently, 'il appartient à un seul Socrates d'accointer la mort d'un visage ordinaire, s'en aprivoiser et s'en jouer' (iii:4,810). There are times when Montaigne seems only aware of the distance between his own acts and those of his hero. But he could, at least, always appreciate the latter's extraordinary feats (iii:9,951); and, in this way, whenever Montaigne so wished, Socrates could assume an exemplary role, capable of touching all men, whatever their abilities. As a tutor worthy of emulation, Socrates listened to other men's talk before allowing his superior knowledge and reasoning power to intervene with good advice (i:26,149). As a soldier, at a time of defeat, he presented to the world a self 'nullement different du sien ordinaire, sa vcüe ferme et reglée' (iii:6,877)—thus preserving both his own life and the lives of those who were with him. Such a show of courage was, in Montaigne's view, peculiarly appropriate to any man exposed to the dangers of civil war, as were all Frenchmen during the Wars of Religion. Moreover, in old age, Socrates remained remarkably sensitive to the power of love, thus proving, in Montaigne's words, that 'Socrates estoit homme; et ne vouloit ny estre, ny sembler autre chose' (iii:5,870).

Persuaded by the variety of the models of behaviour which Socrates offered later generations, Montaigne had no difficulty in extending his relevance over many areas of opinion. Socrates's views on man's limitations, for instance, are quoted repeatedly in the *Apologie* (ii:12), most often (and increasingly in the last additions to the *Essais*) in support of Montaigne's own opinions: 'C'est à l'advis de Socrates, et au mien aussi, le plus sagement jugé du ciel que n'en juger point' (ii:12, 516). His adherence to the laws of his country, even to the point of

death, had special relevance for sixteenth-century Frenchmen, and
Montaigne lost no opportunity to stress this in *De la coustume et de ne
changer aisément une loy receüe* (I:23,117), in the *Apologie* (II:12,562)
and in *De l'utile et de l'honneste* (III:1,773), to quote but one example
from each book of the *Essais*. Even on delicate subjects such as prayer
and oracles, Montaigne does not hesitate to quote Socrates's own views
and experience as a guide to his contemporaries whom he enjoins to pray
frequently, and to refrain from discussing religious matters, just as
Socrates did (I:56,307). The latter's serene and smiling countenance is
presented as proof of the fact that 'la vertu est qualité plaisante et gaye'
(III:5,822). His insistence on the need to settle one's own conscience,
before accusing or punishing others of misdeeds, is used as a means of
encouraging men to turn their minds in upon themselves at a time when
such private preoccupations were swamped by swift, wholesale, public
condemnations (III:8,908). It is as though Socrates's opinions are so
much in the forefront of Montaigne's mind that they are ever ready to
confirm a point already made, or to clinch an argument: 'Et les foibles,
dict Socrates, corrompent la dignité de la philosophie en la maniant'
(III:8,910). There seems no way of arguing with such unquestionable
authority; and, just in case one were tempted to do so, Montaigne inserts
the emphatic, 'et Socrates l'ordonne' (I:26,169), thus giving an irrefutable air to his comments. So frequently are the Greek's views
quoted that one begins to feel that his opinions are a necessary adornment
to the discussion of any topic.

Plato (in a sense both Socrates's creator and his pupil) is similarly
used. 'Suivant le precepte de Platon' (I:26,162), 'selon Platon' (II:12,
517), 'comme dit Platon' (I:26,155), 'comme Platon preuve' (II:12,
507): such expressions abound in the *Essais*. And yet, Montaigne is by
no means as complimentary towards the pupil as he had been to his
master. He uses the reader's natural expectancy of Plato as a great mind
to set up an ideal which he later proves to be false. An instance of this is
his insertion into the essay, *Des menteurs*, of Plato's view on memory as
'une grande et puissante deesse' (I:9,35), which is subsequently
revealed as a somewhat doubtful gift.[3]

Unlike Socrates, Plato is never seen, by Montaigne, as a person.
He always represents a mind or a method, and as such—given Socrates's
exceptional character, and Montaigne's poor view of human reason—he
is more frequently subject to natural human error. Though both figures
qualify to be called 'divine': in the case of Socrates the adjective is more
readily applied to his 'god-given' character; while Plato earns divine

honours on account of the soaring nature of his thought. And here again, the praise of Plato is more ambiguous. This is the principal way in which Montaigne distinguishes between two figures who exerted such an influence over him. Most of his strictures on Plato occur in the *Apologie* (ii: 12) where, full of mischief, he declares rather magnanimously that he cannot take Plato's notions on logic very seriously, (or even Aristotle's for that matter). They were no doubt formed, he conjectures, 'par jeu et par exercice' (ii: 12,488). A page or two later he similarly states: 'Je ne me persuade pas aysement qu'Epicurus, Plato et Pythagoras nous ayent donné pour argent contant leurs Atomes, leurs Idées et leurs Nombres' (ii: 12,491).[4] In the essay *Des livres*, even Plato's method of using dialogues comes under sharp attack. Montaigne warns us that he is treading on sacred ground when he advances 'cette sacrilege audace', which finds the dialogues long-winded and overburdened with 'ces longues interlocutions, vaines et preparatoires' (ii: 10,394).[5] In the context of discussing his own impatient response to certain forms of writing, his complaints about Plato seem not only consistent but also judicious.

Naturally, in the domain of method, Montaigne cannot reasonably continue to distinguish between Plato and Socrates. They become one and the same. And there are times when Montaigne seems to contradict his earlier view that platonic dialogues are long-winded and frequently obscure. Even in the *Apologie* (ii: 12,489), while explaining in detail how the method works and why people have responded to it diversely, he seems to be approving its use. As he analysed Plato's approach to various subjects more closely, he recognised that, if you have to write about religion or republics for the common good—a task which, as Montaigne reminds us, the *person* Socrates refused to undertake, though the *spokesman* Socrates is the chief narrator of *The Republic*—then it was doubtless necessary to adopt a variety of different stances: 'Quand il faict le legislateur, il emprunte un style regentant et asserverant, et si y mesle hardiment les plus fantastiques de ses inventions, autant utiles à persuader à la commune que ridicules à persuader à soy-mesme' (ii: 12, 492). He is further prepared to accept Plato's point that it is justifiable to use poetic effects and to feed people's minds 'plustost de mensonges profitables que de mensonges ou inutiles ou dommageables'.

While both Plato and Socrates were considered by Montaigne as of one mind regarding all advice concerning human behaviour—summed up in both instances in the adage 'Fay ton faict et te cognoy' (i: 3,18)—it is primarily to Socrates that he turns when he wants to explore his own self and to defend the nature and extent of his analysis. In *De l'exercita-tion*, for example, when he is arguing for a more positive kind of self examination than the mere recital of faults committed—constituting the act of confession between a man and his priest—the figure of Socrates suggests itself to him as the best instance of what he understands by self-exposure. That is to say, a controlled analysis of mental activity explored through lively conversation among friends: 'de quoy traitte Socrates plus largement que de soy? A quoy achemine il plus souvent les propos de ses disciples, qu'à parler d'eux, non pas de la leçon de leur livre, mais de l'estre et branle de leur âme' (II:6,359).

It seems that Socrates's inward search, and ultimate discovery of the limits nature had imposed upon him, provided Montaigne with much more than a source of inspiration. We know that Montaigne devoted more and more time in his later years to a study of Plato's works; and there, in the person of Socrates, he found experience which seemed exactly parallel to his own. Here was a man, whose wisdom was re-nowned through centuries of enquiry into the human mind, and whose authority gave a sense of value to Montaigne's own humble efforts. Whenever Montaigne's mind turned towards problems of detailing inner experience and exposing his private self to public gaze, he thought of Socrates. In *Sur des vers de Virgile* (III:5,824), while elaborating upon the statement 'je suis affamé de me faire connoistre', and stressing the need to attain such accuracy in describing his self that no one could misunderstand him, he remembers Socrates's way of handling the same problems and thereby gains confidence. In both the *Apologie* (II:12,478) and *Du repentir* (III:2,787), when he is preoccupied with the difficulties of rendering an accurate account of the complex mental processes involved in even a humdrum, day to day existence, he notes how easy it is to perform heroic deeds, and how astonishingly hard it is to think about himself and communicate that thought. Yet, he reminds us, this is precisely what Socrates had achieved. And this presence at Montaigne's side, as he reflects on self-analysis, is both a source of strength, providing as it does confirmation of the rightness of Montaigne's self-appointed enterprise, and a remarkably potent means of persuasion for the reader already dazzled by the very sound of Socrates's name. Self-knowledge implied a recognition of limited capacity, and even a despising of self, and by comparing his own findings with those of Socrates, Montaigne convinced himself of the need to publish them. *De l'exercitation* ends with this challenging acclaim: 'Qui se connoistra ainsi, qu'il se donne hardi-ment a connoistre par sa bouche' (II:6,360).

Both men were grappling with similar problems of learning to work with the psychology of self; of trying to find a language which could define precisely the often abstract nature of what they wanted to communicate;[6] and, finally, of searching to avoid the technical vocabulary used and abused by professional philosophers.[7] For Montaigne and Socrates, 'philosophy' was frequently defined as empty speculation; and, thus defined, it was a domain to be regarded with a certain scorn, since its main preoccupations were divorced from what they saw as real life: 'comme dict Socrates en Platon, qu'à quiconque se mesle de la philosophie, on peut faire le reproche que faict cete femme à Thales, qu'il ne void rien de ce qui est devant luy' (ii: 12, 520). While it is inevitable that Montaigne should thus disdain philosophy in an essay which sets out to expose man's ineptitude in this field, it is also true that his concerns, like those of Socrates, were directed towards more practical ends. In fact, Montaigne specifically draws attention to the non-specialist emphasis of Socrates's teaching, in the well-known essay *De l'institution des enfants* (i: 26, 158) which offers a pragmatic approach to counterbalance and justify his ridiculing of pedantic, professional conceptions in the previous essay *Du pedantisme* (i: 25).

How far then are general affinities in thought, and similar recognition of the difficulties of communication reflected in Montaigne's detailed response to Socrates's methods of handling ideas, defining concepts, and bringing his listeners around to an understanding of the exact issues involved in any statement they might have been incautious enough to advance? As we shall see, his appreciation of the Socratic method seems to accord fairly closely with some modern views on the subject,[8] while at the same time coming near to certain judgements expressed by that expert and prolific translator of Plato—Louis le Roy.[9]

It is possible that a coincidence of views, wittily set down, first attracted Montaigne's attention. Socrates's succinct opinion on whether to marry or not 'lequel des deux on face on s'en repentira' (iii: 5, 829); his response to glittering display of riches, 'combien de choses je ne desire point' (iii: 10, 986–7), and to the person who returned unchanged after a long voyage, 'je croy bien, dit-il, il s'estoit emporté avecques soy' (i: 39, 234); and especially, his smart repartee even on questions of death, 'a celuy qui disoit à Socrates: les trente tyrans t'ont condamné à la mort. Et nature a eux, respondit-il' (i: 20, 90): these are all instances which Montaigne finds worthy of repetition. Like many of his own phrases, they put an end to discussion. Their maximum effect depends, in large part, on their air of spontaneity which, in turn, calls for a speaker and an admiring group of listeners, or a writer capable of simulating such an easy exchange of views between himself and his readers.

Montaigne recognised that he shared with Socrates a similar paradoxical attitude towards the power of reason: on the one hand, they both acknowledged, and insisted upon, the inadequacy of man's reasoning faculties; on the other, they were both persuaded of the supremacy of reason over all else. Since Montaigne's comments on the Socratic method try to take account of these two apparently-opposed fundamental positions, they might occasionally seem contradictory. Because man's reasoning power is inadequate, it follows that what he can say about anything at all must be limited, and is probably best advanced in a tentative and inconclusive way: 'la raison humaine est un glaive double et dangereux.' Et en la main mesme de Socrates, son plus intime et plus familier amy, voyez à quants de bouts c'est un baston' (II: 17,638). Thus, the best of all thinkers, Socrates, in the *Timaeus* and elsewhere, does not claim to advance certain knowledge: for such a gift does not belong to mortal man. He simply puts forward possible explanations, expressed only in a humble way, approximating to the truth. The ideas he offers are as reasonable and as adequate as the next man's, and he will speak about them 'comme un homme à un homme' (II: 12,487). Montaigne then quotes, at some length, Cicero's translations of Socrates's ideas transmitted through Plato, emphasising the temporary, approximate nature of his thought, and insisting on the fact that it was principally the undecided character of Socrates's thought which so impressed his immediate followers and which led them to express themselves as modestly as Cicero did in the *Tusculan Disputations*, 'Je m'expliquerai comme je le pourrai: non que mes paroles soient des oracles certains et incontestables rendus par Apollon Pythien; faible mortel, je cherche par conjecture à découvrir la vraisemblance' (II: 12,487). Hypothesis, groping expressions, and genuine diffidence: we have many times encountered the same guarded approach in the *Essais*, and for similar reasons.

The same caution also guided both Montaigne and Socrates in their handling of moral concepts. When Montaigne reflects on ways of defining constancy (*De la constance*, I: 12,46), Socrates's treatment of the same problem is evoked, and his mockery of Laches's definition of fortitude—as standing firm against the enemy—is used to demonstrate the inadequacy of any simple or obvious definition, and to underline the ever-shifting nature of moral terms. Essays devoted to *De la vertu* (II: 29), *De la gloire* (II: 16), and *De l'yvrongnerie* (II: 2), display the same care to hedge round every distinction with further qualifications and plenty of supporting material. The watchword used by both Montaigne and Socrates, and which sums up their conception of moral problems, is DISTINGUISH. They urged men to distinguish different levels of argument, changing moods, and new contexts. They sought to teach them to discern the motives underlying human actions. Socrates thought that it was the job of a wise man to distinguish virtues and vices. But Montaigne made a more discriminating claim—very modestly expressed: 'nous autres, à qui le meilleur est toujours en vice, devons dire de mesme de la science de distinguer les vices: sans laquelle bien exacte le vertueux et le meschant deviennent meslez et incognus' (ii: 2,322). His ability to perceive such niceties had already been demonstrated in the opening paragraphs of *De la punition de la couardise* (i: 16, 70), where he studiously set out 'les fautes qui viennent de nostre foiblesse, et celles qui viennent de nostre malice'.

If you are convinced about the complexity of man's nature—and Montaigne reports Socrates as saying 'qu'il ne sçait à la verité que c'est que l'homme et que c'est l'une des pieces du monde d'autant difficile connoissance' (ii: 16,527)—then it follows naturally that the only honest way of recording your thoughts on man is to do so modestly. Moreover, when such uncertainty is admitted, then oblique presentation of findings seems the most appropriate manner of engaging your listener's (or reader's) interest. Montaigne does not always approve of Plato's methods, and sometimes links his writings with those of less formidable minds, where it is impossible to distinguish between philosophy and poetry: so obscurantist are the intentions of philosophers who try to protect themselves from accusations of ineptitude. Nevertheless, this coupling of philosophy and poetry has a less critical turn, even though Montaigne, as elsewhere in the *Apologie*, cannot resist presenting the argument ironically. They are similar arts in so far as they both resort to indirect ways of leading the reader to an apprehension of the truth: however complex, however obscure, and however trifling that truth might prove to be.

Par cette varieté et instabilité d'opinions, ils nous menent comme par la main, tacitement, à cette resolution de leur irresolution. Ils font profession de ne presenter pas tousjours leur avis en visage descouvert et apparent; ils l'ont caché tantost sous des umbrages fabuleux de la Poësie, tantost soubs quelque autre masque: car nostre imperfection porte encores cela, que la viande crue n'est pas tousjours propre à nostre estomac: il la faut assecher, alterer et corrompre: ils font de mesmes: ils obscurissent par fois leurs naïfves opinions et jugemens, et les falsifient, pour s'accommoder à l'usage publique. Ils ne veulent pas faire profession expresse d'ignorance et de l'imbecillité de la raison humaine, pour ne faire peur aux enfans; mais ils nous la descouvrent assez soubs l'apparence d'une science trouble et inconstante. (II: 12, 527–8)

Behind obliqueness lies admission of human inadequacy.[10]

Such diffidence is not always so frank, as we have had occasion to demonstrate in earlier chapters. Both Montaigne and Socrates enjoyed making an art out of their modesty. They both made remarkable use of what has most properly been called 'artful diffidence';[11] and, in their extraordinary displays of insufficiency, they both transferred attention away from the weaknesses of human reasoning towards a confidence in their own superior powers. With undisguised glee Montaigne recounts the story of Socrates's cool deflation of Hippias. Socrates listens, bides his time, and occasionally profers a question, delicately turned and devastatingly timed, waiting for Hippias to condemn himself from his own mouth about his experience in Sparta. What Montaigne most admires is Socrates's skilful understatement, allowing Hippias only to guess at his real opinion: 'Et au bout de cela Socrates, luy faisant advoüer par le menu l'excellence de leur forme de gouvernement publique, l'heur, et vertu de leur vie, luy laisse deviner la conclusion de l'inutilité de ses arts' (I: 25, 143).

Socrates's superiority is unquestioned. Indeed, it has been argued that he wins his arguments all too easily.[12] They usually stem from some paradoxical statement, so apparently difficult as to defy ready elucidation. A typical principle for Socrates is the thesis that virtue is knowledge: an idea which is developed in the *Euthydemus*, and which Montaigne explicitly refers to in *De l'art de conferer* (III: 8, 906). It is Socrates who chooses the premiss, and who, through his questions, carefully chosen and relentlessly exploited, both tests the truth of the premiss and controls the course of the discussion. His superior powers of analysis virtually dictate definitions, and almost (one might say) anticipate conclusions before the discussion is under way—and, at any rate, long before his companions have realised whither the argument is tending.[13] As we have shown, Montaigne himself valued the advantages of paradoxical statements and used them frequently.[14] What he lacked—and he was painfully aware of the lack—was the context of live discussion in which the precise nature of their ambiguities could be made plain. In *De l'art de conferer* (III:8), he spelt out the problems which he continually encountered through being forced into a writing medium; whereas the cut-and-thrust of intelligent dispute, and the active participation of two or more minds engaged in keen debate, would have handled the problems more effectively and, probably, in greater depth. It was much more complicated to have to supply both speaker and listener. It was more difficult for him, and more awkward for the reader, to take account of the multiple aspects of a theme, or to follow the tangled web of arguments presented obliquely. And he draws attention to the untidiness of his style because that very untidiness was part of his answer to the constraints imposed upon him by the medium in which he worked. It was the nearest he could get to spoken language, and to the spontaneous effects which arise naturally in verbal dispute. In the *Phaedrus*, Socrates examined at some length the differences between spoken and written language; stressing the advantages of the former; and drawing attention to what he calls the bastard nature of the latter, which, like a dead language, cannot answer the questions it poses, and is bandied about indiscriminately, and often fallaciously, by all and sundry.[15] Montaigne's sentiments are exactly similar; and, for this reason, he prized contradictions, and conscientiously wrote them into his *Essais*, anticipating all possible responses from a variety of readers. 'Les contradictions donc des jugemens ne m'offencent ny m'alterent; elles m'esveillent seulement et m'excercent' (III:8, 901), he wrote, continuing on the same page: 'quand on me contrarie, on esveille mon attention, non pas ma cholere; je m'avance vers celuy qui me contredit, qui m'instruit'. He accorded the same gratitude to such mental interruptions as Socrates gave to his friends who challenged his line of reasoning. Both men positively enjoyed having to deal with new demands imposed by their own mental energies, or by those of others. They revelled in the opportunity of exercising to the full their considerable reasoning power: 'ce que Socrates receuilloit, tousjours riant, les contradictions qu'on faisait à son discours, on pourroit dire que sa force en estoit cause, et que, l'avantage ayant à tomber certainement de son costé, il les acceptoit comme matiere de nouvelle gloire' (III:8, 903). Montaigne, too, was impressed by the inevitable victories won by Socrates.

To Montaigne's mind, the success of the Platonic dialogues owed much to an ability to vary styles: now speaking with grace in a plain and popular fashion (II:17, 621); now rigorously defining abstract terms; and now constructing an interchange which mingled subjects of love with

those on rhetoric in a 'fantastique bigarrure',[16] slipping from one theme
to another with 'une merveilleuse grace à se laisser ainsi rouler au vent,
ou à le sembler' (III:9,973). Montaigne emulated such graceful passages
of apparently artless spontaneity, which conveyed convincingly the
effect of voices speaking aloud.

The art of the dialogue was one which Montaigne's contemporaries had cultivated with varying degrees of success.[17] Their efforts had
exposed the difficulties of simultaneously assuming liveliness of tone,
spontaneous effects, and probing thought. In his introduction to the first
edition of his translation of the *Phaedo* in 1553, Louis le Roy set out
what he thought to be the main advantages of using the dialogue form.
His explanations might well have encouraged writers, anxious to make
their way in the literary world, to attempt dialogues in French—as, for
example, Bruès whose *Dialogues contre les Nouveaux Academiciens* (which
provided much source material for Montaigne's *Apologie*) appeared in
1557.[18] Le Roy's explanations, and Bruès's practice, might also have
warned someone as perspicacious as Montaigne that it was difficult in
dialogues to escape formality. We do not know whether Montaigne
used Le Roy's translations of Plato: he certainly used Ficino's large
Latin rendering of the Greek, and he knew the *Phaedo* well.[19] But
whether or not Montaigne had read the 1553 French translation, it is
worth quoting Le Roy's comment on the dialogue form since it seems to
have been a fairly typical French sixteenth-century response;[20] and,
moreover, it gives us a clear background against which to view Montaigne's own assessment.

> Au reste Platon à escrit par Dialogues, esquelz il introduit com-
> munément Socrates, qui n'assume rien, dispute beaucoup de choses
> affirmativement et negativement, s'enquiert de toutes, demande
> l'opinion des assistants sans dire la sienne, et sans rien resoudre,
> usant le plus souvent d'induction pour venir d'un semblable en
> l'autre, et de plusieurs particuliers colliger l'universel. Laquelle
> maniere d'escrire à grand'efficace, et rend les disputations plus
> intelligibles, comme si on les faisoit lors, et n'estoient prinses
> d'ailleurs: gardant mesmement la dignité des personnes introduytes,
> et accommodant à chacun propos convenables pour la varieté qui
> cause un merveilleux plaisir.[21]

Here, the main features of Socrates's method are neatly summed up: his
deliberate assertions that one must assume nothing until it has been
proved; the fact that the tenor of his reasoning is such that the accent

is on the search rather than upon solutions; the movement from a variety
of particulars towards general definitions; and, finally, the realisation
that the same fundamental issues can be attacked from a number of
vantage points by using a variety of speakers whose words are appropriate to the character of each.[22]

Other readers of Plato were very well aware of the power of dissimulation which resided in Socrates's questioning technique. Philippe
Canaye describes it in this way, pointing out how Socrates seems to be
asking for information, while, all the time, placing the strain of learning
upon those who consented to talk with him:

> Et qui lira les discours de Socrates dans Platon et Xenophon, il
> trouvera que tout est plein d'une telle dissimulation qu'il semble bien
> souvent qu'il veuille plustost recevoir instruction de celuy à qui il
> parle, que de faire professer de l'enseigner. Et par ce moyen il
> gaignoit le coeur de ceux qui avoient la patience de l'escouter, de sorte
> que de leur plein gré, et sans resistance quelconque, il les menoit où
> il vouloit.[23]

It is not surprising that Montaigne, too, perceived the enormous
advantages to be gained from such enviable control over other people's
minds.

Naturally, and especially in the *Apologie*, Montaigne was most
attracted by the inconclusive nature of Socrates's method. Abundance of
questions seemed to keep the argument for ever on the move, 'tousjours
demandant et esmouvant la dispute, jamais l'arrestant, jamais satisfaisant' (ii:12,489), abandoning displays of accumulated knowledge in
order to assume a spirit of enquiry. Indeed, knowledge resided in the
quest for knowledge. Montaigne develops this idea through the
metaphor of the midwife who assists at the birth of the child, making its
passage into the world easy, nourishing it, strengthening and fortifying
its members, allowing them to thrive and to flourish until they, in their
turn, are capable of taking over a more creative role. Socrates is the
midwife, and his children are the questionings which go on in the minds
of friends as his enquiries direct their thoughts and foster ideas.

> Socrates disoit que les sages femmes, en prenant ce mestier de faire
> engendrer les autres, quittent le mestier d'engendrer, elles; que luy,
> par le tiltre de sage homme que les dieux lui ont deferé, s'est aussi
> desfaict, en son amour virile et mentale, de la faculté d'enfanter, et se
> contente d'aider et favorir de son secours les engendrants, ouvrir leur

nature, graisser leurs conduits, faciliter l'issue de leur enfantement,
juger d'iceluy, le baptizer, le nourrir, le fortifier, le maillotter et
circonscrire: exerçant et maniant son engin aux perils et fortunes
d'autruy. (ii: 12, 489)

Montaigne clearly sees that the burden of learning was placed squarely
on the shoulders of Socrates's companions, and that the role of the
master was to create the conditions in which discoveries could best be
made. These conditions not only depended on an unending spate of
questions from Socrates. They also demanded that the latter play a dissimulating role; that he should protest his ignorance and a genuine
desire to be enlightened; and that he should hide his own superior gifts,
and give his friends the impression that they were really discovering
things for themselves and instructing him. And indeed they were: for in
these ways they were led willingly and unknowingly along routes which
Socrates could foresee but never obviously described. They were surprised into discovery, so to speak. That Montaigne appreciated the value
of engaging in such deceits must now be fairly obvious from the number of
roles he himself was prepared to play in the *Essais*. His commendation
of such tricks is also made explicit in *De l'art de conferer*, where he spells
out what he considers to be Socrates's motives in the *Euthydemus* and the
Protagoras: 'Il m'est advis qu'en Platon et en Xenophon, Socrates
dispute plus en faveur des disputants qu'en faveur de la dispute, et, pour
instruire Euthydemus et Protagoras de la connaissance de leur impertinence plus que de l'impertinence de leur art. Il empoigne la premiere
matiere comme celuy qui a une fin plus utile que de l'esclaircir, assavoir
esclaircir les esprits qu'il prend à manier et exercer' (iii: 8, 906). The
method becomes the philosophy. Neither Montaigne nor Socrates seem
concerned to supply a new set of opinions for outdated ones, but rather
to shake men out of their mindless assumptions, and to awaken them to
genuine intellectual curiosity. While both agreed that man's reasoning
power is very limited, they were both equally impatient of stupidity.
For them, to use Gulley's phrase: 'knowing what is good is a necessary
and sufficient condition of being and doing good'. The way to become
courageous is to find out what courage is; and such knowledge lies in the
process of discovery.

The matter could be expressed in terms frequently used by earlier
humanists. We have in the *Essais*, just as in some at least of the *Dialogues*
of Plato, a blending of eloquence and philosophy. Since Petrarch, men
had sought to link again these two arts which had been so rigorously

separated by Aristotle.[24] Their joining together had become a major subject of discussion for Renaissance writers; and, perhaps, two sixteenth-century French examples will suffice to show the nature of this problem. Peter Ramus claimed that he had provided writers with the necessary equipment for achieving a fusion of eloquence and philosophy: the words he uses are 'esprit guidé' and 'trouver et diriger l'esprit'.[25] And Louis le Roy argued, in all the prefaces to his translations from the Greek, that increased knowledge of ancient sources would bring about this long desired harmony. The desire at least was institutionalised with the founding of the Chair of Rhetoric and Philosophy at the College de France in 1571; and Le Roy was its first incumbent.[26] It is very tempting to argue that the *Essais* provided the first convincing proof of their union.

*   *   *

As previous critics of Montaigne have tended to stress the frank and open aspects of the *Essais*, it seems appropriate to offer, as a kind of coda to my book, a collection of responses to Montaigne's work, written or published in the century following his death. Did writers immediately recognise his oblique approaches to truth? Did they take any account of the 'harmony' Montaigne achieved?[27]

The first fleeting reactions to the *Essais* were not very interesting, but, in 1613, as he was about to abandon his reading of the *Essais* for ever, Jean-Pierre Camus wrote a lengthy *Apologie*[28] on their behalf; and, as Alan Boase has justly claimed, 'as a piece of literary criticism, it shows more insight than many famous writers on Montaigne since'.[29] Camus —who had absorbed the *Essais* as thoroughly as Montaigne had previously digested Plato—loved their diversity, their apparent spontaneity and frankness about self, and their conversational style: 'La simple et grossiere naïveté de nature'.[30] He found that, every time he read the *Essais*, he discovered something new, and not only about Montaigne's habits of thought, but—more significantly—about himself: 'Plus vous irez avant, plus vous vous cognoistrez, car sçachez que c'est le miroir de tout le monde'. This does not mean that Camus considered all men to be alike, but simply that a proper reading of the *Essais* is so demanding, and imposes such attention to detail, that it brings not only a desire for self-knowledge but also a way of achieving it: 'Je tiens qu'un homme, pour habile qu'il soit, n'y sçauroit mordre à plain à la premiere lecture; il y faut de l'attention et de la subtilité pour le pénétrer'.[31] Among his contemporaries, Camus seems to have come closest to an understanding of Montaigne. He saw that the study of self, in differing contexts, was the central preoccupation of the *Essais*, and that such a study depended upon an indissoluble harmony of form and content—a manner which constantly impinged on the reader's attention.

Apart from remarks about the old-fashioned nature of many of Montaigne's words, it was the potentially more puzzling aspects of his style which aroused frequent comment in the early years of the seventeenth century. Vital d'Audiguier, for instance, uses Montaigne as his authority when he promises to 'traicter une chose et parler d'une autre';[32] while De Lancre blames Montaigne's equivocations, and seems to get his purpose the wrong way round, 'Laissant ainsi toutes choses en doubte, quoy qu'il semble hardiment et absolument les décider'.[33] The problem of deciphering Montaigne's thought accurately was also discussed by Dominicus Baudius, a friend and correspondent of Lipsius. In an acute appreciation of Montaigne, whom he calls 'noster ille heros', he acknowledges his genius, and the diversity of subjects and style in the *Essais*, noting his power to move the reader and to arouse diverse interpretations. The latter, he maintains, derive principally from Montaigne's ability to express splendidly complex thoughts in everyday, humble words.[34]

Similar discerning admiration came, unexpectedly, from a pious Protestant—Jonatan de Sainct Sernin—exiled in London, who began meditating the *Essais* with a view to writing his own 'Essais'.[35] The few he did write were published in 1626, and, although they demonstrate clearly that he himself was absolutely incapable of reproducing Montaigne's style, they nevertheless record an intelligent and sensitive reaction to the problems posed by the *Essais*. He recognises the *Essais* as a search for knowledge of self, and he sees the contradictions, and the variations in mood, tone and opinions, as proof of the difficulty of knowing oneself.[36] He also detected that Montaigne's oblique manner is not an involuntary untidiness, but the only means of coming close to solving the difficulties involved in any search for self-knowledge: 'Montaigne n'a d'autre fin que d'essayer et esprouver son esprit, et partant nous met en lumiere ce qu'il enfante confusement et sans ordre'.[37] Enlightenment through confusion seems to me an excellent way of summing up Montaigne's impact, and this point is made very persuasively by Charles Sorel who, after examining the 'artifice' which lies in the structure of some essays, adds 'enfin ce n'est point là une lecture pour les Ignorans et des Aprentifs, ny pour des Esprits foibles'.[38] Yet, not all Montaigne's readers in the seventeenth century were to respond in this manner. Indeed, in the seventeenth century, the *Essais* were rarely studied dispassionately, How could they be, since the demands they make on any reader are so personal?

Two major obstacles stood in the way of a full appreciation of Montaigne's methods. The first presented itself in the person of Pierre Charron, whose three books of *De la Sagesse*[39] borrow liberally from Montaigne, but rearrange his ideas with such a love of order and desire to link knowledge of self with propaganda for catholicism—'arrangé et ajancé avec jugement, et a propos' as Charron himself puts it[40]—that the original thought, which depended on superficially untidy and exploratory expression, is lost, or severely transformed through exhortation.[41] The second obstacle was erected by the formalistic approach to style, incarnated in the first half of the century in Guez de Balzac. He was among the first to criticise Montaigne for his style. While grudgingly conceding that his digressions were mostly agreeable, and that 'en certains endroits il porte bien haut la Raison humaine', Balzac castigated the *Essais* as 'un corps en pièces; ce sont membres couppez'.[42] It was, he added, not entirely Montaigne's fault, but rather the crude state of the French language in the sixteenth century which inevitably produced flaws, now fortunately banished by progress.

It is, nevertheless, true that this formal approach to style was not accepted by all Balzac's contemporaries.[43] Indeed, by about 1660, Balzac had himself become a figure of fun; and it is largely through a freer and more sophisticated view of style, developed by the Méré brothers,[44] and above all by Pascal, that the true influence of 'l'incomparable auteur de *l'art de conferer*' filtered into men's writing and thinking habits. Pascal saw that Montaigne's power of persuasion lay in his conversational, natural style which not only quickly seduced the reader, but also set his own thinking mechanisms to work: 'La manière d'écrire d'Epictète, de Montaigne et de Salomon de Tultie [Pascal himself] est la plus d'usage, que s'insinue le mieux, qui demeure plus dans la mémoire, et qui se fait le plus citer, parce qu'elle est toute composée de pensées nées sur les entretiens ordinaires de la vie' (*Pensée* 18). Significantly also, *Pensée* 64 links self-discovery with Montaigne: 'Ce n'est pas dans Montaigne, mais dans moi que je trouve tout ce que j'y vois'. A study of Montaigne turns men's minds in upon themselves, just as in *De l'institution des enfants* (1:26,150) Montaigne had found that a study of Plato did: 'La verité et la raison sont communes à un chascun, et ne sont non plus à qui les a dites premierement, qu'à qui les dict apres. Ce n'est pas non plus selon Platon que selon moy puis que luy et moy l'entendons et voyons de mesme'. Pascal detected, however, nascent problems even within

Montaigne's most important gifts : a preoccupation with self, which could become excessive and exclusive; and a formidable mental equipment, which might be more tempted to persuade than to arrive at the truth. The *Entretien avec Monsieur de Saci*, while distorting the *Apologie* for polemical purposes, makes it clear that reading the *Essais* is permissible for someone as intelligent and as right-thinking as Pascal: but what of lesser brethren ?

Montaigne's style had helped formulate some key ideas in seventeenth-century aesthetic attitudes : the stress on the natural, and also on carefully conceived methods appropriate to the occasion, the *genre*, and the thought; the regard for wit, urbanity, and what was called the 'je ne sais quoi'; together with the conviction that the greatest art and the greatest pleasure lay in the power to suggest rather than to state, and that this power frequently came from the use of dissimulation. For years before and after Pascal wrote and talked about the *Essais*, handbooks on rhetoric and social behaviour had been telling their readers that, 'le raisonnement est quelquefois caché soubz l'histoire';[45] that 'le plus grand art qu'il y ait, c'est de sçavoir cacher l'Art : c'est par là qu'on ravit les hommes en admiration, leur faisant croire que l'on parle bien naturellement et sans affectation aucune';[46] and, moreover, that 'le grand art consiste à ne pas tout dire sur certains sujets; à glisser dessus plutôt que d'y appuyer; en un mot à en laisser penser aux autres plus qu'on n'en dit'.[47] All these instructions placed a considerable responsibility upon the reader; and it was precisely for this reason that the good men at Port Royal were concerned about the influence of Montaigne. His manner in the *Essais* delighted the reader, and involved him, as Pascal had demonstrated, so intimately that the 'Solitaires' were positively afraid of the effects produced on untrained minds; either these would be sucked into excessive self-reflexion, or they would acquire the ability to call everything into question—even God's word. Both responses were considered equally disastrous, and the source of such dangers had to be attacked. The author of a manuscript now in the Bibliothèque Nationale,[48] who seems to have known Nicole and other members of the Port Royal circle, gives a good idea of the extent of Messieurs' admiration for Montaigne, and the degree of their alarm at his influence. He notes, for instance, 'les beaux esprits l'admirent auiourdhuy';[49] and, he adds later, 'Monsieur Paschal estimoit Montaigne pour son stile et son sens. Il disoit qu'il luy avoit appris à escrire'.[50] The Chevalier de Méré, he states, 'travaille sur le fonds de Montagne';[51] Gabriel Naudé found inspiration in the *Essais* more than in any other work; and 'M. Nicole dit qu'il y a mille belles choses dans Montaigne, mais qu'il le faut lire avec discernement'.[52]

Pierre Nicole and Antoine Arnauld were reluctant to let their occasional approval of Montaigne show through their comments, criticisms, and distortions of his thought, in *La Logique ou l'Art de penser*.[53] This work was inspired by Pascal's fragment *De l'esprit géométrique*, and was designed to give their pupils the necessary mental equipment to reason well, to judge other writers' reasoning power, to distinguish the true from the false, and in particular, to detect the devious methods of persuasion used by Montaigne. He seems constantly in the minds of the authors of this work which is concerned to attack false rhetoric and to defend a purer art of thinking and writing.[54] Montaigne is the dissimulator *par excellence*; and he is presented as the main spokesman and defender of that abominable sect of liars—the Pyrrhonists.[55] He is never shown other than as a man who affects to be sincere, especially when writing about the self; and even then, Nicole and Arnauld observe, 'il est facile de voir que tout cela n'est qu'un jeu et un artifice qui le doit rendre encore plus odieux'.[56] His love of disputation 'est encore un defaut qui gâte beaucoup l'esprit',[57] since, they contend, nothing is more capable of distancing a man from truth and leading him into confusion. The very virtues of disputation, as stressed by Montaigne, are condemned as the source of bad thinking. Since the function of this form of discourse is to excite and arouse the mind, it excites the passions simultaneously—and even more effectively. The consequence is thinking clouded by passion, and here Nicole and Arnauld direct a specific attack against the means used to arouse thought in the *Apologie*, where Montaigne is seen to be indulging in even more devious practices. In order to persuade, he offers as true evidence sentiments in which he himself does not believe: 'et il est inexcusable de se jouer ainsi de ses Lecteurs, en leur disant des choses qu'il ne croit pas'.[58] For Nicole and Arnauld, it is intolerable that truth should be so close to lying. Yet, though they expose some of the oblique methods used by Montaigne to get his reader's mind into play, their demonstration merely serves to confirm Montaigne's success. Such methods might be morally wrong, but their power is manifest in the vigorous protests the two Jansenists felt constrained to make. It is significant that Bérenger's subsequent defence of Montaigne[59] merely indicates those passages where Nicole and Arnauld have deliberately distorted his words, before allowing Montaigne to speak for himself. Large chunks of the *Essais*, and all *De l'institution des enfants*, are quoted to make the point that Montaigne's art of thinking is useful and efficient.

It suffices to cite part of the opening paragraph of *Sur des vers de Virgile*:
'Il faut avoir l'ame instruite des moyens de soustenir et combattre les
maux, et instruite des reigles de bien vivre et de bien croire, et souvent
l'esveiller et exercer en cette belle estude' (III: 5, 818).

Nevertheless, writers searching for Truth continued to find their
response to the *Essais* somehow non-rational and almost violent. They
were fascinated by the ways in which Montaigne communicated his ideas,
and they tried to analyse the extent of the emotional disturbance these
means aroused. Malebranche is a valuable critic in so far as he was aware
that Montaigne, by getting at our feelings, gets at our minds. He is at
once as impatient of the method as he is affected by it. Recognising its
strength, he knows that within his own great design some account must
be given of it, since it challenged his own commitment to the supremacy
of reason. 'Cet Autheur a un certain air libre, il donne un tour si naturel
et vif à ses pensées, qu'il est mal-aisé de le lire sans se laisser préoccuper.
La négligence qu'il affecte lui sied assez bien, et le rend aimable à la
plûpart du monde sans le faire mépriser . . . L'air du monde et l'air
cavalier soûtenus par quelque érudition, font un effet si prodigieux sur
l'esprit, qu'on l'admire souvent, et qu'on se rend presque toûjours à ce
qu'il décide, sans oser l'examiner, et quelque fois même sans l'entendre.
Ce sont nullement ses raisons qui persuadent'.[60] It is no wonder that the
Essais were put on the Index in 1676.

Montaigne's impact is certain: but the way he awakens our
emotions is very difficult to diagnose, as Malebranche suggests.[61] It has
been the aim of this book to try to analyse how one person's responses
to the *Essais* have been alerted and interested by the oblique approaches
of their author. In these final paragraphs, through a rapid survey, I have
tried to suggest that, in the seventeenth century, men perceived the fact
(some only faintly) that Montaigne's method of communication is an
integral part of his search for, and his discovery of, Truth. No one realised
this more keenly than the eighteenth-century 'philosophe' whose manner
of writing and thinking comes so close to Montaigne's own: Denis
Diderot. His comments on Montaigne deserve to be repeated and set
beside Montaigne's own description of the Socratic method, as a fitting
end to this book.

Diderot

Un auteur paradoxal ne doit jamais dire son mot, mais toujours ses
preuves; il doit entrer furtivement dans l'âme de son lecteur, et non
de vive force. C'est le grand art de Montaigne, qui ne veut jamais

prouver, et qui va toujours prouvant, et me ballottant du blanc au noir, et du noir au blanc.[62]

Montaigne

Le conducteur de ses dialogismes, Socrates, va tousjours demandant et esmouvant la dispute, jamais l'arrestant, jamais satisfaisant. (II : 12, 489)

NOTES

INTRODUCTION

1   See, for example, the following works: Robert Griffin, *Coronation of the Poet. Joachim Du Bellay's Debt to the Trivium*, University of California Press, 1969; Alex L. Gordon, *Ronsard et la Rhétorique*, Droz, 1970; and M. Dassonville's edition of Ramus's *Dialectique* (1555), Droz, 1964.

2   Some works published since this study was completed suggest that more attention is now being paid to the importance of self-conscious writing in the sixteenth century. See J. C. Lapp's *The Esthetics of Negligence*, Cambridge University Press, 1971; B. C. Bowen's *The Age of Bluff*, University of Illinois Press, 1972; and R. A. Sayce's *The Essays of Montaigne. A Critical Exploration*, London, 1972. However, none of these works is specifically concerned with those 'secret' ways by which Montaigne seeks to persuade his readers, and which constitute the subject of my book.

CHAPTER 1

1   The word 'Rhapsody' was frequently used by sixteenth- and seventeenth-century writers who understood its meaning as 'a written composition having no fixed form or plan', J. Webber, *The Eloquent 'I': style and self in seventeenth-century prose*, Madison, 1968, pp 126–7. W. Ong in his article 'Wit and Mystery: a Revaluation in Mediaeval Latin Hymnody', *Speculum*, vol 22, NO. 3, July, 1947, pp 310–41, sees it as 'a stitching together of things already read'. The word is used by Boaistuau in this sense in his *Theatre du monde, avec un brief discours de l'excellence de l'homme*, Paris, 1561, in the preface *Au Lecteur*, sig. ã iv: 'de sorte que si tu luy veux imposer le nom de Rapsodie ou recueil de diverses auctoritez, tu ne luy feras point d'iniure'. Montaigne owned a copy of this work.

2   The articles of Henry E. Genz 'First Traces of Montaigne's progression towards Self-Portraiture', *Symposium*, vol 16, 1962, pp 206 ff, and J. P. Boon 'La Pensée de Montaigne sur la mort a-t-elle évolué', *Modern Language Notes*, vol 80, 1965, pp 307 ff; 'Montaigne: Du Gentilhomme à l'Ecrivain', *Modern Philology*, vol 64, 1966, pp 118 ff; and 'Evolution et esthétique dans les *Essais* de Montaigne', *Philological Quarterly*, vol 47, 1968, pp 526 ff, have most recently called into question the rigid chronological approach advocated by Pierre Villey, especially in his monumental *Sources et Evolution des 'Essais' de Montaigne*, Paris, 2nd ed. 1933, 2 vols, *passim*. The works of Hugo Friedrich, *Montaigne*, Paris, 1968 (French ed.) and M. Baraz, *L'être et la connaissance chez Montaigne*, Paris, 1968, also set relatively little store in a strictly chronological approach to the *Essais*.

3   *The Praise of Folly*, translation used, London, 1887, p 5.

4   *L'Heptaméron*, *préface*, p xi of the Garnier edition.

5   *Discours politiques et militaires*, Paris, 1587, sig. ã ij^v.

6   *Ibid*, sig. iiij^v.

7   To quote but two examples: Boaistuau, *op. cit.* preface, sig. ã iv., and G. Bouchet, in the preface to the *Serées*, Poictiers, 1585, sig. b vi.

8   Plutarch, *Œuvres morales*, translated by Amyot, Paris, 1572, p 138^v. Montaigne uses this chapter as the source of an anecdote in *Divers evenemens de mesme conseil* (I:24).

9   Monluc, for instance, only records his virtues once his military career has been prematurely terminated.

10   Plutarch, *op. cit.* p 141^v. It seems that Montaigne had taken heed of Plutarch's final warning: 'on ne peult endurer patiemment ceulx qui en escrivant ou en lisant se donnent le tiltre de sages, et est on bien aise d'ouir ceulx qui se nomment amateurs de sagesse, ou qui disent qu'ils profitent en l'estude de sapience, ou telle chose semblable, qui est modeste et non subiecte à aucune envie' (*op. cit.* p 141). These words could be taken as a fairly accurate summary of the hesitant, tentative approach always advocated by Montaigne.

11   See in the work of M. Gribaldus, *De methodo ac ratione studendi, libri tres*, Lyon, 1544, and our discussion below, chapter 3, pp 42, 56.

12   See the studies of J. Plattard, *Montaigne et son temps*, Paris, 1933, and of Dezeimiris who discusses Montaigne's annotations of N. Gilles in a series of articles in the *Revue de l'Histoire littéraire de la France*, vol 16, 1909; vol 19, 1912; vol 20, 1913; vol 21, 1914; and of Quintus Curtius, *Ibid*, for vol 23, 1916; vol 24, 1917; vol 25, 1918; and vol 26, 1919.

13   See also later in *De la gloire* (II:16,602).

14   Boon points out in 'Montaigne: Du Gentilhomme', *art. cit.* p 118, how Du Bellay in the second preface to *L'Olive* felt the need to

defend himself 'contre la faulse persuation de ceux qui pensent l'exercice de lettres deroger à l'estat de noblesse'.

15   Professor S. Dresden has drawn attention to the important role of the reader in the *Essais*, see his article 'Le dilettantisme de Montaigne', *Bibliothèque d'Humanisme et Renaissance*, vol 15, 1953, pp 45 ff.

16   See particularly *Du démentir* (ii : 18,649).

17   It is interesting to note Philippe Canaye's advice in *L'Organe, c'est à dire l'instrument du discours*, Geneva, 1589, pp 727–8, where he outlines the advantages of writing ambiguously.

18   J. B. Gelli, *Les Discours fantastiques de Justin Tonnelier*, Lyon, 1566, pp 10–11. The plainest of men is overheard by his nephew who reports his words.

19   Estienne Pasquier, *Œuvres*, Amsterdam, 1723, 2 vols, ii : col. 516. Charles Sorel in his *Bibliothèque Françoise*, Paris, 1664, p 72 was to return to this subject again, see our Chapter 8, n. 38. His comments are discussed by Alan Boase, *The Fortunes of Montaigne*, London, 1935, p 24. P. Ballaguy 'La sincerité de Montaigne', *Mercure de France*, vol 245, 1933, pp 547–75, seems not to have fully understood what Montaigne meant by sincerity—which involves a complete revealing of self and not a simple retailing of facts which are known to be true. It is this second kind of truth, limited to happenings and deeds, upon which Monluc bases his lengthy discussions in his *Commentaires*, Pléiade ed. 1964; see Book I, pp 21–2, p 31 'car je ne veux escrire par ouyr dire', p 50, and so on.

20   G. Bouchet, *op. cit.* sig. b iv, and P. de Lestoile, *Journal pour le regne de Henri III*, 1574–1589, ed. Gallimard, 1943, p 31. Henri Estienne, according to the eighteenth-century editors of his *Apologie pour Hérodote* (Paris, 1735) was referring to Montaigne when he reports an anecdote and its author as 'ennemi mortel des mensonges'. It seems unlikely that this could refer to Montaigne since Estienne made the comment in the first edition of his work published in Lyon in 1566, p 169.

21   La Boëtie, *Œuvres complètes*, ed. P. Bonnefon, Bordeaux, 1892, p 159.

22   O. Landi, *Paradossi*, translated and imitated by C. Estienne in *Paradoxes*, Poitiers, 1553, p 55. Landi is, of course, thinking of the professional fool, of the type used by Shakespeare in *King Lear*. There are, however, obvious affinities between his stance in that play, and the role adopted by Erasmus and Montaigne in their works.

23   E. Du Tronchet, *Finances et thresor de la plume Françoyse*, Paris, 1572, p 91.

24   See also Du Tronchet's remarks, *op. cit. Epistre*, sig. ã iij–iiij.

25   Professor Mansell Jones first pointed out this positive character

of Montaigne's defensive writing in *Three French Introspectives from Montaigne to André Gide*, Cambridge, 1937.

26   Such a lack of conscious control is extended to all man's activities in *De l'art de conferer* (III : 8,922).

27   Montaigne owned a copy of the *De Docta Ignorantia*, see Villey, *Sources et Evolution, op. cit.* vol I, p 112. Petrarch, too, in his most well known moral work—the *De Remediis*—had noted that wisdom consisted in admitting that one was not wise. Edition used, Poitiers, 1534, p 7ᵛ.

28   Lefèvre d'Etaples in his panegyric on Nicholas of Cusa. Sig. ãã ii of N. Khrypffs' *Haec accurata recognitio trium voluminum operum clariss. P. Nicolai Cusae*, 1514.

29   H. C. Agrippa, *Declamation sur l'incertitude, vanité et abus des sciences*, Paris, 1582; French translation by L. de Mayerne Turquet.

30   F. Sanchez, *Quod Nihil Scitur*, ed. used, Lyon, 1581. His title indicates, he says (p 3), a mode of knowledge; p 10, he claims Socrates the wisest (a) because he said he knew nothing, (b) because he wrote nothing. On Sanchez and Montaigne, see F. Strowski's discussion in his article 'Un contemporain de Montaigne : Sanchez le Sceptique', *Bulletin Hispanique*, vol 18, 1906, pp 79 ff. It would be an easy task to find general statements approving ignorance in Landi, Jacques Yver and many other writers contemporary with Montaigne. I have, however, found no writer of that time willing to absorb ignorance into himself in the way that Montaigne does. Landi, *op. cit.* p 31, Jacques Yver, *Le Printemps*, Paris, 1572, pp 307ᵛ–8.

31   Plutarch, *op. cit.* p 140ᵛ.

32   Joachim du Bellay, *Deffence et Illustration de la Langue Françoyse*, éd. critique, H. Chamard, Paris, 1904, p 314.

33   *The Praise of Folly, op. cit.* pp 87 ff.

34   *Ibid*, pp 121, 129.

35   *Ibid*, p 113.

36   A similar view is suggested by E. V. Telle in his article 'Le mot "Essai" chez Montaigne', *Bibliothèque d'Humanisme et Renaissance*, 1968, vol 30, pp 225 ff, where an interesting and detailed discussion of the passage from 'essai' to 'effort' and on to 'arrêt' may be found.

CHAPTER 2

1   The point is further elaborated in the *Apologie* (II : 12,569–70), where Montaigne, after noting 'En la parole la plus nette, pure et parfaite qui puisse estre, combien de faulceté et de mensonge a lon fait naistre ?', turns his attention to the multiplicity of questionable interpretations of the Bible.

2   Charles de la Ruelle, *Succinctz adversaires . . . contre l'Histoire et professeurs d'icelle*, Poictiers, 1574, p 43.

3   Florimond de Raemond, *L'Anti Christ et l'Anti Papesse*, Paris, 1599, p 136. See also Alan Boase's article, 'Montaigne annoté par Florimond de Raemond', *Revue du Seizième siècle*, vol 15, 1928, pp 237 ff.

4   Erasmus, in *Ratio studii ac legendi . . . auctores*, n.p. 1511, envisaged plenty of skills from a variety of sources, but he placed the accent on the student's performance as did most sixteenth-century writers; see, for example, P. Porteau's discussion of Verrepaeus in *La vie pédagogique au temps de Montaigne*, Droz, 1935, pp 128 ff.

5   Ruelle, *op. cit.* pp 47–53, for his attack on Erasmus. Even those writers who seem most distant from the spirit of Montaigne—Ramus and Le Roy, for example—were striving to attain similar ends through different means. See our discussion in Chapter 8, p 163.

6   W. H. Woodward, in his introduction to *Desiderius Erasmus Concerning the aim and method of Education*, New York, 1964 (reprint), pp 119 and 123 ff, has some interesting comments on this point.

7   Gelli, *Discours*, *op. cit.* p 10, makes his 'rustic' talk in similar fashion about his style: 'en un style si bas, et mal tissu; comme n'estant continué de droit fil, mais souvent interrompu'.

8   It is easier for Montaigne to demonstrate an 'unnatural' style and to define the 'natural' by contrast, as it were. It would be interesting to know, for example, how far Montaigne's images are ordinary, learned, cliché-ridden or personal.

9   'J'ay, de ma part, le goust estrangement mousse à ces propensions qui sont produites en nous sans l'ordonnance et entremise de nostre jugement' (ii : 8,366).

10   Montaigne is so confident in his consciousness that he does not note the degree of nostalgia in the development in *Du repentir* (iii : 2, 793–5).

11   See Grahame Castor's discussion, *Pléiade Poetics*, Cambridge, 1964, p 48.

12   P. Du Plessis Mornay, *Memoires*, Paris, 1624–51, 4 vols, vol I, p 7.

13   In the longest essays Montaigne takes great care to ensure that the reader follows the argument. In the *Apologie*, for instance, he clearly announces his intentions at the beginning of each section (ii : 12,426, 430,469,482,514,517,518,571).

14   It is interesting to compare similar writing habits in Cardanus. See, for example, the equally inconsequential 'Or à fin que ie revienne à mon propos', in *De la Subtilité*, Paris, 1556, p 1ᵛ, etc.

15   There are some valuable comments on Montaigne's familiar prose in A. Lorian 'Montaigne—De l'impératif', *Zeitschrift für Romanische Philologie*, vol 80, 1964, pp 54–97.

16   Apart from the many dialogues written in Italian, Pontus de

Tyard and Jacques Tahureau were two of the most prominent sixteenth-century authors of dialogues. Although Estienne Pasquier used the dialogue form only once in *Monophile*, he nevertheless advocated its use: 'Il me semble que les Dialogues sont fort propres pour communiquer nos conceptions', *Œuvres, op. cit.* col 31.

17   It is little wonder that Montaigne should have expressed a preference for communication by means of letters. They provided, as his contemporary Habert has shown (*Style de composer des lettres missives*, Paris, 1587), the most extensive range of diverse tones, and allowed for the passage from one tone to another without the conscious barrier of rules necessitated by more formal writing. See also Du Tronchet's *Lettres missives*, Paris, 1583, p 325 on the need to adopt different styles for different readers.

18   My italics. Pierre Fabri, *Le grand et vrai art de Pleine Rhetorique*, six editions between 1521 and 1544. I quote from the modern edition, Paris, 1889, p 197.

19   *Ibid*, p 204 'avant que l'en prenne la plume pour escripre, l'en doibt considerer la personne à qui l'en escript'.

20   Montaigne shows himself aware of the subtleties involved in different styles of speaking in France, See *De la praesomption*, II:17,622.

21   F. Gray, *Le style de Montaigne*, Paris, 1958, pp 24–95.

22   See Lestoile, *op. cit.* p 483 'Le 20 janvier [1587] le roi fait venir par devers lui, au Louvre, le président le Faure et d'Anguéchin, son procureur en la cour des aides, les blâma aigrement et avec injures atroces de ce qu'ils avaient envoyé Sardini prisonnier en la conciergerie du Palais, à cause que de sa privée autorité il avait fait imprimer l'édit du doublement des daces qui avait été publié et registré, ce requérant et consentant le procureur général du roi, combien que par le dit arrêt eût été dit et fait écrire par le greffier en mots exprès qu'il avait été publié de l'exprès commandement du roi et après plusieurs itérées jussions, pour faire paraître qu'ils l'avaient laissé publier par force par les cardinaux et autres que le roi y avait envoyés exprès à cet effet'.

23   Bonaventure des Periers, *Nouvelles*, Paris, 1558, p 72.

24   *L'Heptaméron, ed. cit.* p 260.

25   Such features of style can be found in P. de Mexia, *Diverses Leçons*, Paris, 1557; J. Des Caurres, *Œuvres morales*, Paris, 1584; and Louis le Roy, *De la Vicissitude et variété des choses humaines*, Paris, 1576; just to quote some obvious examples.

26   'simplement plaisans' is a compliment and not a dismissive comment as Professor M. Screech has suggested, 'An aspect of Montaigne's Aesthetics', *Bibliothèque d'Humanisme et Renaissance*, vol 24, 1962, pp 576 ff.

27   E. Moët sums up this attitude very neatly 'Il voudrait bien qu'on

le prît pour un grand écrivain sans le savoir; au lieu qu'il est véritable-
ment et essentiellement homme de lettres', *Des opinions et des jugements
littéraires de Montaigne*, Paris, 1859, p 34.

28   For the importance of aesthetics in Montaigne's moral world,
see the work of E. Ruel, *Du sentiment artistique dans la morale de
Montaigne*, Paris, 1901, and also Alan Boase, *Fortunes, op. cit.* p xxxv.

29   For comment on Montaigne's essentially aesthetic approach to
some ancient authors, see W. G. Moore's article on Montaigne's
handling of Lucretius 'Lucretius et Montaigne', *Yale French Studies*,
vol 38, 1967, pp 109 ff.

30   A guide to Montaigne's increasing awareness of the importance
of aesthetics can be seen from J. Coppin's study *Etude sur la grammaire
et le vocabulaire de Montaigne*, Paris, 1925, p 108: 'Même ses corrections
de grammaire ou de langue manifestent chez lui des soucis d'artiste
plutôt que des scrupules du grammarien'.

31   Fabri, *op. cit.* pp 169 ff, discusses such phrases in detail and offers
this example as a model: 'Qui ayme justice, il hayt malice, et se garde
de malefice'.

32   These antitheses were written for the first publication of the
Essais. It is interesting to note that Montaigne multiplies similar
contrasts on the same theme in his last additions to this essay (1:20,91)
'Le continuel ouvrage de vostre vie c'est bastir la mort. Vous estes en la
mort pendant que vous estes en vie. Car vous estes apres la mort quand
vous n'estes plus en vie'. Sponde, Du Plessis, Chassignet, and any writer
who pillaged Seneca, Cicero and the Bible, used the same technique of
antithesis and accumulation. See my article 'Prose Inspiration for Poetry:
J. B. Chassignet', in *The French Renaissance and its Heritage*, London,
1968, pp 139 ff.

33   In any case, Montaigne abhorred the 'nouveautés des beaux
esprits' (III:5,850). Gray, *op. cit.* p 57, note 36, does cite one instance
where Montaigne's formulation seems unhappily contrived.

34   See Carol E. Clark's article 'Seneca's Letters to Lucilius as a
source of some of Montaigne's imagery', *Bibliothèque d'Humanisme et
Renaissance*, vol 30, 1968, pp 249 ff.

35   Traditionally, he likens his borrowing technique to the bee's
flight from flower to flower (1:26,150).

36   Seneca, *Epistulae morales Ad Lucilium*, Loeb ed. 3 vols, vol I, 20
and 23, pp 133, 159.

37   Another example would be from *De la ressemblance des enfans aux
peres* (II:37,755), where the satire depends on more complex structures
which accumulate, each succeeding statement matching stylistically, but
contradicting the one before.

38   Noteworthy is the notorious sequence of animal stories in the

Apologie (ii : 12), and the dazzling display of drugs and opinions in *De la ressemblance des enfans aux peres*, ii : 37, 752–5.

39   *Opera quae extant . . . Pyrrhoniarum hypotyposes libri III*, Paris, 1569, translation and annotation by Henri Estienne.

40   Note the large number of pages given to the discussion of the various forms of syllogism in George Trebizond for example, *De Re Dialectica Libellus*, Paris, 1558.

41   *Dialectique* (1555), ed. M. Dassonville, Droz, 1964, p 144.

42   Most contemporary writers argued forcibly that diversity in style was needed for maximum persuasion. Examples are Amyot, *Œuvres morales, op. cit.* preface, sig. ã iij; Mexia, *Diverses Leçons, op. cit.* i : 10; N. Franco, *Dix plaisans dialogues*, Paris, 1579, *Epistre*, ĩi. 2ᵛ.

43   Sebillet's *Paradoxe* is printed pp 263 ff, in his *Contramours*, Paris, 1581. The passage I refer to starts on p 268.

44   See Paré's description of the siege of Metz, in 'Apologie et Voyages', *Œuvres*, 1585, f LLliiᵛ.

45   Montaigne's use of the image deserves a full length study; this is being undertaken by Carol E. Clark. Her article 'Montaigne and the Imagery of Political Discourse in sixteenth-century France', *French Studies*, 1970, p 337 should be consulted and M. Baraz 'L'Image dans les *Essais* de Montaigne', *Bibliothèque d'Humanisme et Renaissance*, vol 27, 1965, pp 361.

46   The curiously measured account of oriental widowhood which gains its effect precisely from the almost dead-pan tone 'ce qui se fait et en cette maniere' (ii : 29, 685–6) would be another good example.

47   It is interesting to note that Courcelles, *Rhetorique, op. cit.* p 21ᵛ, advocates change of tone 'de sorte qu'il soit tantost grave, tantost legier et inconstant', as the best means of catching the attention of your audience in narration.

CHAPTER 3

1   P. Fabri, *Le grand et vrai, op. cit.*, Courcelles, *Rhetorique, op. cit.*, and Ramus, *Dialectique, op. cit.* I quote from the more accessible French texts, which frequently are elaborate adaptations of Latin editions. See Roy E. Leake Jr., his article on Fouquelin's *Rhetorique* of 1557, which he shows to be an adaptation of Talon's Latin edition, and not a translation as was originally thought. *Bibliothèque d'Humanisme et Renaissance*, vol 30, 1968, pp 85 ff.

2   A. Fouquelin, *La Rhétorique françoise*, Paris, 1557, p 10; Fabri, *op. cit.* pp 189 ff; Ramus, *op. cit.* p 150 ff; and Gribaldus, *op. cit.* chapter XII.

3   'Sed eruditissimum longe, si per aliam rem alia indicetur', Quintilian, *Institutio Oratoria*, Loeb ed. 4 vols, III, Book IX, chapter 2, pp 434–6. Most of Book IX is devoted to a discussion of the art of dissimulation.

4   Fabri *op. cit.* p 41; Courcelles, *op. cit.* ch. 5, pp 15 ff; Agrippa, *De l'incertitude, op. cit.* p 49, uses the same facts to point to a different conclusion which fits in well with his main thesis 'cest discipline de rhetorique n'est autre chose, qu'une manière ou artifice de bien flatter et amadouer, ou pour le dire plus clairement, de bien mentir, à fin de persuader sous un faux voile ou masque de belles paroles . . .' Montaigne was not unaware of such moral strictures. It is interesting to note that Jacques Tahureau considered the bulk of Agrippa's writings to be 'mocqueries', that is to say, he frequently wrote the opposite of what he thought and his readers recognized this. *Les Dialogues*, Paris, ed. F. Conscience, 1870, pp 156–7.

5   Ramus, *op. cit.* p 151.

6   Bonaventure des Periers, *Cymbalum Mundi*, Lyon, 1538. Text used, ed. by Peter Nurse, Manchester, 1958. See also Professor M. Screech's article on Des Periers' title 'The Meaning of the title *Cymbalum Mundi*', *Bibliothèque d'Humanisme et Renaissance*, vol 31, 1969, pp 343 ff.

7   Pierre de la Primaudaye, *Academie Françoise*, Paris, 1580, 3rd ed. p 5, 'J'ay delibéré de faire comme ceux qui iöuent sur un theatre, lesquels soubs des masques empruntez representent les vrays personnages . . .' Jacques Yver uses the same technique in his *Printemps, op. cit.* p 5.

8   Du Plessis Mornay, *Memoires, op. cit.* I, pp 18 ff.

9   *Œuvres, op. cit.* col 528. In view of this remark it is surprising that Pasquier did not understand what Montaigne meant by *Diversion*.

10   *The Praise of Folly, op. cit.* p 6.

11   *Colloquies*, ed. used Paris, 1720, 4 vols, II, NO. 9, 'L'art de bien mentir'; and p 169, 'La langue a été donnée à l'homme pour s'en servir prudemment et pour dire ce qui est à propos: or il n'est pas toujours à propos de dire la verité'.

12   *The Civile Conversation of M. Steeven Guazzo*, London, 1581 (first 3 books) and 1586 (4th Book); Reprint 1967, 2 vols, I, p 27.

13   B. Castiglione, *The Courtier*, Everyman ed. p 51.

14   Philibert de Vienne, *Le philosophe de Court*, Paris, 1547, pp 95 ff. The praise of methods of dissimulation in rhetoric should not be confused with moral interpretations of disguising, thoroughly disapproved of by writers like Du Tronchet, *Lettres, op. cit.* p 8, or Nicolas Margues in his *Description du monde desguisé*, Paris, 1563, *passim*.

15   This point was indirectly suggested by Moët, *Les opinions littéraires, op. cit.* p 23. 'La méthode qu'il préfère est celle qui se dissimule', and p 25, 'On arrivera au but par une route plus longue, sans doute, mais plus attrayante'.

16   Pasquier complained that Montaigne 'prenoit plaisir de desplaire plaisamment', *Œuvres, op. cit.* col 515, although Pasquier himself

advocated oblique methods of persuasion: 'Il advient ordinairement que sous l'escorce d'une fable nous descouvrons la verité' *op. cit.* cols 523 ff.

17   See Friedrich's discussion of Montaigne's use of anecdote, *Montaigne, op. cit.* p 215.

18   See also the very pointed series of reversals that Montaigne uses in his satire on doctors and their judgements (II : 37, 753 ff).

19   This technique is not very far removed from Bacon's shrewd comment 'The nature of an use is best discerned by considering what it is not, and then what it is; for it is the nature of all human science and knowledge to proceed most safely, by negatives and exclusives, to what is affirmative and inclusive'. *Reading on the Statute of Uses*, 1600; ed. used, *Works*, London, 1879, 2 vols, I, p 598.

20   Consider also *Nous ne goustons rien de pur* (II : 20, 657) where feelings of pain and pleasure, laws and politics, are set upon the same plane to reinforce the point made in the title.

21   For example, R. de Lucinge 'Qui pourroit trouver l'Histoire en forme de Dialogue, cette maniere d'entreparleurs nous fait plus diligens à en remarquer la tissure', *La Maniere de lire l'Histoire*, Paris, 1614, p 20. T. Sébillet's *Contramours, op. cit.* is a translation of Fregoso's dialogue on love; the latter's *Le Ris de Democrite* and *Le Pleur de Heraclite*, Paris, 1547 was naturally written in this form; as were most courtesy books (Castiglione and Guazzo) and, very obviously, the work of Guy de Bruès, *Les Dialogues*, Paris, 1557. Pasquier maintained that this form was best suited to works designed to give pleasure only, *Œuvres, op. cit.* col 8.

22   Bruès' work is similarly ambiguous. See the difficulties of interpretation in P. Paul Morphos' critical edition of the *Dialogues*, John S. Hopkins Studies in Romance Languages and Literature, Extra vol XXX, Baltimore, 1953.

23   Innocent Ringhieri's *Dialogue de la vie et de la mort*, Lyon, 1557— a work owned by Montaigne—is the most blatant example I have come across.

24   Guazzo, *op. cit.* p 41 discusses and demonstrates the advantages of getting to truth through the contradictions of another.

25   The advantages of disputation, particularly as far as alerting the mind is concerned, were firmly advanced by Maldonat, whom Montaigne consulted. See M. Prat, *Maldonat et l'université de Paris au XVIe siècle*, Paris, 1856, pp 277 & 279.

26   Fregoso, *Le Ris, op. cit.* Democrite's long discourse of some sixty pages ends with this praise of 'Amour sainct et vertueux'. Referring to *De l'incertitude de nostre jugement*, Boase suggests 'It would be a mistake to take this contrast as a mere literary exercise. Its primary function is a satisfaction of the emotions by a dramatic device'. *Fortunes, op. cit.* p xxvii.

27   Note Montaigne's own experience in *De l'art de Conferer* (III :

8,901) 'les contradictions donc des jugemens ne m'offencent ny m'alterent; elles m'esveillent seulement et m'exercent'.

28   He seems to have been persuaded of this view as early as the first
version of the *Apologie* (ii: 12,545–6) although here the view is posed
more negatively. Burton seems to have adopted a similar approach for
similar reasons, see Webber, *The Eloquent 'I'*, *op. cit.* pp 105 ff.

29   See, for example, *Des livres* (ii: 10,389).

30   For a more detailed discussion, see chapter 7.

31   Another instance would be his essay on suicide (ii: 3) where he
shows us the motives for suicide, examines many cases in detail, but
ultimately one does not get the impression that Montaigne has solved
anything, even for himself. He writes about suicide because most
moralists did in the sixteenth century and the subject fascinated him.

32   Friedrich, *Montaigne*, *op. cit.* p 297 notes that theatrical terms
often come from ancient sources, and this fact might well be relevant to
our discussion.

33   Ramus, *Dialectique, ed. cit.* p 150.

CHAPTER 4

1   Baraz notes the importance of paradoxes used in this kind of
context in his article 'Sur la structure d'un essai de Montaigne',
Bibliothèque d'Humanisme et Renaissance, vol 23, 1961, pp 273–4: 'Pour
glorifier le beau incarné, Platon avait fait l'éloge du laid silène, Montaigne fera celui de la répugnante gravelle'. Montaigne must have noted
the use of opposites made by Sextus Empiricus. The latter's sceptical
system depended on opposing to every proposition an equal proposition.
Montaigne did not adopt a similar method to avoid having to arrive at
conclusions, as did Sextus, but in order that the truth might emerge.

2   As a lawyer he would have been trained to get at the truth through
arguing by opposites, see M. Gribaldus, *De Methodo, op. cit.* cap. 6, p 33,
'Per contraria et oppositiones veritatem melius invenire'. Modern critics
who have given some attention to Montaigne's use of the paradox
include Yves Delègue 'Du Paradoxe chez Montaigne', *Cahiers de
l'Association Internationale des Etudes Françaises*, vol 14, 1962, pp 241 ff;
P. Porteau 'Sur un paradoxe de Montaigne', *Mélanges offerts à P.
Laumonnier*, Paris, 1935, p 333; and Floyd Gray, *Le Style, op. cit.* p 80.
For more general discussions on the paradox see Walter Kaiser, *Praisers
of Folly*, Cambridge Mass., 1963; Rosalie Colie, *Paradoxia Epidemica*,
Princeton, 1966; and Sister Geraldine 'Erasmus and the Tradition of
Paradox', *Studies in Philology*, vol 61, 1964, pp 41 ff.

3   Pasquier's paradoxical writings can be found in his *Œuvres, op.
cit.* cols 103, 249, 1053; and Peletier's in his *Œuvres poétiques*, Paris,
1547, pp 86ᵛ–88ᵛ.

4   *Œuvres, op. cit.* col 585. Pasquier, while professing not to understand Montaigne's method of diversion is not averse to using the same paradoxical methods as the *Apologie* which seem to fall well within Montaigne's definition of diversion. Reasoned contrasts were to become the main dialectical method of Pierre Charron who refers to the legal origin of such forms of argument: 'les oppositions et les contradictions raisonnées sont les vrais moyens d'exercer cet office de juge', *De la Sagesse*, Bordeaux, 1601, Part II, paragraph 4b.

5   Porteau, *art. cit.* quotes G. M. Bruto's *La Institutione di una fanciulla nata nobilmente* (Antwerp, 1555) to support his comment that paradoxes 'secouent l'apathie du lecteur. Elles stimulent son intelligence. Elles échauffent son zèle combatif, sa mémoire et sa raison', p 346. See also his comments on the usefulness of sustaining two contrary opinions in *Montaigne et la pédagogie, op. cit.* pp 196 ff. This tradition is also discussed by Walter Ong, *Ramus and the Decay of Dialogue*, New York, 1958, pp 37 ff.

6   Pasquier, *Œuvres, op. cit.* cols 43–6: 'Entre autres choses, j'ai voulu passer sur ses Paradoxes, par lesquels Ciceron se vante, terrasser la commune opinion de la populace. Qui n'est pas à mon jugement oeuvre de trop grand merite; car y a t-il rien si aisé, que de combattre sur le papier, telles opinions qui sont ordinairement brusques et sans fondement de raison? C'est pourquoy aprés avoir fait en moy un long divorce du pour et contre de plusieurs choses, il m'est entré en la pensée qu'il y auroit matiere de faire des Paradoxes plus hardis, qui y voudroit mettre la main. Et pour le premier je voudrois, par forme de jeu, soustenir que les Paradoxes des anciens n'estoyent Paradoxes'.

7   Writers include J. Passerat and his praises of nothing, *Nihil*, Paris, 1587; and A. Hotman, 'Paradoxe de l'Amitié et de l'Avarice', published in *Opuscules*, Paris, 1617, pp 113 ff.

8   C. Dornavius, *Amphitheatrum sapientiae socraticae jocoseriae, hoc est, Encomia et Commentaria Autorum qua veterum, qua recentiorum prope omnium: quibus res, aut pro vilibus vulgo aut damnosis habitae, styli patrocinio vindicantur, exornatur: opus ad mysteria naturae discenda, ad omnem amoenitatem, sapientiam, virtutem, publice privatimque, utilissimum*, Hanoviae, 1619. Mc Kerrow's edition of the *Works* of Thomas Nashe (London, 1904, 1905, 1908, 1910; reprint, Oxford, 1958) lists many paradoxical works, vol III, pp 176 ff.

9   V. L. Saulnier makes an attempt to distinguish between these forms in his article 'Proverbe et paradoxe du XVe et XVIe siècles', published in *Pensée humaniste et tradition chrétienne aux XVe et XVIe siècles*, Paris, 1949, pp 98 ff.

10   In a letter quoted by E. M. Simpson: *A study of the Prose Works of J. Donne*, Oxford, 1949, p 148.

11   Ed. London, 1647, sig. A 4.

12   First noted by George Boas, *The Happy Beast in French thought of the seventeenth century*, Baltimore, 1933, p 10. Landi's work has frequently been referred to by critics; it was used in some detail by W. G. Rice for his article 'The Paradossi' of Ortensio Landi', *Michigan Essays and Studies in Comparative Literature*, VIII, 1932, pp 59 ff.

13   Ed. Paris, 1553, sig. A ii.

14   Quoted from Dolet's translation, Lyon, 1543, pp 99–100.

15   Guazzo's comment on this subject can be taken as typical: 'Behold . . . with howe great pleasure and admiration we reade the Paradoxes of divers wittie and learned writers . . . and therefore I am of opinion, that in things of most difficultie, consisteth most excellencie and admiration', *Civile Conversation, op. cit.* p 91.

16   A. E. Malloch, 'The Techniques and Function of the Renaissance Paradox', *Studies in Philology*, vol 53, 1956, p 203.

17   See A. E. Pease's comments in 'Things without Honor', *Classical Philology*, vol 21, 1926, pp 27 ff, where he sees paradox and encomia as being at the origin of the modern essay.

18   *Paradossi*, ed. Lyon, 1543, paradox XIV, sigs. G4^r–6^r.

19   Montaigne's development here should be set in the tradition of religious writing where paradoxes were extremely common. Examples which illustrate this trend might be Luis de Granada, Du Plessis Mornay, and Jean de Sponde, as well as moral writings inspired by Seneca. See my article 'Prose Inspiration for Poetry', *art. cit.*, *passim*. These parallel sources are ignored by Friedrich both in his book, *op. cit.* chapter VI, and in his recent articles 'Montaigne et la Mort', published in *Preuves* (NOS. 204, 205, février and mars, 1968) which differ hardly at all from his original chapter.

20   *Epistulae Morales, ed. cit.*, 26, p 187.

21   A parallel case where paradox is used to win men over to death through an increasing intimacy can be found in Du Plessis Mornay's *Excellent Discours de la vie et de la Mort*, La Rochelle, 1581. It is a work which also leans very heavily upon Seneca's *Letters* for inspiration.

22   Compare Du Plessis Mornay, *Excellent Discours, op. cit.* p 3, 'Nous appellons vie, une mort continuelle, et mort, l'issue d'une mort vivante, et l'entrée d'une vie eternelle'; p 21^v, 'Nostre vivre n'est qu'un mourir continuel. A mesure que nous vivons, nous mourons: à mesure que nous croissons, nostre vie descroit'.

23   *Epistulae*, 78, 'morieris, non quia aegrobas, sed quia vivis'.

24   For an idea of the strength of this tradition see Walter Ong's article on paradox and wit in the poetry of Adam de St. Victor and St. Thomas Aquinas, *Speculum, art. cit. passim*.

25   *Epistres*, Paris, 1582. My quotations are taken from pp 80^v–81.

26   Delègue, *art. cit.* pp 241 ff, has some interesting views on this aspect of Montaigne's use of the paradox. Frank Bowman also discusses the effect of Montaigne's use of extremes in his admirable little book *Montaigne*, London, Arnold, 1961, pp 30–2.

27   Petrarch sums up the traditional position in *On his own Ignorance*, trs. by P. Kristeller, in *Renaissance Philosophy of Man*, p 101, 'He promises one the knowledge of Himself. When He grants this to me, it will appear superfluous to busy myself with other things that are created by Him'. A typical reaction, more contemporary with Montaigne, can be found in Lipsius, *De Constantia*, Antwerp, 1584, p 89.

28   See the next chapter for a detailed discussion of Montaigne's use of assertion.

29   Landi shifts his ground in a similar fashion to Montaigne. In his discussion of the paradox 'Qu'il vault mieulx estre ignorant que sçavant', he uses Socrates on the one hand as a symbol of those who have died because of their wisdom (p 37), and on the other as a model to follow in so far as he despised learning. (p 40).

30   But Montaigne does not develop his ideas of the truest wisdom—that is God's wisdom—in as detailed a way in *De la vanité* as he does in the *Apologie* (II: 12,480).

31   Pasquier, *Œuvres, op. cit.* cols 523 ff. There is the same kind of contempt for wisdom in La Noue's *Discours*.

32   *Paradossi, ed. cit.* paradox XXX, sigs. O i^r–7^r.

33   See Merleau Ponty's comment *Signes* IX, p 254, 'Le mot d'étrange est celui qui revient le plus souvent quand Montaigne parle de l'homme. Ou 'absurde!' Ou 'monstre'. Ou 'miracle'.'

34   He even ostentatiously profits from this knowledge as he explains in the *Apologie* (II: 12,445) where he tries to justify the extent and nature of his anecdotes: 'Nous admirons et poisons mieux les choses estrangeres que les ordinaires'.

CHAPTER 5

1   John Florio, *The Essayes of Michael Lord of Montaigne*, London, 1603, preface.

2   See particularly 525C–F for the methods to be pursued in writing 'Advanced exercises in composition', translated in W. H. Woodward's *Desiderius Erasmus, op. cit.* p 171. Porteau discusses the utility of commonplaces, *La pédagogie, op. cit.* pp 179 ff.

3   One of the early translations of the *Disticha Catonis*—*Le Cathon en françoys*, Lyon, 1527, was undertaken 'pource que auiourdhuy plusieurs seioyssent des briefves parolles et sentences'.

4   The bibliography contained in Mario Praz, *Studies in Sixteenth and Seventeenth century Imagery*, (2nd ed. Rome, 1964) though very

inaccurate, still provides the most complete description of French emblem books yet available.

5   *Œuvres morales*, Paris, 1584, sig. ã iij^v.

6   M. Gribaldus, *De methodo, op. cit.* Of the other works available Abraham Fraunce's *The Lawiers Logicke, exemplifying the Praecepts of Logike by the Practice of the Common Lawe*, London, 1588, gives the most complete list of commonplaces. For a swift modern survey, see Sister Lechner, *Renaissance concepts of commonplaces*, New York, 1962.

7   Translated by Margaret Phillips, *Adages*, London, 1968, p 171.

8   One could, of course, argue that such additions which Montaigne made on his own copy of the *Essais* were intended as alternatives only. There is plenty of evidence in the rest of the *Essais*, however, to suggest that he preferred to accumulate and retain all such thoughts.

9   Sister M. K. Elaine in an article on the 'Moral Force of Montaigne's Proverbs', *Proverbium*, vol 3, 1965, gives a complete list. Unfortunately, her discussion of Montaigne's use of them does not advance much beyond Villey's comments, *Sources et Evolution, op. cit.* II: 296–9.

10   Pasquier, *Œuvres, op. cit.* col 517.

11   See Guazzo's comment on the pleasure to be derived from difficulty, cited in the previous chapter, note 17.

12   Seneca, *Epistulae*, III, NO. 94 'On the Value of Advice', p 31.

13   *Meditations*, translated by Meric Casaubon, and dedicated to Archbishop Laud, London, 1634, pp 40–1.

14   *Ibid*, pp 71–2.

15   *Ibid*, p 151.

16   *Ibid*, p 126.

17   *Ibid*, p 139.

18   Xylander's Latin translation of the *Meditations* came out in Lyon in 1559, and in 1570 appeared the first vernacular translation, a version in French by Pardoux Duprat. A. S. L. Farquharson, *The Meditations of the Emperor Marcus Antoninus*, Oxford, 1944, pp xlii ff, discusses the diffusion of the printed text in Europe from these early printed editions onwards; pp lxxiv–v he notes that the work seems to have been composed as consolation and encouragement, two words which also partly describe the function of the *Essais* for Montaigne.

19   Montaigne's protestations against witchcraft, against its admirers and its adversaries, is a protest against attitudes to an old superstition which has been given a new lease of life. This view is analysed in detail by Alan Boase in his article 'Montaigne et la Sorcellerie', *Humanisme et Renaissance*, 1935, pp 402 ff.

20   Montaigne had personally protested violently against the number of witch trials in Lorraine, for example, where the Provosts of Nancy, and in particular Nicolas Remy 'the scourge of witches', had since 1571

been engaged in the pursuit and punishment of several hundred witches.

21   There is evidence from this essay that Montaigne knows at least the work of Bodin (*De la Démonomanie des sorciers*, Paris, 1580) and of Johan Weyer (*De l'imposture et tromperie des diables*, Paris, 1567), and that he was familiar with the main talking points which preoccupied writers—the real or imaginary transportation of bodies, the use of drugs, self-accusation, threats, torture and so on.

22   This wish can sometimes lead him into the most gross exaggerations as in *De la solitude* (1:39,235).

23   Agrippa, *De l'incertitude et de la vanité des sciences humaines*, *op. cit.*; and L. le Roy, *De la Vicissitude, op. cit.*

24   Seneca, *Epistulae*, III, no. 94 'On the Value of Advice', pp 27–8.

CHAPTER 6

1   Professor Boase informs me that the Matignon correspondence at Monaco (which includes a large number of the known letters of Montaigne) gives a good idea of what a 'gouverneur de province' heard from his officers day by day and month by month. During Montaigne's first two years as Mayor of Bordeaux, the letters suggest that even in the South-West of France the fighting was largely sporadic.

2   This was a common complaint, see for example, Le Roy's comment about the upside down nature of the world in his edition of Aristotle's *Politiques*, Paris, 1568, p 546: referring to the seditious Romans, he says 'Et tous les maulx qu'ilz faisoyent, ilz les appeloyent par noms nouveaux et inusitez: Car les temeraires estoyent nommez deffenseurs vertueux de leurs amys: et la tardité et froideur ilz nommoyent une honneste crainte: et la modestie, pusillanimité couverte l'indignation precipitée, virilité et hardiesse: la consultation et deliberation prudente, tergiversation palliee'.

3   See chapter II, p 21 for a more detailed discussion of this point.

4   The full titles of these pamphlets are *Le Reveille matin des François et de leurs voisins*, n.p. 1574, and *Le tocsain contre les massacreurs et auteurs des confusions en France*, Reims, 1577.

5   Villey, *Sources et Evolution, op. cit.* I, p 69.

6   Le Roy, like Montaigne, lamented the injustice of his times but maintained that laws must on no account be changed.

7   *Politiques, op. cit.* p 543.

8   The *privilège* of 1574 suggests that the composition of *L'Organe* was strictly contemporary with the *Essais*.

9   Canaye, *préface aux Lecteurs*, no pagination.

10   Canaye, *op. cit.* pp 587 ff.

11   *Ibid*, p 273.

12   *Ibid*, p 751.

13   Geoffrey Atkinson discusses the popularity of this work in *Les Nouveaux horizons de la renaissance française*, Droz, 1935, pp 424–5. I quote from the Slatkine reprint of the 1566 edition of the *Apologie*.

14   *Apologie, op. cit.* preface to the *Seconde Partie*; an idea expanded in later editions, see reprint pp 113–6.

15   Titus Livius, *The History of Rome*, Bohn translation, London, 1880, preface, p 3. See also A. D. Leeman's discussion in *Orationis Ratio*, Amsterdam, 1963, p 194.

16   The advantages of this method have been demonstrated by Atkinson, *op. cit. passim*, and by R. Lebègue, 'Montaigne et le paradoxe des Cannibales', *Studi in onore di B. Revel*, Florence, 1965, pp 359 ff. On the other hand, deficiencies of the method are shown up by René de Lucinge, *La Manière, op. cit.* p 34^v, 'Lipsius s'est fort peiné de mouller nos guerres civiles de point en point sur le modelle de celles de Cesar et de Pompee dans Rome. Mais il n'a pas donné au blanc pour la generale similitude, ny de si pres que sa visee avoit choisi : Car les exemples des choses si reculees de nos temps, ne se peuvent si bien mesurer que l'on n'y trouve merveilleusement à redire'.

17   It must be pointed out that not only did contemporary practice generally show the advantages of the comparative method, contemporary theory advocated its use, and critics continued to do so well into the seventeenth century. See le sieur de Richesource who suggests that parallelisms 'charment l'imagination des auditeurs', *Le Masque des Orateurs*, Paris, 1667, pp 26–7.

18   Pasquier, *Œuvres, op. cit.* cols 55–6.

19   Estienne, *Apologie, op. cit.* sig. ã iii^v of 1566 ed., the idea is expanded in later editions, see reprint, pp 16–18.

20   For a full discussion of the ramifications of this myth, see A. Lovejoy and G. Boas, *Primitivism and Related Ideas in Antiquity*, Baltimore, 1935.

21   Atkinson, *op. cit.* p 142.

22   The status given to all things Greek can be gauged from Henri Estienne's *Project du livre intitulé de la preexcellence du langage François*, Paris, 1579, where the best claims he can make for French are that as a language it equals the Greek.

23   Etiemble 'Sens et Structure dans un essai de Montaigne', *Cahiers de l'Association Internationale d'Etudes Françaises*, 1962, NO. 14, pp 263 ff.

24   Lestoile's oblique comparison comes nearest : 'le roi montrait son front à la Ligue, couvert d'un sac de pénitent et d'ermite, au lieu que Cesar opposait l'authorité de son visage armé à ses légions mutinées', *Journal, op. cit.* for the year 1586, p 457.

25   The 'people' in the *Essais* are not always free from criticism; see II : 10,990–1 & 996–7.

26   Lestoile, *op. cit.* p 388.

27   Atkinson, *op. cit.* p 198, cites numerous pamphlets written on the cruelties of the Christians against the Turks.

28   'Apostat ennemy' is the typical reaction to Julian. Le Roy's assessment of the Roman Emperor in *De la Vicissitude, op. cit.* p 75 can be taken as current.

29   We cannot know for certain exactly when Montaigne composed the essays of Book III. Although my argument does not depend on giving essays specific dates I have had in mind Villey's suggested datings: *De l'utile et de l'honneste* (1586), *Du repentir* (after 1584), *De la vanité* (1586–8), and *De mesnager sa volonté* (after 1587).

30   A famous example of such a view can be found in the fourth chapter of Machiavelli's *The Prince*.

31   Most exhortatory literature in the sixteenth century used such parallels; one of the first works in French to do so was Guillaume Budé's *L'Institution du Prince*, composed about 1519 and first printed in 1547.

32   For a more detailed discussion of the importance of Socrates for Montaigne, see Chapter 8.

33   Villey, *Sources et Evolution, op. cit.* I, p 162. Montaigne himself praises Lipsius as 'le plus sçavant homme qui nous reste' (II: 12, 562).

34   The *De Constantia* was first published in English in London, 1595. Guillaume du Vair's *De la Constance et Consolation es calamitez publiques* (Paris, 1594) follows the same paralleling pattern, closely modelled on Lipsius and Montaigne.

35   Stradling's translation, p 20.

36   *Ibid,* pp 31 ff.

37   *Ibid,* pp 78–9.

38   *Ibid,* p 125.

39   *Ibid,* pp 2–3.

40   *Ibid,* p 41.

41   *Ibid,* p 125.

42   The first English translation was in 1594.

43   The civil wars drew Montaigne inexorably towards an appreciation of, and yearning for, Stoic virtues which he sometimes confuses with his idea 'style soldatesque'; see Chapter 7 for an elaboration of this last point.

CHAPTER 7

1   See the following studies: N. Dow, *The Concept and Term 'Nature' in Montaigne's 'Essais',* Philadelphia, 1940; H. Weber 'Montaigne et l'idée de nature', *Saggi e Ricerche,* V, Pisa, 1964, pp 41 ff; S. J. Holyoake, 'The Idea of "Jugement" in Montaigne', *Modern Language Review,* April, 1968, pp 390 ff ; R. C. La Charité, *The Concept of Judgment in*

Montaigne, The Hague, 1968; G. Castor, *Pléiade Poetics, op. cit.*, pp 150–1, 153, 159–61, 167; I. D. McFarlane 'Montaigne and the Concept of the Imagination', *The French Renaissance and its Heritage*, London, 1968, pp 117 ff; and H. Friedrich, *Montaigne, op. cit.* chapter VI. Jean-Yves Pouilloux's brief and provocative work: *lire les 'Essais' de Montaigne*, (Paris, 1969) shows awareness of the significance of contexts, but hardly discusses them.

2   J. Zeitlin pertinently notes in the Introduction to his translation of the *Essais*, New York, 1934–6, 3 vols, I, p li, that while it is well to recognise the value of Villey's contribution and his principle of development in the essays 'we may ask whether the development is not in intellectual breadth and literary art rather than in moral character'.

3   See Dow, *The Concept and Term 'Nature', op. cit., passim.*

4   Pliny gave a very extended account, which Montaigne uses, in Book VII of his *Natural History*; and Pasquier's *Lettre en forme de Paradoxe pour les bestes brutes, Œuvres, op. cit.* pp 251 ff, covers the same ground. Boas, *The Happy Beast, op, cit.* should also be consulted.

5   Montaigne discusses the number of history books he read and the delight he found in them in *Des livres* (II : 10).

6   J. Plattard, *Montaigne et son temps, op. cit.* p 131 ff.

7   It is interesting to compare the general nature of Montaigne's comment to the more particularised satire of Lestoile 'C'est l'exercice ordinaire d'un ligueur et la marque infaillable d'un catholique zelé, d'avoir tousjours la messe et la religion en la bouche, l'athéisme et la brigandage au coeur, et le meurtre et le sang aux mains', *Journal, op. cit.* p 624.

8   E. Marcu 'Quelques invraisemblances et contradictions dans les *Essais'*, *Cahiers de l'Association Internationale des Etudes Françaises*, vol. 14, 1962, p 241, asks the question, 'Is this passage ironical?' It is, perhaps, best answered by Pierre Charron who, in chapter 59 of the first book of his *De la Sagesse* (1968 Slatkine reprint, 3 vols, 1, pp 414–6), quotes in full the same passage from the *Essais* and sets it beside an extended comment which describes the military profession as 'L'art et l'experience de nous entredesfaire, entretuer, de ruiner et perdre nostre propre espece, semble desnaturé, venir d'alienation de sens'. The diatribe covers two pages.

9   Well-known and detailed discussion of the theme of instability can be found in Le Roy's *De la Vicissitude, op. cit., passim*; and in La Primaudaye's *Académie, op. cit.* pp 77 ff. The ease with which an author's tone could rise to warm eloquence can be demonstrated from the writings of De Lancre who was as impressed as Montaigne by the inconstancy of things: 'Ainsi les mers nous portent, et les vents nous transportent, nous soufflent et ressoufflent dans leur flux et reflux, l'air qu'on y prend

et les vapeurs qu'on reçoit nous mouillent, nous brouillent, et nous detrempent dans l'humidité de tant d'eau', is a typical passage in *Tableau de l'Inconstance des mauvais anges et demons*, Paris, 1613, p 32.

10 Pierre Breslay, *L'Anthologie ou Recueil de plusieurs discours notables*, Paris, 1574, p 28ᵛ.

11 Du Plessis Mornay, *Excellent Discours*, *op. cit.* p 17ᵛ and Guazzo, *Civile Conversation*, *op. cit.* I, pp 214 ff.

12 For a fuller discussion of 'cuyder' see R. Lebègue's article 'Le cuyder avant Montaigne et dans les 'Essais', *Cahiers de l'Association Internationale des Etudes Françaises*, Vol. 14, 1962, pp 275 ff.

13 The articles of Boon, especially 'Montaigne: Du Gentilhomme à l'Ecrivain', *art. cit.*, and that of S. J. Holyoake 'Montaigne and the concept of "bien né" ', *Bibliothèque d'Humanisme et Renaissance*, vol. 30, 1968, pp 483 ff, are relevant here.

CHAPTER 8

1 These two great minds have often been linked rather incidentally. To my knowledge there has been no serious study of the influence of Socrates on Montaigne. F. Kellerman's article 'Montaigne's Socrates', *Romanic Review*, vol. 45, 1954, pp 170–7, discusses briefly the impact of Socrates's personality upon that of Montaigne. The abiding presence of Socrates for Montaigne has been stressed by Baraz in his book *L'être et la connaissance*, *op. cit.* p 43.

2 Sources of information on Socrates available to Montaigne were extensive. There was the rather tortuous transmission through Cicero and Xenophon, as well as anthologies and sixteenth-century handbooks such as *Les plus illustres et plus notables sentences, receuillies de Platon*, published by A. Brière after a French translation of *The Banquet*, Paris, 1556. There was, in addition, Ficino's big Latin translation of Plato's works, Le Roy's numerous renderings into French, and Plutarch's 'Daemon de Socrates' available in Amyot's translation of the *Œuvres morales* in 1572.

3 The fact that Plato's view is added later to the essay gives even more support to the idea of using a great mind in order to deflate some generally held notion.

4 Montaigne launches a similar attack on their pictures of the underworld; see II: 12, 497–8, 499, 520.

5 Louis le Roy, too, is aware of the difficulties of handling this form by inferior minds; this often leads to 'Questions et oppositions, qu'ilz accumuloyent l'une sur l'autre sans ordre, sans elocution, et sans jugement'. *Trois oraisons de Demosthene*, Paris, 1551, sig. B. ij.

6 See E. A. Havelock's discussion of this problem in *Preface to Plato*, Oxford, 1963, *passim*.

7 This view of Socrates is maintained by Michael J. O'Brien, *The*

Socratic Paradoxes and the Greek Mind, University of North Carolina Press, 1967, p 222.

8   I have relied principally on the work of Havelock, *op. cit.*, O'Brien, *op. cit.*, N. Gulley, *The Philosophy of Socrates*, London, 1968, and R. Robinson, *Plato's Earlier Dialectic*, 2nd ed. Oxford, 1953.

9   Since Montaigne used Le Roy's translations and commentaries on Aristotle he might well have looked into his renderings of Plato. For an opposite view see Villey, *Sources et Evolution, op. cit.* I, p 193.

10   For other references to poetry and philosophy in the *Apologie* see II : 12, 518, 538.

11   Or 'artful reserve' as O'Brien calls it, *op. cit.* p 108.

12   *Ibid*, pp 87–90.

13   R. Robinson, *op. cit.* pp 8–9.

14   See chapter 4.

15   *Phaedrus*, Heineman ed. Harvard, 1960, pp 565–6, 'Writing Phaedrus, has this strange quality, and is very like painting; for the creatures of painting stand like living beings, but if one asks them a question, they preserve a solemn silence. And so it is with written words; you might think they spoke as if they had intelligence, but if you question them, wishing to know about their sayings, they always say one and the same thing. And every word, when once it is written, is bandied about, alike among those who understand and those who have no interest in it'.

16   Montaigne is referring to the *Phaedrus*.

17   Examples of dialogues can be found among the writings of Bruès, Tahureau, Pasquier, Sebillet and Ringhieri. For details of their works see Chapter 2, note 15.

18   Bruès' *Dialogues* are very stilted, in practice close to a set of monologues.

19   He used the *Phaedo* extensively in *Que philosopher c'est apprendre à mourir*, I : 20.

20   Similar comment can be found in Philibert de Vienne, *op. cit.* pp 95 ff.

21   Le Roy, *Phedon*, *op*, *cit*. pp 8–9. It is interesting to note that later in his life Le Roy did not find the Socratic method always quite so straightforward as his description here suggests. 'Platon introduisant Socrates en ses escriptz, le faict disputer par dialogues; refutant l'opinion des autres, sans declarer la sienne : et use de plusieurs inductions, et autres argumens subtilement deduictz : ce qui en rend l'intelligence plus difficile, comme ayant en aucuns endroictz apparence d'ambiguité et es autres de superfluité', *Les Politiques* [of Aristotle] *op. cit.* pp 172–3.

22   Compare Montaigne's remarks on this last point : 'Platon me semble avoir enjoué cette forme de philosopher par dialogues, à escient, pour loger plus decemment en diverses bouches la diversité, et variation de ses propres fantaisies' (II : 12, 489–90).

23   Canaye, *op. cit.* p 670.

24   For a detailed discussion see J. E. Seigel, *Rhetoric and Philosophy in Renaissance Humanism*, Princeton, 1968.

25   Ramus, *Dialectique, ed. cit.*, p 61, 'la vérité des choses comprises és ars est ainsi naturellement proposée à l'esprit comme est la couleur à la veüe, et ce que nous appelons enseigner n'est pas bailler la sapience ainsi seulement tourner et diriger l'esprit à contempler ce que de soy mesme il eut peu apercevoir s'il fut là tourné et dirigé'.

26   Ong, *op. cit.* pp 26 and 283.

27   The following survey owes a great deal to Alan Boase's important study, *The Fortunes of Montaigne, op. cit.* I am naturally concerned to give far more emphasis to responses to Montaigne's style than Professor Boase had space to develop in his all-embracing work. I also consulted P. Villey's *Montaigne devant la posterité*, Paris, 1935, and Boase 'The Early History of the *Essai* title in France and Britain', *Studies in French Literature presented to H. W. Lawton*, Manchester University Press, 1968, pp 67 ff.

28   The Apology was couched in letter form. It is to be found in vol VIII of Camus' *Les Diversitez*, Paris, 1613, pp 406–60.

29   Boase, *Fortunes*, p 114.

30   *Diversitez, op. cit.* vol IX, p 469; see also, II, pp 460 ff.

31   *Ibid*, vol VIII, p 437.

32   *Le vray et ancien usage des duels*, Paris, 1617, p 88. I suspect that Montaigne is frequently used as a good excuse by authors who have not had the time to set their thoughts in an order that would forestall criticism. Such seems to be the case of Antoine de Laval, *Dessein des professions nobles*, Paris, 1613, preface, sig. ẽ ij.

33   *De l'incredulité et mescreance du sortilège*, Paris, 1622, p 340.

34   A lengthy comment on Montaigne and his style is appended to a poem addressed to Mlle de Gournay in his *Poematum*, Leiden, 1607, pp 360 ff. For information on Baudius, see Boase, *Fortunes*, pp 21–3, and V. L. Saulnier 'Les dix années françaises de Dominique Baudier', *Bibliothèque d'Humanisme et Renaissance*, vol 7, 1945, pp 139 ff.

35   My attention was drawn to this work by Boase, *Fortunes*, p 3, note 1.

36   *Essais et Observations sur les Essais du Seigneur de Montaigne*, London, 1625, address to the 'Noblesse de la Grande Bretagne'; 'En quoy, il semble, qu'il s'est voulu sonder et cognoistre soy-mesme, surquoy il se trouve bien empesché le plus souvent, et se contredit en plusieurs lieux, ce qu'il confesse luy-mesme, disant que son esprit est variable et inconstant, le quel ne peut se contenter, et que maintenant une chose luy est agreable, et bientost apres il change d'opinion contraire. Nous monstrant en cela, combien l'homme est un sujet ondoyant et inconstant, et combien il est difficile de se cognoistre soy-mesme'.

37   *Ibid*, [no pagination].

38   C. Sorel, *La Bibliotheque, op. cit.* p 77. It is also worth quoting in full an earlier comment on Montaigne's studied deceits: 'J'adjousteray qu'encore que plusieurs de ses Discours contiennent autre chose que ce qui est promis par le Titre, cela n'arrive pas à tous, et que lors qu'il l'a fait, il a semblé que c'estoit par affectation plustost que par inadvertance, afin de nous montrer qu'il ne pretendoit pas faire un Ouvrage reglé à l'ordinaire. Cela se connoist par l'enchaisnement bigearre de ses Entretiens, où parlant d'une chose à propos d'une autre, il en enfile plusieurs diferentes en suite. Il s'estoit possible imaginé qu'un homme pouvoit bien faire cecy dans ses meditations particulieres, ainsi qu'on le fait dans les conversations ordinaires, que quand elles ne seroient qu'entre deux ou trois personnes, leurs discours varient extremement, de sorte que si on les mettoit par écrit, on verroit que les derniers ne répondroient gueres aux premiers. Il a voulu imiter cela exprez pour nous donner un Ouvrage libre et non encore veu, tellement que ce qu'en dit le sieur Chanet, ne nous persuadera pas, qu'il l'ait fait par un défaut de jugement. Quelquefois aussi il a caché son dessein dans ses Titres, comme par exemple dans son troisieme Livre, ayant remply un Chapitre presque entier de Discours contre les Medecins, il faut croire qu'il a voulu empescher qu'on ne connust d'abord ce qu'il desiroit traicter [*Ressemblance des enfans aux peres*]. En ce Chapitre et en d'autres, il y peut aussi avoir de l'artifice, bien loin d'y avoir de l'ignorance.' *Ibid*, pp 72–3.

39   First published in Bordeaux in 1601.

40   Quoted from the first edition, preface, sig. ẽ iv-2.

41   The extent of Charron's borrowing has been studied by A. Delboulle, 'Charron plagiare de Montaigne', *Revue d'Histoire Littéraire de la France*, vol 7, 1900, pp 284 ff.

42   Collected ed. of *Œuvres*, Paris, 1665, 'Dissertations critiques', NO. XIX, p 658, 'De Montaigne et ses Escrits'. From the same premiss of order, Balzac criticised Ronsard and Ariosto.

43   Although some love of method was predominant in the way even devotees of Montaigne responded to the *Essais*. See G. Naudé, *Bibliothèque Politique*, Paris, 1624, p 16, whose praise of Charron demonstrates the degree to which he prized method.

44   See Boase's discussion, *Fortunes*, pp 326 ff, and E. B. O. Borgerhoff, *The Freedom of French Classicism*, Princeton, 1950, pp 84 ff.

45   Père du Bosc, *L'Honneste Femme*, Paris, 1632, 'Advis au Lecteur'.

46   C. Sorel, *De la connoissance des bons livres*, Paris, 1671, p 270.

47   D. Bouhours, *La Manière de bien penser dans les ouvrages*, ed. used, Paris, 1743, p 481; Bouhours, who has just been quoting Montaigne, expresses here sentiments frequently repeated in the seventeenth century.

48   N.a.fr.4333. It is a kind of chatty diary, written about 1670.

49   *Ms. cit.* f 18. Numbered among these were Mlle de Scudéry and the Marquise de Sablé. See Méré *Lettres*, Paris, 1659, 2 vols, II, p 604; and Grace Norton, *The Influence of Montaigne*, London, 1908, p 27.

50   *Ms. cit.* f 94.

51   *Ibid*, f 52ᵛ.

52   *Ibid*, f 98. Claude Irson, *Nouvelle methode pour apprendre facilement les principes et la pureté de la langue françoise*, Paris, 1666, p 269, makes a similar comment on Montaigne: 'Il faut lire le livre du premier [Montaigne] avec précaution'.

53   First published in 1662, it enjoyed a certain success; subsequent editions are listed in *La Logique ou l'Art de Penser, ed. crit.* by P. Clair & F. Girbal, Paris, 1965—this is the most recent presentation of the work, from which I quote. Nicole and Arnauld were prepared to make positive use of Montaigne on several occasions, see for example, p 232.

54   Montaigne is used as the main evidence in this attack on false rhetoric, a work which falls well within a clearly defined tradition stemming from Pico della Mirandola's own assaults on Rhetoric to those misgivings of François Lamy's *Connoissance de soi-mesme*, Paris, 1700. For a discussion of this battle in France in the second half of the seventeenth century, see Peter France, *Racine's Rhetoric*, Oxford, 1967, pp 20–1.

55   *La Logique, op. cit.* p 19.

56   *Ibid*, p 267.

57   *Ibid*, pp 269–70.

58   *Ibid*, p 273.

59   G. Bérenger, *Réponse à plusieurs injures* . . . . *contre Michel de Montaigne*, Paris, 1668.

60   *Œuvres complètes*, Paris, 1962, 20 vols. *Recherche de la verité*, vols I-III, II, iii, V, p 359 ff.

61   Malebranche's analysis was to be developed more generally for false rhetoric by François Lamy, who in *Connoissance de soi-mesme, op. cit.* sums up the deceits which Montaigne used as 'l'art d'aller à l'esprit par le coeur et d'aller au coeur par l'imagination' cited in France, *Racine's Rhetoric*, p 20.

62   *Œuvres complètes*, Ed. Assézat et Tourneaux, vol II, pp 272-3. I wish to thank Dr Peter France for first drawing my attention to these words of Diderot, and to the article of Georges May, 'Diderot, artiste et philosophe du décousu', *Europäische Aufklärung. Herbert Dieckmann Zum 60 Geburtstag*, Munich, 1967, pp 165 ff.

BIBLIOGRAPHY

PRIMARY SOURCES

AGRIPPA, H. C. *Declamation sur l'incertitude, varieté et abus des sciences*, Paris, I. Durand, 1582.

ARISTOTLE *Politics* (trs. L. le Roy, *Les Politiques d'Aristote*, Paris, M. de Vascosan, 1568).

ARNAULD, A. & NICOLE, P. *La Logique ou l'art de penser* (crit. ed. P. Clair & F. Girbal, Paris, 1965).

D'AUDIGUIER, V. *Le vray et ancien usage des duels*, Paris, P. Billaine, 1617.

AURELIUS, M. *Meditations* (crit. ed. A. S. L. Farquharson, London, 1934 and Oxford, 1944).

BACON, F. *Works* (ed. London, 1879) 2 vols.

BALZAC, G. DE *Œuvres*, Paris, T. Jolly, 1665, 2 vols.

BAUDIUS, D. *Poematum*, Leiden, T. Basson, 1607.

BÉRENGER, G. *Réponse à plusieurs injures. . . contre Michel de Montaigne*, Paris, I. d'Houry, 1668.

BOAISTUAU, P. *Theatre du monde, avec un brief discours de l'excellence de l'homme*, Paris, pour V. Sertenas, 1561.

BODIN, J. *De la Démonomanie des Sorciers*, Paris, I. du Puys, 1580.

BOUCHET, G. *Serées*, Imprimé sur la copie faicte à Poictiers, 1585.

BOUHOURS, D. *La manière de bien penser dans les ouvrages d'esprit*, Paris, S. Mabre-Cramoisy, 1687.

BRESLAY, P. *L'Anthologie ou Recueil de plusieurs discours notables*, Paris, I. Poupy, 1574.

BRUÉS, G. DE *Les Dialogues*, Paris, A. Wechel, 1557.

BRUTO, G. M. *La Institutione di una fanciulla nata nobilmente*, Antwerp, C. Plantin, 1555.

BUDÉ, G. *L'Institution du Prince*, Lyon, G. Gazeau, 1547.

CAMUS, J. P. *Les Diversitez*, Paris, C. Chappellet, 1613.

CANAYE, P. *L'Organe, c'est à dire l'instrument du discours*, Geneva, I. de Tournes, 1589.

CARDANUS, H. *De la Subtilité*, Paris, C. L'Angelier, 1556.

CASTIGLIONE, B. *The Courtier* (ed. Everyman).

CATO *Le Cathon en françoys*, Lyon, O. Arnoullet, 1527.

CHARRON, P. *De la Sagesse*, Bordeaux, S. Millanges, 1601. (Slatkine reprint, 1968, 3 vols).

COURCELLES, P. DE *Rhétorique*, Paris, G. Le Noir, 1557.

CUSA, N. See N. Khrypffs, *Haec accurata recognitio trium voluminum operum clariss. P. Nicolai Cusae*, n.p. 1514.

DES CAURRES, J. *Œuvres morales*, Paris, G. de la Nouë, 1584.

DES PERIERS, B. *Nouvelles*, Lyon, R. Granjon, 1558.

DES PERIERS, B. *Cymbalum Mundi*, Lyon, B. Bonnyn, 1538.

DORNAVIUS, C. *Amphitheatrum sapientiae socraticae jocoseriae . . .*, Hanoviae, 1619.

DU BELLAY, J. *Deffence et Illustration de la Langue Françoyse* (ed. crit. Paris, 1904).

DU BOSC, J. *L'Honneste Femme*, Paris, P. Billaine, 1632.

DU PLESSIS MORNAY, P. *Excellent Discours de la vie et de la mort*, La Rochelle, 1581.

DU PLESSIS MORNAY, P. *Mémoires*, Amsterdam, L'Elzevier, 1624–51, 4 vols.

DU TRONCHET, E. *Finances et thresor de la plume françoyse*, Paris, W. Du Chemin, 1572.

DU TRONCHET, E. *Lettres missives*, Paris, N. Bonfons, 1583.

DU VAIR, G. *De la constance et consolation es calamitez publiques*, Paris, M. Patisson, 1594.

ERASMUS *Ratio studii ac legendi . . . auctores*, n.p. 1511.

ERASMUS *Adages* (trs. M. Phillips, London, 1968).

ERASMUS *Colloquies* (ed. Paris, 1720, 4 vols).

ERASMUS *The Praise of Folly* (ed. London, 1887).

ESTIENNE, H. *Project du livre intitulé de la preexcellence du langage françois*, Paris, M. Patisson, 1579.

ESTIENNE, H. *Apologie pour Hérodote* (ed. Paris, 1735).

FABRI, P. *Le grand et vrai art de Pleine Rhetorique* (ed. Paris, 1889).

FOUQUELIN, A. *La rhétorique françoise*, Paris, A. Wechel, 1557.

FLORIO, J. *The Essayes of Michael Lord of Montaigne*, London, V. Sims, 1603.

FRANCO, N. *Dix plaisans dialogues*, Lyon, I. Beraud, 1579.

FRAUNCE, A. *The Lawiers Logicke*, London, W. How, 1588.

FREGOSO, A. *Le Ris de Democrite*, Paris, G. Corrozet, 1547.

GELLI, J. B. *Les Discours fantastiques de Justin Tonnelier*, Paris, G. le Noir, 1566.

GRIBALDUS, M. *De methodo ac ratione studendi, libri tres*, Lyon, A. Vincentium, 1544.

GUAZZO, S. *The Civile Conversation*, London, R. Watkins, 1581.

HABERT, P. *Style de composer des lettres missives*, Paris, C. Micard, 1587.

HOTMAN, A. *Opuscules*, Paris, Vve M. Guillemot, 1617.

IRSON, C. *Nouvelle methode pour apprendre facilement les principes et la pureté de la langue françoise*, Paris, P. Baudouin, le fils, 1666.

LA BOËTIE, E. DE *Œuvres complètes* (ed. Bordeaux, 1892).

LAMY, F. *Connoissance de soi-mesme*, Paris, A. Pralard, 1700.

LANCRE, P. DE *Tableau de l'inconstance des mauvais anges et demons*, Paris, J. Berjon, 1613.

LANCRE, P. DE *De l'incredulité et mescreance du sortilège*, Paris, N. Buon, 1622.

LANDI, O. *Paradossi* (trs. Poitiers, J. de Marnef, 1553).

LA NOUE, F. DE *Discours politiques et militaires*, Basle, F. Forest, 1587.

LA PRIMAUDAYE, P. DE *Academie Françoise*, Paris, G. Chaudière, 1580.

LA RUELLE, C. DE *Succinctz adversaires . . . contre l'Histoire et professeurs d'icelle*, Poitiers, Bouchetz frères, 1574.

LAVAL, A. DE *Dessein des professions nobles*, Paris, A. L'Angelier, 1613.

LE ROY, L. *De la vicissitude et variété des choses humaines*, Paris, P. L'Huilier, 1576.

LE ROY, L. *Trois oraisons de Demosthène*, Paris, M. de Vascosan, 1551.

LESTOILE, P. DE *Journal pour le regne de Henri III, 1574–89* (ed. Paris, 1943).

LIPSIUS, J. *De Constantia*, Antwerp, 1584 (trs. J. Stradling, London, R. Johnes, 1595).

LIVY *The History of Rome* (trs. London, 1880).

LUCINGE, R. DE *La manière de lire l'Histoire*, Paris, T. du Bray, 1614.

MALEBRANCHE. *Œuvres* (ed. Paris, 1962, 20 vols).

MARGUES, N. *Description du monde desguisé*, Paris, T. Richard, 1563.

MÉRÉ, CHEV. DE *Lettres*, Paris, D. Thierry & C. Barbin, 1682, 2 vols.

MEXIA, P. DE *Diverses Leçons*, Paris, J. Cavelier, 1557.

MONLUC, B. DE *Commentaires* (Pleiade ed. 1964).

NASHE, T. *Works* (ed. Oxford, 1958, 4 vols).

NAUDÉ, G. *La Bibliothèque politique*, Paris, Vve de G. Pelé, 1642.

NAVARRE, MARGUERITE DE *L'Héptameron* (ed. Garnier, n.d.).

PARÉ, A. *Œuvres*, Paris, G. Buon, 1585.

PASCAL, B. *Pensées* (ed. Brunschvig, Garnier, 1958).

PASQUIER, E. *Œuvres*, Amsterdam, 1723, 2 vols.

PASSERAT, J. *Nihil*, Paris, S. Prevosteau, 1588.

PETRARCH *De Remediis* (ed. Paris, D. Ianot, 1534).

PLATO *Les plus illustres et plus notables sentences, recueillies de Platon* (publ. by A. Brière after his translation of *Le Banquet*, Paris, G. Guillard, 1556).

PLATO *The Dialogues* (trs. Jowett, Oxford, 1875, 5 vols).

PLUTARCH *Œuvres morales* (trs. Amyot, Paris, M. de Vascosan, 1572).

QUINTILIAN *Institutio Oratoria* (ed. Loeb, 4 vols).

RAEMOND, F. DE *L'Anti Christ et l'anti Papesse*, Paris, A. L'Angelier, 1599.

RAMUS, P. *Dialectique* (ed. M. Dassonville, Droz, 1964).

Le Reveille matin des François et de leurs voisins, n.p. 1574.

RICHESOURCE, J. S. *Le Masque des Orateurs*, Paris, Académie des Orateurs, 1667.

RINGHIERI, I. *Dialogue de la vie et de la mort*, Lyon, R. Granjon, 1557.

SAINT SERNIN, J. DE *Essais et observations sur les Essais du Seigneur de Montaigne*, London, E. Allde, 1625.

SANCHEZ, F. *Quod Nihil Scitur*, Lyon, A. Gryphium, 1581.

SÉBILLET, T. *Contramours*, Paris, 1581.

SENECA *Epistulae morales ad Lucilium*, (ed. Loeb. 3 vols).

SEXTUS EMPIRICUS, *Opera quae extant . . . Pyrrhoniarum hypotyposes libri III*, Paris, M. le Jeune, 1569.

SOREL, C. *La Bibliotheque françoise*, Paris, Cie des abonnés du Palais, 1664.

SOREL, C. *De la connoissance des bons livres*, Paris, A. Pralard, 1671.

TAHUREAU, J. *Les Dialogues* (ed. Paris, 1870).

Le tocsain contre les massacreurs et auteurs des confusions en France, Reims, J. Martin, 1577.

TREBIZOND, GEORGE OF *De Re Dialectica Libellus*, Paris, T. Richard, 1558.

VIENNE, P. DE. *Le Philosophe de Court*, Lyon, J. de Tournes, 1547.

WEYER, J. *De l'imposture et tromperie des diables*, Paris, I. du Puys, 1567.

YVER, J. *Le Printemps*, Paris, A. L'Angelier, 1572.

SECONDARY WORKS*

BOOKS

BARAZ, M. *L'être et la connaissance chez Montaigne*, Paris, 1968.

BOASE, A. M. *The Fortunes of Montaigne*, London, 1935.

BOWMAN, F. *Montaigne*, London, 1961.

FRAME, D. *Montaigne: A Biography*, London, 1965.

FRIEDRICH, H. *Montaigne*, Paris, 1968.

GRAY, F. *Le Style de Montaigne*, Paris, 1957.

GUNDESHEIMER, W. *Louis le Roy*, Droz, 1966.

JONES, P. MANSELL *Three French Introspectives from Montaigne to André Gide*, Cambridge, 1937.

---

* I cite only those modern works on Montaigne which I have found especially useful in writing this study.

KAISER, W. *Praisers of Folly*, New York, 1964.

MICHA, A. *Le singulier Montaigne*, Paris, 1965.

ONG, W. J. *Ramus and the Decay of Dialogue*, Cambridge, Mass., 1958.

PORTEAU, P. *La vie pédagogique au temps de Montaigne*, Paris, 1936.

RUEL, E. *Du Sentiment artistique dans la morale de Montaigne*, Paris, 1901.

THIBAUDET, A. *Montaigne*, Paris, 1963.

VILLEY, P. *Les sources et l'évolution des 'Essais' de Montaigne*, 2nd. ed. Paris, 1933, 2 vols.

WEBBER, J. *The Eloquent 'I': style and self in seventeenth-century prose*, Madison, 1968.

ARTICLES

AUERBACH, E. 'La condition humaine', *Mimesis*, Anchor Books, 1953.

BESPALOFF, R. 'L'Instant et la liberté chez Montaigne', *Deucalion* 3.

BOON, J. P. 'La Pensée de Montaigne sur la mort a-t-elle évolué?', *Modern Language Notes*, vol 80, 1965, pp 307 ff.

'Montaigne: Du Gentilhomme à l'Ecrivain', *Modern Philology*, vol 64, 1966, pp 118 ff.

'Evolution et esthétique dans les *Essais* de Montaigne,' *Philological Quarterly*, vol 47, 1968, pp 526 ff.

CLARK, C. E. 'Seneca's Letter to Lucilius as a source of some of Montaigne's imagery', *Bibliothèque d'Humanisme et Renaissance*, vol 30, 1968, pp 249 ff.

'Montaigne and the Imagery of Political Discourse in sixteenth-century France', *French Studies*, 1970, p 337.

CROLL, M. W. 'Attic Prose: Lipsius, Montaigne, Bacon', *Schelling Anniversary Papers*, New York, 1923, pp 117 ff.

'Juste Lipse et le mouvement anticicéronien à la fin du XVIe et au début du XVIIe siècle', *Revue du Seizième siècle*, vol 2, 1914, pp 200 ff.

'Muret and the History of Attic Prose', *Publications of the Modern Language Association*, vol 39, 1924, pp 254 ff.

'The Baroque Style in Prose', *Studies in English Philology. A Miscellany in Honor of F. Klaeber*, University of Minnesota Press, 1939, pp 427 ff.

DELÈGUE, Y. 'Du Paradoxe chez Montaigne', *Cahiers de l'Association Internationale des Etudes Françaises*, vol 14, 1962, pp 241 ff.

DRESDEN, S. 'Le dilettantisme de Montaigne', *Bibliothèque d'Humanisme et Renaissance*, vol 15, 1953, pp 45 ff.

ETIEMBLE 'Sens et Structure dans un Essai de Montaigne', *Cahiers de l'Association Internationale des Etudes Françaises*, vol 14, 1962, pp 263 ff.

FRIEDRICH, H. 'Montaigne et la mort', *Preuves*, Fév-Mars, 1968, pp 17 ff, 26 ff.

HOLYOAKE, S. J. 'Montaigne and the concept of "bien né" ', *Bibliothèque d'Humanisme et Renaissance*, vol 30, 1968, pp 483 ff.

'The Idea of "Jugement" in Montaigne', *Modern Language Review*, 1968, pp 340 ff.

JASINSKI, R. 'Sur la composition chez Montaigne', *Mélanges d'histoire littéraire offerts à H. Chamard*, Paris, 1951.

MCFARLANE, I. D. 'Montaigne and the Concept of the Imagination', *The French Renaissance and its Heritage*, London, 1968.

PORTEAU, P. 'Sur un paradoxe de Montaigne', *Mélanges offerts à P. Laumonnier*, Paris, 1935, pp 333 ff.

SAYCE, R. 'Baroque Elements in Montaigne', *French Studies*, vol 8, 1954, pp 1 ff.

'L'Ordre des Essais de Montaigne', *Bibliothèque d'Humanisme et Renaissance*, vol 18, 1956, pp 7 ff.

'Montaigne et la peinture du passage', *Saggi e Ricerche*, vol 4, Pisa, 1963, pp 9 ff.

STAROBINSKI, J. 'Montaigne et "la relation à autruy" ', *Saggi e Ricerche*, vol 9, Pisa, 1968, pp 77 ff.

TELLE, E. V. 'A propos du mot *Essai* chez Montaigne', *Bibliothèque d'Humanisme et Renaissance*, vol 30, 1968, pp 225 ff.

TRINQUET, R. 'Problèmes posés par la révision de la Biographie de Montaigne', *Cahiers de l'Association Internationale des Etudes Françaises*, vol 14, 1962, pp 285 ff.

WEBER, H. 'Montaigne et l'idée de nature', *Saggi e Ricerche*, vol 5, Pisa, pp 41 ff.

INDEX